BOWS ON THE
LITTLE DELTA

GLENN ST. CHARLES

BOWS ON THE
LITTLE DELTA

Glenn St. Charles

Author of *Billets to Bow*

Bows on the Little Delta and Billets to Bow are designated
"Quiver Series" books of the Pope & Young Club. Over time,
the Quiver Series will contain a select few rare and unique
manuscripts which honor the true spirit of hunting with the
bow and arrow and document our bowhunting heritage.

The Quiver Series

Published by Glenn & Margaret St. Charles
19807 1st Avenue South, Seattle, Washington 98148-2493

ISBN 0-9651394-1-7
Library of Congress Catalog Card Number 97-91878
Copyright © 1997 Glenn & Margaret St. Charles

Printed in the United States of America.

To my beloved family
who kept the home fires burning
during my many and long
"Walks in the Woods."

Little Delta Bowhunters, 1959.
From left: Fred Bear, Dick Bolding, Bob Kelly, Russ Wright, and Glenn.

TABLE OF CONTENTS

ACKNOWLEDGMENTS

Margaret St. Charles who began recording these stories in the 1950s,
and has worked tirelessly to see this book become a reality;

Holly Jensen our assistant, both personally and professionally, for help with
editing and proofreading, and for overseeing the production of this book;

and
Larry Jensen
Rose Malinoski
G.H. "Mal" Malinoski
Dick Mauch
Dick McIntyre
Jack Reneau
Jay G. St. Charles
Joe R. St. Charles
for their consultations and advice in support of this project.

CREDITS

Artwork
Charles H. Denault
Tyler Jensen
C.W. Palmer

Photography
Grace Bartlett
Chuck Bartlett
Pat Marino
Arlyne Rhode
Roger Sandford

Letters & Pictures

Dick Bean
Fred Bear
Catherine and Lloyd Beebe
Dick Bolding
"Wild Bill" Childs
Keith Clemmons
John O. Cook, III ("Buzzi")
Billy Ellis
Frank Glaser
Bob Kelly
Dick Latimer

G.H. "Mal" Malinoski
Rose Malinoski
Carol Mauch
Dick Mauch
Margaret St. Charles
Jay G. St. Charles
Joe R. St. Charles
Frank Scott
Chester Stevenson
Jim Stuart
Bert Wallis

I'm with the man, Glenn St. Charles. He has seen the guts of bowhunting in this country long before many of us were born. When he talks of any period in time, even into the future, I listen. He prefers to hunt alone. If you want him around at noon, you carry his lunch.

One who has been there,
Jack H. Williams

FOREWORD

by Billy Ellis

The old order is passing. Swiftly receding into memory are the days of strong, earnest men who followed an atavistic yearning to pit their skills against wild animals. In those days, to be designated "hunter" was the highest honor that could be bestowed while today sport hunting is under constant assault by various groups of Quixotic malcontents.

Some of us have been lucky enough to briefly glimpse or share a campfire with those living anachronisms in buckskin coats with hand-made bows and gale-burned faces. Glenn St. Charles is one of them.

In this book, Glenn speaks of those by-gone days. Some halcyon, some full of struggle with the elements, but all suffused with the joy and wonder of the wilderness. You will wander on bowhunting journeys through raw and lonely lands on man's greatest quest; bowhunting the beautiful, cunning, and sometimes dangerous big game animals of North America, with a bow.

You will also learn of the history of this quest; of the great and near-great who have taken the last trail but who left their moccasin prints for us to follow. This book is a compilation, not of mere words, but a reverent conveyance of in-born knowledge coupled with the unfathomable joy of archery.

This book will live as a major classic of archery literature because, to Glenn St. Charles, traditional archery and traditional values are one and the same. His life has spanned the better part of this century, but he also comes from a time far away. A time when a man's word was his bond; when the quality of the finished product was more important than the wage earned; when the success of a hunting trip was measured in warm companionship rather than in game brought to bag. When a gentler, kinder spirit pervaded America, God created Glenn St. Charles.

There have never been many "legends" in bowhunting circles. Many aspire, but few are chosen. A person becomes a "legend" when the strength of his character causes a whole movement to become better and stronger until it rises to a higher philosophical plain. Glenn St. Charles has done that for his beloved sport of bowhunting. In this century, our legends have been Ishi, Pope and Young, and Bear and St. Charles.

Listen now to the words of our elder; listen to the thunder in the mountains, the click of the caribou's hoof as the wind sweeps the barren grounds; and hear the bear's roar.

Glenn St. Charles speaks to our hearts of these things.

FOREWORD

by Richard Mauch

My close personal relationship with Glenn began in 1962, when we attended a meeting of the minds at Bear Archery Company in Grayling, Michigan. Afterward, Glenn elected to fly with me in my Comanche to my home in Bassett, Nebraska. Eventually I would get him to an airport for his return to Seattle. The flight over some of the most populated areas in the United States concerned him and prompted him to ask if I had sufficient replacement rubber bands aboard in case the engine conked out!

After a couple days in Bassett touring the surrounding country, we flew on to Denver where he took a flight on to Seattle. This trip to my ranch proved to be one of many Glenn was to make throughout the ensuing years.

Founding the Pope and Young Club was no doubt Glenn's greatest challenge. It became apparent in the early fifties that bowhunting would need credibility in the eyes of the public to survive. He almost singlehandedly took on the doubters, the likes of the Humane Society and the gun hunting clan, who constantly badgered our wildlife agencies to get rid of us before we got any kind of a foothold. With the advent of the Pope and Young Club and their trophy lists, the DNR had the proof needed to put to rest any doubts that they and the public had.

As P&Y Records Committee Chairman from February 1968 to February 1972, I was ever aware of Glenn's foresight, leadership and forcefulness. I remember well the 1972 Directors' Board meeting at the

Regency Roadway Inn, Denver, Colorado. As the first day Directors' meeting wound down, Glenn raised the question as to what to do with the trophy heads that were on display at the Clarence Love Indoor Archery Lanes nearby. He suggested that the trophies be displayed on the walls of the hotel banquet room for all to admire. The unanimous consensus of the rest of the directors and officers was that this was not necessary, that the banquet attendees would view them at the Love location. They voted the idea down. His wife Margaret recalls that Glenn, in their room that night, was very disappointed and convinced that the directors were not correct in their assessment of the whole situation. Surely these magnificent animals deserved more respect and should be displayed in the banquet hall. The next morning when Glenn opened the Directors' meeting he questioned his own judgment in even bringing the trophy head display up for discussion. For now, while he was running the show, they would hire a truck and get those heads over to the banquet hall and put them on the walls. Without a word from anyone, it was done! The heads were in the banquet room for all to see.

Glenn was awarded NFAA's highest award, the Compton Medal of Honor, in 1958. He became a member of the prestigious Boone and Crockett Club in 1980. The 30th Anniversary of the Pope and Young Club in Seattle, Washington, 1991, saw Glenn inducted into The Archery Hall of Fame and presented with Pope and Young Club's most prestigious Ishi Award, thus taking his rightful place in history among the other giants of our archery tradition. It was also during these ceremonies that the considerable contributions of Glenn's wife Margaret and his other family members were recognized. Certainly it is because of their love and support for more than four decades that Glenn has been able to accomplish all he has for our sport.

Glenn is very accessible — to him, everyone is a VIP. He is indeed a mover and a shaker. He has touched many lives. I am proud to call Glenn St. Charles one of my closest friends.

PREFACE

by Glenn St. Charles

Herein this book are hunting stories, many of which are the way it was before high-tech gadgetry, tree stands, baiting, camo, scents, and trophy hunting. 1930-1950 most bowhunters used self wood longbows and shot the instinctive way. A few sight shooters came from the ranks of the National Archery Association (NAA). There were enough of them to spawn the equipment controversy which continues to this day. Laminated longbows came on the scene in the early '50s.

We were bowhunting pioneers. Nothing much had been written about the sport. We would write the books. Guides were untried and, even though briefed on what was to be expected of them, were quick to pull the trigger when an animal with an arrow in it didn't drop in its tracks. Early on, bowhunting to most of us simply meant a "walk in the woods" in search of a game animal. No significance was placed on gender. Anything that was taken with a bow was considered quite an achievement. The media was our friend and reported our success nationally and with truth. Public acceptance seemed to revolve around the fact that bowhunting gave the animals a fair chance.

As the saga of the Little Delta hunts unfold, you will read for the first time how the area was discovered and hunted by me and my companions, Keith Clemmons and Dick Bolding in 1957; also the events leading up to the 1958-1959 Fred Bear hunts there. There were no guides.

Alaska, the last frontier, was a U.S. Territory until July 4, 1959 when it became a state. I was in Fairbanks at the Ladd Air Force Base when the Alaska flag was lowered and the Stars and Stripes was raised. It was quite a ceremony — a lot of tears! Many square-jawed folks obviously did not want this to happen. Significant too, Texas became the second largest state in the Union!

A thumbnail bowhunting history of Washington State pretty much parallels what it was like throughout the rest of the country. The challenges that we faced along the way were taken care of by good leaders who had no conflict of interest. The advent of the compound bow was to change the course of bowhunting and the archery industry. Under the heading of progress and the quest for money, this high-tech industry has swept traditional values aside and all but eliminated a primitive sport.

Other concerns are: our image — how the non-hunting public perceives bowhunting, and the current breakdown of the moral fiber of society which is affecting hunting and the outdoor experience. No longer are hunting camps and trailheads safe without being attended. Land owners are experiencing unwanted trespass and need more control. This costs money. Prime hunting, that a handshake and a bottle of whiskey could get you, could now cost you — bring money and credentials.

It's all in this book as seen through the eyes of one who has been there from the beginning and writes from actual experience. Graphics and text depict behavior that was acceptable for the times.

This book was written entirely by me. There were no ghost writers, no public relation folks looking over my shoulder, no enhancements.

1
BACKGROUND

Soon after the turn of the century the St. Charles family, consisting of my father Phillip Joseph (PJ) St. Charles, mother Coral Barbara Rouse (her maiden name), brother Ray, and sister Gladys, moved from Alpena, Michigan to Seattle, Washington. My father was a timber cruiser by trade and reasoned that the vast forests of the northwest was where the timber industry would find its ultimate future, and that was where he could best provide for the family. I was born in Seattle, December 15, 1911. For several years, my dad cruised timber in the forests of the Cascade Mountains near Seattle. Time in school for me was for the most part like other pre-teenagers. Sports were marbles and spinning tops.

In 1921, my dad's work took him to the Kanisku National Forest of northern Idaho. The family moved to Spokane, Washington, to be closer to his work. For the next three years, I had occasion to spend some time with my dad and brother, Ray, touring the logging areas in a Reo Power Wagon, the only dependable truck to hold up on the terrible roads we travelled. We watched logging crews yard-in logs by donkey engine and cable to existing ponds or ponds made by temporarily damming up small creeks. From these ponds, each day's log harvest was floated across country through large wooden water troughs called flumes, to the nearest river where the logs literally flew out into the water, sometimes from hundreds of feet above. From there, the logs floated downstream and were snatched out of the river by sawmill crews for processing into lumber. I spent time in the timber cruising

Glenn, a toddler with his teddy bear. He was born in Seattle, Washington, in 1911.

Glenn, on the colt he eventually rode to a one-room school in the Horse Heaven Hills near Kiona, Washington.

camps with my dad and a chain man who, by compass and a 100-foot chain, kept my dad's lumber evaluation on track. The estimated height, base diameter, and the usable top diameter of each tree was the formula that gave them the needed answer. Two large tents housed us and a cast iron kitchen range, all brought in by pack horse over remote forest trails. While my dad and the chain man were at work, I took care of the camp chores, washed dishes, cut wood, and kept a back burner crock of sourdough happy, bubbling, and burping by feeding it potato peelings. Pancake batter was cooked directly on the stove top. I fished the streams and ponds and harvested a grouse occasionally with my 22 single shot "Stevens Favorite" rifle. This kept the "pot" busy; the "pot" being a large cast-iron skillet for deep-frying. We used gobs of butter. The native animals were there, moose, elk, deer, and bear. I spent many hours observing their movements and behavior. Little did I know at the time, that this was to be the backdrop for much of my life; of hunting and time in the woods.

At age ten, I spent about a year on a wheat ranch in the Horse Heaven Hills near Kiona in southcentral Washington. There I had access to horses and rode one a mile to and from a one-room school house. The huge combines that harvested the wheat were drawn by teams of 20 mules — Missouri Mules — the best, but ornery. They could kick a stall to shreds in seconds and occasionally put a handler in the hospital. The work was tough and in very hot country. There were occasional sand storms so severe you could not see the hand in front of your face. You did not want to be caught out in one of these away from the house.

In 1924, we moved from Spokane back to a residence at Laurel Beach near Fauntleroy, a suburb of Seattle. My dad decided to give up timber cruising and went into the real estate business. I was then in the seventh grade at Fauntleroy Grade School and aside from the learning part, was into soccer, baseball, and plying the waters around the islands on Puget Sound in a sailing canoe.

It is August, 1926. Picture, if you will, a near cloudless day — a gravel beach on Puget Sound about 10 miles south of Seattle, Washington. The salt water at high tide is gently lapping at the tangled mass of drift logs and seaweed that has come ashore. Pristine, practically untouched islands lay across the mile stretch of water against the backdrop of the Olympic Mountains, now drained of their snowfields by the late summer sun. Seabirds out there dive for small fish fry just under the surface of dead calm water. Seagulls are darting here and there in their everlasting search up and down the beaches looking for any morsel to satisfy their insatiable appetites.

Suddenly, this peaceful setting is broken by the screaming of a mass of diving seagulls. As happens many times in the afternoon of each day, a housewife from one of the little houses that dot the shoreline has just dumped a load of garbage over the nearby seawall. Garbage, you say — yes, garbage that is not all that bad — no plastic, no aluminum. The steel and tin cans of those days soon wasted away in the corrosive salt water. Bottles almost certainly break up with each change of the tide. Garbage collection in those days was more of a luxury than a necessity. Sleek scavengers, cruising over the sea bottom, were taking care of the rest of the goodies out of reach of the birds above — *sand sharks!*

This racket has attracted a few teenagers from the nearby houses. They carry long spears tipped with barbed points, or bows and arrows. They walk along the 1-1/2-foot thick cement seawall, peering into the 5-foot depth of the clear blue-green water for anything that moves. Bows are of hazelnut branch, strung with meat wrapping twine. Arrows are willow shoots plucked from the edge of a nearby creek. They are tipped with sharpened headless nails — not very lethal, and very expendable. Put these all together — they are the tools of the day for an exciting pastime for these youngsters of yesteryear.

I was one of those teenagers with the bow and arrow. Little did I know at the time that this was the first of a long life of concern and pleasure with the bow and arrow.

Scouting was the next thing to get my attention — Troop 291, headquartered at the nearby Fauntleroy Community Church and Recreational Center. A gym and a manual training room was available. It was complete with all the basic woodworking tools — tools that would soon put me to the test.

From the Boy Scout manual I learned about the yew wood tree — how it made good archery bows. This could be tied in with the quest for an archery merit badge. The trees grew quite profusely in the mountains nearby and all over the Puget Sound region. From one tree near my home, some branches and a small log or two were cut. James Duff's book on bows and arrows from the local library told me that the wood had to be seasoned for two or three years. We couldn't wait for that. We used a lot of limbs in the green — crude bows, but bows nevertheless that served our purpose. Our main shooting ground was a huge sand-pit bowl nearby. Yes, we had fun!

The scout program offered an eastern state address where one could purchase a partially worked Tennessee Cedar stave. A spoke-shave and rasp fit my needs and soon, shaving here and there, a sem-blance of a bow emerged. I found myself shooting this bow with every spare moment I could find. My shooting ground was a sandy beach. My targets were pieces of bark and any object where there was a sand back-ground. I was just simply flanging arrows. Nobody taught me how.

This activity led to more orders among the scouts for cedar staves. I began showing others how it was done. Eventually, Troop 291, under the leadership of Rusty Burke, engaged in archery competition with Troop 65, led by Clark Schurman. This went on for the next two years. This involvement led to my having a couple of stints of teaching archery at Camp Parsons, the area's Boy Scout summer camp on Hood's Canal on the Olympic Peninsula. (1927-28)

Located in the rain forest of the Olympic Mountains, Camp Parsons was an encampment almost the likes of an army operation. It consisted of a parade ground surrounded by six huge tents and a big log lodge. Each tent held eight scouts with cots and all their belongings. They were there for two weeks at a time. The lodge was headquarters for the operating personnel and served as the mess hall.

I was one of the Rangers, the older scouts and those who had been there before. We were the instructors and had separate quarters nearby.

Boy Scouts on duty at Camp Parsons. Sandy Stewart, left, and Glenn.

Glenn, a Boy Scout.

At 16, attending West Seattle High School.

We taught such things as mountain climbing, survival, boating, fishing, trail building and archery. The latter was my bag. I would take six or eight scouts into the woods where we would harvest material for our archery equipment. For bows, there was yew, vine maple, cherry and dogwood. Arrows were reeds we plucked from the numerous creek beds nearby. We tried to keep wood ahead in camp that was seasoning. When our green materials were brought in, we would set them aside for drying and seasoning and use material from the year before.

Hatchets, knives and rasps were our main tools. The bows were very crude but served the purpose. Part of our program was making bowstrings. Linen was our bowstring material. Turkey feathers worked very well by tying and gluing them to the arrow shafts. We had no fletching jigs. The nock end of an arrow for the string slot was reinforced by simply making a wrap of linen thread at the base of the slot. It was all very crude, but worked well enough to pass the tests for the archery merit badge. Competitions were held — there was a lot of pride shown in the accomplishment. It was truly a grassroots effort — through the years many future archers and bowhunters were born.

June, 1929 summer vacation, Alan "Mutt" Webster and I hitchhiked to Colfax, Washington, a town near the Idaho border — wheat and alfalfa hay country. We applied for work at the local farm bureau and were hired by an elderly Dutch couple, owners of a hay farm nearby. Their children had long flown the coop and were learning to become teachers, lawyers, whatever. These folks needed help with the hay harvest. After being comfortably located in their bunkhouse, we were given a tour of the farm. They raised all their own vegetables and a variety of fruits. They had pigs (homemade sausage!), chickens, dairy cows, and a creamery to take care of the milk products — cream, cottage cheese, and hard cheese. It was all like right out of Holland! The work, yes, we had work! While the old gentleman ran the mower, Mutt and I shocked the hay, loaded it into a wagon, and hauled it to the barn, load after load. We learned how to slop the pigs, milk the cows, run the creamery, and make the ice cream. Boy, oh boy, did we ever eat! The Mrs. was delighted to have a couple of characters like us to feed — pies for every meal. We should have gained pounds. The work kept us trim and the pay was good. August came; time to head home for school. It was a difficult parting — the whole experience I could never forget. My bows and arrows didn't make the trip. They were not the kind of equipment one would hitchhike with.

Then came the fall of 1929 — Black October — the stock market crash triggering the worst depression the country has ever known. It was then that I was lucky enough to get an after school job to help supplement my dad's income and to finish high school which now became more of a priority than archery. However, my bow was always handy for practice sessions whenever possible.

High school had its ups and downs. A strange thing happened to me which had little meaning at the time, but later — WOW! I went to a county fair with friends. While there we were enticed into a fortune-teller's booth. We all had a good laugh when the soothsayer read my future. She said: "I see sticks — piles of sticks. Some day you will spend much of your life being involved with lots of sticks." *How about that for a coincidence!!*

It's now 1930 — high school graduation time. Immediately after the graduation ceremony, four of us climbed into a Model T Ford and headed for Story, Wyoming, where the parents of Sandy Stewart, one of my best friends, owned the Kilbourne Ranch. There we were to engage ourselves in developing the ranch into a vacation retreat for dudes. Although my zest for archery had cooled a bit, I did have bows and arrows along — you never know if some critters out there might need my attention or, if for no other reason, just to watch my arrows fly.

The trip was a long, grueling experience over dirt roads. Flat tires and breakdowns plagued us every bit of the way. A leaking radiator dictated that one of us had to sit on the fender with a five gallon can of water, pouring constantly into the radiator as we went down the road to where we could get it repaired. We had no money for such a major repair. We luckily found a farmer who needed some fence-building. A half day delay, but this took care of our repair needs and we were again on our way.

We finally reached the ranch, set up shop in the main vine-covered log cabin and took stock of our needs. Acquiring enough food for four ravishing characters was going to be a problem. Rabbits were plentiful and fish in the nearby pond helped considerably. We needed more. Our next door neighbors operated a fox farm. Fox feed was meat from wild horses (mustangs) that they acquired from the wide open prairies near Decker, Montana, about 35 miles north. To earn needed money for food, we joined in the round-up. These truly cowboy experiences I remember as if they happened only yesterday. The fox farm bought about 50 head of the mustangs for a dollar apiece. These wild horses had never known any form of control.

The main old building, Kilbourne Ranch, Story, Wyoming.

As for our riding horses supplied by the farm — they were something else! Picture, if you will, wild-eyed stock, fresh off the winter range, fat, and full of gas generated by green grass. Saddling these critters was a chore, but getting aboard was an effort in futility and when you finally did you KNEW the first quarter mile or so would be "hanging-on time," the horses snorting and blowing at both ends — literally "breaking in two" with each jump! Once our mounts cooled and we were settled in our saddles, it was just a matter of seeing to it that the mustangs got through the proper gates and pastures on their way south. The first downpour brought the brims of our Sears cowboy hats down around our ears. Oh well, so much for quality. It was a very tired bunch of city guys and wild-eyed animals that finally arrived at the fox farm.

We were allowed to pick a few of these wild ponies for our own use, the price $2 each. The rest of the wild horses were dispatched and cut up for fox feed. We also helped with this and were allowed to take any of the good cuts we wanted for our own use. Not exactly USDA stamped, but it was better than no meat at all. Yes, we survived on this fare along with sacks and sacks of onions marinated in vinegar.

18-year-old Glenn holding colt down for branding at the Kilbourne Dude Ranch.

Breaking our horses to ride and pack produced a lot of bumps and bruises. They were smart enough to charge wildly through small patches of trees to scrape us off their backs, or they would stop suddenly and let us sail off into thin air. It must be noted, that city-bred folks should not be trying to break a bunch of wild horses to ride or pack. It certainly lends to considerable time mounting and hitting the dirt — we called it "learning by the seat of our pants."

All the while, we were putting up log and stone cabins. Progress was slow but sure. Occasionally, time was taken off to take advantage of the excellent fishing in nearby Piney creek and explore the local area. Due to my early association with the bow and arrow, I was very much interested in the Indian history that was evidenced all around us. This was where the Sioux Chief Red Cloud raised so much hell with the settlers — The Fedderman Massacre near Fort Phil Kearney (1866). The scene of the Wagon Box Fight (1867) was only a half mile away. Flint arrowheads and spear points were plentiful near by. Buffalo skulls and horns lay about the sagebrush prairie — almost too plentiful to worry about picking them up. I did retrieve a few. It took us three summers to put up enough buildings to start booking dudes. Each of these summers, I would take leave of my work in Seattle and head for Wyoming.

Stone cabin Glenn helped build in July/August 1930, Kilbourne Ranch, Story, Wyoming.

Dudes headed out of the mountains.

The dudes came from the eastern states. To us, it was odd that they knew little about the west. They wondered if the Indians still attacked the people around Seattle, a little fishing village. Oh well, while there was some communication and media at that time, 1933-34, many of the folks in the east were out of touch and didn't keep up with the times. We knew communication was poor but we actually hadn't realized it was that poor.

We had established high-lake fishing camps and just plain old camps in the Big Horn Mountains for these dudes. Long rides, 10 to 15 miles a day, did much to keep their backsides in a very sensitive state and this would immobilize them for awhile, but it was very good experience for the easterners with few opportunities such as we provided.

An episode I remember well: We were bringing out a pack train to the ranch. We noticed a big black cloud of smoke rising in the sky behind us — a forest fire! As we closed to within a mile or so of the ranch, a fast moving pack train went up the trail by us — obviously firefighters, their many horses loaded with equipment and food. The head man, who was the game warden, sheriff and whatever you needed, had apparently conscripted every man in the area and he wanted the four of us. We agreed, but begged off long enough so we could secure the dudes, get a little food and fresh horses. The warden said he would furnish fresh horses and would meet us in an hour and a half at his place at the foot of the trail. This took place, the horses were great and talk about hightailing it out of there we did! Nightfall soon caught up with us. We were utterly amazed at how these horses could continue the pace they did in pitch black darkness through the woods, their noses almost scraping the ground. It was a very long night. We were 20 miles in when we arrived at the fire site. Tents had been pitched — the temporary corrals roped off for the horses. The fire would have to wait till morning — it was a humdinger!

We were in for a long haul and it was obvious that something would have to be done for more food. I was delegated to care for the horses and have some responsibility for rounding up more food. Yes, but how? We could not spare anyone to go back and get the rifle that we had forgotten so that we could take a deer or an elk. The creek we were camped on was full of fish, schools of them. It was only about a foot deep. There was some of our food, but how to get it? I would put four flies on a line and catch four fish about every cast — not exactly sport fishing but served the purpose for the time. It was a tiring job, and I was running out of flies. Perhaps there was another way. I would

On the fire line.

try to rig up a bow and arrow. A branch of something was acquired, strung with a fish line and, around the campfire at night, a bunch of willow shoots were rigged into arrows. One of the younger fellows was delegated to help me with the fishing. I would shoot an arrow into a fish, impeding it enough so that my helper downstream could retrieve it. The arrow acted as a flag which he would carefully grab and toss the fish up on the bank. It worked! To make a long story short, we ate lots of fish, got the fire out with no casualties and returned to our ranch.

The dude ranch was a success. However, before moving on, I would like to remember and record some of the experiences of the times and places around Story, Wyoming: The Big Horn Mountains are spectacular. High, white cliffs, plateaus of lodgepole pine thickets, wildlife everywhere, cattle roaming the lower hillsides, creeks and lakes brimming with cutthroat and mackinaw trout — large — I mean six or seven pounds; the awesome view from Red Cloud Lookout stretching out over the Powder River Plain below; the tales told by the old timers about the Johnson County Cattle War that swirled around them, ending in 1892; the Crow Indians squatting on the sidewalks of Sheridan dressed in their native garb, staring with piercing black eyes at apparently nothing from beneath their stiff-brimmed, tall black hats. The Crows were the favored ones and moved about in nice cars. Then, there

Indians at Sheridan Rodeo, Wyoming, 1931.   *Sioux Chief*

was the Sheridan, Wyoming Rodeo with the proud Northern Cheyennes (Sioux), apparently still paying for their alleged troublesome nature during the Indian Wars (1860's), now poor and driving horse-drawn wagons to the rodeos. When an unlucky steer became disabled from the rodeo games, the Cheyennes would rush out onto the grounds, dispatch the hapless beast and cut it up before the very eyes of the startled spectators. Soon the meat could be seen hanging in small strips between the wagons to dry — jerky it was called — the black flies never missed a piece of it. Come nightfall, the area within the acres of colorful tipis was lit up by huge fires. The thunderous beat of drums filled the night air. These evenings were truly exciting and gave one a sense of the frontier the likes of which you might not find anywhere else.

How about the Saturday night dances at Andy's Pavilion in Story, the beaver and muskrat we tried to eat and the ten gallon crock of home brew we kept in the saddle house, cradled over the hole in an old oak commode and kept bubbling by a kerosene lamp below — can't remember that much of it ever got bottled. Sampling with a ladle kept it in check. The ever-present, drunken yellow jackets that covered the top were simply scraped aside. Baseball games — we had them almost every Sunday and fights afterward. And the old wood-fire heated

Crow Indian dressed for rodeo, Sheridan, Wyoming.

Indians camped at Sheridan, Wyoming Rodeo, 1931.

cement swimming pool — I was the part-time lifeguard. Can't remember that I ever had to jump in after anyone. Any part of it could be reached by a pole with a hook on the end. Anyone in trouble was fished out by the swimsuit. Those were the days when the swimsuit had enough material to do just that.

Several trips to and from Seattle were via freight trains. Hobos, railroad bulls (police) and bellowing steam engines were no strangers to us. The Model T we drove out in was demolished on one of our return trips to Seattle. Four of us, travelling at night, were about 35 miles from home when we changed drivers. For lack of luggage space, all but the driver was covered with camping gear, pots, pans, etc. Someone shouted: "All's well, Mutt's at the wheel." About then, the lights went out! We hit the ditch alongside the highway — the car switched ends — turned over and rolled about 60 feet down an embankment! It came to a stop right side up on a dirt road below, headed back where we had come from! No one was hurt. A flashlight revealed that Mutt's pants had taken the brunt of the acid out of the broken battery. The pants disintegrated before our very eyes! Even in our distressed state, we found that we could still laugh. He was able to get into some other clothes before the acid got to his skin. We "camped out" the rest of the night. Morning, long in coming, gave us further clues as to our plight.

Glenn and Marjorie in Model T Ford he and his friends brought from Seattle.

We reloaded what we could find and pushed the car back up the dirt road and to a garage 1/4 mile up the highway. There we were able to assess the damage and replaced some broken magneto boxes. After a little tightening and adjusting here and there and a turn of the key, it started. The old Ford, minus windshield, limped slowly the rest of the way home. Needless to say, it was ready to be retired. Gee, how many times since then have I wished that I had kept that old relic!

It became time to leave all this and get on with our lives. I married Marjorie Ernestine Kneisel of Sheridan, Wyoming and brought her back to Seattle to settle down. It was then that I gradually got back into archery. It is now 1938. My wife, Marjorie, had taken an archery course when attending the University of Wyoming in Cheyenne. She indicated that she would like to have a bow and arrow set for Christmas. In order to meet this request, I contacted Wally Burr, a local bowyer, and bought one of his finest yew, 30 pounds; as sweet a shooting stick as you would ever find anywhere! My wife did not get to shoot it much because I had it most of the time.

Yes, I would have to have one of my own. It was then that I bought a yew stave from Burr and proceeded to whittle, and scrape, copying, measurement by measurement, a fine old yew bow on display in a department store window in downtown Seattle. Three months later I drew my pride and joy. To me, my new crooked stick was beautiful to behold and shoot — it did!

Glenn on target.

Archery was not much in evidence in Seattle at that time and it wasn't to me until I saw an article in the local paper about some of the activities of the one and only archery club, The Seattle Bowmen. They were to hold a target shoot at Mountlake Playfield and wanted partici- pants and spectators. I considered myself a pretty good shot at that time, so I thought I would go and show them how it was done. I went — I shot — I got beat soundly! I guess that would adequately describe that I came in last! Perhaps I had an excuse. It was a formal target tournament — the main event was the York Round. They were shooting 100 yards at 48-inch straw mats. That was not my bag. A swamp behind the 100- and 80-yard targets gobbled up most of my arrows. Many participants were National class shooters, champions the likes of Irl Stamps, Gilman Keasey, Ralph Miller and Belvia Carter.

I did meet a lot of other fine archers, too — among them Kore Duryee, Art Partee, L.D. Hunter, S.L. Michaels, N.A. Pearson and Bert Wallis. Irl Stamps took me under his wing when he saw my utter confusion at trying to hit the bull's eye at that distance. I was simply looking at the target and shooting at it. That is not the way they did it. They "sighted in." "Sighting in" meant placing a little white ball fastened to a metal pin in the ground somewhere between the shooter and the target. This was called a point of aim marker. They would draw and put the point of the arrow on the white marker. Where the marker was placed, of course, depended on the yardage needed to hit the bull's eye. There was a shooting line. The archers were split up into groups. One group would shoot three arrows, then the next group would shoot three arrows. This was repeated until an end of six arrows was shot by each participant. They would then score the target and retrieve their arrows.

In contrast to the bows today, it is interesting to note that most of the shooters would unstring their bows after each six-arrow round was shot, thus allowing the bows to "rest." The all-wood yew and osage bows would fatigue a bit after each shot. Some archers had three points of aim spaced to compensate for the cast let-down of the bow after each arrow. Some would even alternate different bows. The pulling weight of the bow changed, depending on the temperature, yew being the most sensitive. Imagine shooting under these circumstances and still shooting fantastic scores.

Most of the bows on the shooting line were stacked or semi-stacked yew bows, variations of the old English longbow. Almost all of them were made by Kore Duryee and Wally Burr.

2
MILESTONES
ALONG THE WAY

1942 — the war effort in full swing found me working for Coates Electric Company, engaged in the manufacture of submarine parts for the Navy. The sport of archery for everyone was more or less set aside for the duration and so was my crafting of the equipment. Off times, I operated out of a little room in the back of the electric company. Early in 1948 my wife Marjorie passed away, leaving me with many fond memories of my days with her in Wyoming. Our daughter, Linda, was nine years old at that time.

Soon after the war, I left Coates Electric and opened an archery shop and store on Airport Way in south Seattle. It was my first attempt at making a living at archery. While there, I met and married Margaret Lorraine Remick, my present wife and helpmate.

Meanwhile, I made contact with the Bear Archery Company and after several conversations with Fred and the other powers back there, I became a Bear dealer. At the time, they were experimenting with an aluminum alloy as a backing for their static recurve bows. They knew of the Boeing Airplane Company and its role in the war effort, the B-17 Bombers, and the possibility of getting the right surplus aluminum sheeting. Although the war had ended long before, the government still maintained a ban on some commercial uses of aluminum. I found what Bear was looking for at the Boeing surplus and was preparing to ship a carload of it when the ban was lifted.

While prowling the Boeing surplus, I came across another surprising find — sheets of Fiberglas! My experimentation with this proved it to be very good as a bow backing. I toyed with the idea of using it for a line of composite recurve bows. It was then that some changes would be made as to where my store and shop would be located.

Early in 1949 we sold our home and some nearby property in West Seattle and bought five acres of wooded land on the outskirts of Seattle. There, on a state highway, we proceeded to put up a two-story building where we could live, have a workshop and archery store. Our customers thought we were out of our minds — who would find us out there? Yes, it was remote, like you could lay down on the highway for 30 minutes before you would have to move for an oncoming car. It was not uncommon for us to be awakened by hunters sighting in their rifles in the adjacent sand pit.

We found it necessary to move into the building long before it was ready — no doors, windows, no electricity, no sewer and NO WATER! We hauled our drinking water in a wooden wine barrel and wash water in a 300 gallon B-17 Bomber wing tank, mounted on a trailer. The water came from Margaret's parents, three miles away. I hooked the wing tank up to plumbing in the daylight basement where we resided until our living quarters could be completed on the upper level. As for the sewer, the following story relates how we coped:

Margaret watched a chauffeured car pull up to our building which is about 100 feet off the highway. Out stepped an elderly lady — a knock on the side of the building. Margaret, home alone with our infant son Jay, dreaded answering, having a pretty good idea what she wanted since there were no gas stations for miles. Sure enough, she wanted to use our restroom. Margaret had to say we didn't have one. "What DO you DO?" the lady asked. "We use the woods," was the answer. To Margaret's amazement, this lovely elegantly dressed lady replied, "Well, I've done some pioneering in MY day! Will you please show me to your woods?"

Eventually we were able to get the building closed up, wiring in, and a fireplace for heat. It was only then we found ourselves along with our children, Linda and Jay, comfortable enough to get on with building up our archery business. The customers found us alright. They liked the abundance of parking, and a place to shoot, try out their equipment, and picnic with their families.

One thing we hadn't counted on was the zoning. We were not zoned for business. It wasn't long before a sheriff appeared at our door

NFAA Field Tournament at Two-Rivers, Wisconsin. Babe Bitzenburger is in the center. Lady at the right is shooting a Thunderbird bow.

with orders to close up the store. Apparently sensing that something was wrong with his orders, he asked, "Where do you live?" "Here," was the reply. "Well," he countered, "I can't close up your home." He suggested that we apply for a variance. We did and we got it. Two bankers on a scouting trip for customers for their new bank stopped in one day and asked why we hadn't finished the building. The result of this was, they finished the building and presented us with a mortgage.

With the advent of plastic in the late '40s, mass production of bows became possible. This consisted of wood strips laminated with Fiberglas or other like materials. The combination would conform to different shapes and sizes of working recurve bows. The tips, instead of having sharp bends that remained static, were now graceful curves which bent with the limbs at each draw of the bow. This created a very pleasant and non-stacking experience with much less jar. The surplus Fiberglas material that I had purchased earlier lent itself to this process.

In 1952, I designed, by trial and error, a fine shooting recurve we called the "Thunderbird." I set up a small plant near our place of business to build these bows. There were two lengths, 63-inch was the hunter and 67-inch was the field and target bow, some with arrow rests on both sides. They did well. So well, in fact, I became concerned with getting too deep into it — that perhaps it would impact my quality of life. Did I really want to cope with the trials and tribulations of a manufacturing business? Furthermore, dealing with the hazards of Fiberglas dust became a factor with everyone in the business.

A decision had to be made to increase production or quit. After about 400 bows, I shut down the plant — but not before I took two of them to show Fred Bear at the NFAA Tournament at Two Rivers, Wisconsin, in the summer of 1953. Several Thunderbirds were being used by the tournament shooters. Fred did not seem to be too impressed. Understandably, when he was still making his static recurve laminated bows — Grizzlys and Kodiaks. However, 1954 saw Bear Archery introduce its first laminated working recurve bow called the Kodiak II.

Meanwhile, this age of plastics made the self bow woods, yew and osage, rather obsolete. For many of the self wood bowyers, the future looked pretty bleak. Their stock of yew and osage bow wood were in many cases sold for firewood.

The late '60s saw the compound bow enter the scene. At first, it was considered a joke. Not only did it prove otherwise, but it was to change the face of archery for years to come — a face that literally had been cast in stone for centuries. The compound acceptance was very slow until Tom Jennings took it under his wing and made it into a real shooting machine. Most of us got caught up in the concept. It brought on a host of accessories that did not relate to our traditional background. Many of us began to realize what was happening. A whole new sport was developing that was not compatible with nature — the "walk in the woods" concept. This mechanical trend brought back cries for the old values and ways. Now we are seeing more recurves, more longbows and more self bows coming into being. The St. Charles family, during the late '80s, once again combed the nearby mountains for yew wood. We imported osage from the middle west. We are going full circle back to the basics of the old reliable yew and osage that relate to rawhide, sinew, glue, beeswax, and the smell of cedar and burnt feathers.

Our pioneering days in the country are behind us. We no longer wake to the sound of gun hunters sighting in their rifles. The adjacent sand pit is covered by a shopping center. The main highway is so well traveled it is dotted with left turn lanes and traffic lights.

Northwest Archery Company, mid-1950s.

1997 — Our five children live in the vicinity. Jay is making bows in the tradition of the St. Charles family. Joe is into archery history with a museum showplace where people from all over the world come to visit. Suzanne is known for her fine colorful arrows. Linda takes care of the bookwork. Rochelle keeps in touch. As for Margaret and me, we're still hanging in here.

THE BEAR CONNECTION

The meeting with Fred Bear at the 1953 NFAA Field Tournament at Two Rivers, Wisconsin, was planned. We discussed many things. Our talks concerned his interests in the northwest. Fred also wanted to reach out to the northwest in his quest for game other than the local whitetails and bear. He recognized that, in Washington, I was where it was at, and with a little more noseying around in the far north, I could get to where there was much more — and would I please include him.

Meanwhile, I would continue to represent Bear, something I had been doing since 1948. Concerns over the dwindling supply of Port Orford cedar shafts sent me on two trips into Oregon for answers.

Chuck Piper, Fred's partner, accompanied me on one trip into the Port Orford cedar country of Oregon to check with his main Port Orford cedar shaft suppliers, McKinney in Oakland, and Rose City Archery Co. in Powers. It was Friday afternoon when we pulled up to the gate of Rose City Archery. A big white Cadillac was about to leave. I rushed to get the attention of the two fellows in the car. They brushed me off with a polite, "We're closed, sorry. Won't be back till Monday morning." With that, I simply said, "Gee, that's too bad. Chuck Piper of Bear Archery is with me." Their startled counter, in unison: "Come on in!" Out rolled the red carpet! This was typical of the respect Fred and his company had attained in the industry.

The ensuing years found me very much a part of the Bear team. I was compensated, but never on a salaried basis. I insisted upon independence and the freedom of being my own boss.

From 1948 and into the '60s, we operated not only as a Bear dealer, but also a distributor and later, as West Coast Warehouse.

West end of museum.

East end of museum.

3

DISASTER
IN "SIBERIA"

It was the fall of 1950 — Washington hunting season. Jack Ott, Chuck Edwards and I had settled in for a week or two of bowhunting in what we called "Siberia," the far reaches of McCue Ridge in Nason Creek, an archery-only hunting area. It is about three by nine miles straight up and down mountains. Flattened out, it would probably be about the size of Rhode Island.

To those who hunted the Nason Creek Bowhunting Reserve through the years, the area became known as "The Mountain." It was astride the migrating route of mulies out of the Cascade Mountains, reaching into Canada. The big migrating bucks were known as "Mountaingators." The bigger ones, we called "Mossbacks." The cover of buck brush and aspen thickets on the south slope harbored the mulies as they rested.

We were camped in alpine country. A gurgling spring came out of some boulders beside our 11 by 14-foot white sidewall tent, anchored at the base of a slope near the top of the ridge. The land beyond the narrow flat that held our tent sloped on down the tree-studded north side. It appeared we would be in no pain. Not so.

The first day we scouted the area and took a few grouse for supper. Upon returning to camp, it was very evident that a bear had decided to share it with us. Food crates were dislodged, tooth-punctured cans strewn about, powdered soap dribbled all over — in fact you could follow the trail of soap where he had actually run off with it. Even

Jack and Chuck setting up camp in "Siberia," 1950.

Glenn, Chuck, and Jack with grouse for supper.

Exit the bear couldn't find when he got inside the tent.

our old black sheet metal stove, spattered with bacon grease, had been knocked off its pins, and another exit hole ripped in the tent simply because the bear did not bother to look for the wide open entrance when he left.

Obviously we had to take measures to cope — hide food as best we could. We loosened all the tent ropes and pulled up the stakes. Ropes holding the tent at each end were looped over small spruce trees that would give at the slightest tug. After returning from our hunt the next day, we knew he had been back and done a lot of snooping.

Early the next morning, while heading down a well-traveled deer trail about 30 yards from camp, I observed a huge bear pile right in the middle of the trail. Hmmmmm, I mused, this bear sure was making good use of our soap. I continued on a few yards, stopped and thought, that pile doesn't look right. I went back and garnished it with a few pieces of toilet paper and went on my way. Later that afternoon, I joined up with Jack about a mile from camp. We headed for our canvas "barn." When our footsteps could be heard from the tent, out bounded Chuck, deep concern etched in his face. "You guys all right?" he retorted. "Yeah," we replied. "Boy, oh boy! From my observation down that trail, somebody around here is in deep trouble!"

OUTWITTING THE BEAR

It was obvious if we were to continue hunting out of this camp, some drastic measures would have to be taken regarding the bear. Chuck came up with a solution. He would GET that bear! The plan was for all to leave the tent at the same time the next morning. Chuck would stop off the trail about 15 yards away from the tent, hide and wait for the bear. Hopefully, it would be another sunny day, and the bear's shadow would be silhouetted inside the tent as other objects were.

With everything in place the next morning, to get the bear's attention we made a noisy exit. Chuck hid in a clump of nearby brush. Jack and I trekked to the top of the ridge where we would drop over the other side to hunt the mulies in the aspen thickets. We hesitated to take in the scene below — the tent — Chuck in hiding — the bright sun silhouetting the objects in the tent. A movement near the tent entrance caught the eye. Sure enough, the culprit was back. The bear stood up, looked all around and headed inside. The bear's moving shadow could be seen on the tent walls.

Chuck moved to a shooting position and made the shot. *A loud crash!* Then a most astounding thing happened! The *whole camp* disintegrated before our very eyes! A moving force, surely! In seconds, a ball of canvas headed for the lower slope. The bear, in a hurry to leave, had apparently caught his chin on a clothes line. He was kicking, clawing, *bellering!!* Chuck was screaming, "I GOT HIM! I GOT HIM!" Such a din, you could hardly imagine. Who was getting who became an issue, when the ball of canvas lodged against a tree. Chuck rushed into the mess and out came the roaring bear! Chuck was knocked to the ground and the terrified bear took off for parts unknown, apparently none the worse for wear.

Jack and I, by now, were headed back to the scene. After getting Chuck back on his feet, we sorted through the mess — no blood, nothing. The whole thing was an utter disaster. Yes, we did find the arrow intact, *inside the old black stove!* So much for trying to do in our harassing bear!

BEAR PROOF CABINS?

As a result of this bear episode, it became generally accepted that if you were to have a good hunting camp where bears abound, it would have to be in a more permanent camp than canvas tents.

In 1951, Bob Kelly, Bob Arvine, Bill Jardine and I decided to build a cedar shake cabin in the lower reaches of McCue Ridge — about 2,000 feet lower in elevation than the area we called Siberia. We were far enough along with the "Chalet" to begin hunting out of it in the fall of 1952. We figured that if we got one or two years out of it at most that it would be all worthwhile. It still stands today — 46 years later!

In 1955, we decided we needed a hunting cabin on Thompson Ridge to cover the migration route off the lower end of McCue Ridge, about 2-1/2 miles southeast, as the crow flies, from the "Chalet." As there was no cedar in the area, it was made of fir logs, a one-story affair. We had considerable help from Ronnie Raume and ex-logger Wayne Hathaway in handling the logs. A family of pine martens watched our every move from their nest in the top of a 20-foot tall fir stump. We thought they were cute until Howard Vallentyne hung a deer nearby. That night they ravaged the carcass, eating most of the exposed choice parts. As if that wasn't enough, a week later one of the martens squeezed its way into the cabin in the middle of the night. Bob Arvine felt it as it crossed his bunk. With a howl, he leaped to the floor from his top quarters. Flashlights lit up the place and before someone had presence of mind to open the door to let the terrified critter out, the interior was in shambles.

Through the years, many a bowhunter footprint has led to and from these cabins. Everyone was welcome. Chuck Kroll came from as far away as Michigan to hunt the mule deer migration from Canada to their wintering grounds.

The timber in Nason Creek has been logged except for patches around the "Chalet" and the "Fort." The logging company respected their existence. As for being *bear proof,* the "Fort," yes. The "Chalet," no — even though we put an opening in the bottom of the door, the bear did not recognize it as an exit and would bash his way through one of the shake walls!

Bob Kelly and Bob Arvine at the cedar Chalet, 1952.

The Fort, 1955.

Inside the Chalet — Margaret's sister Rosie taking a turn at dishwashing atop the "Toad."

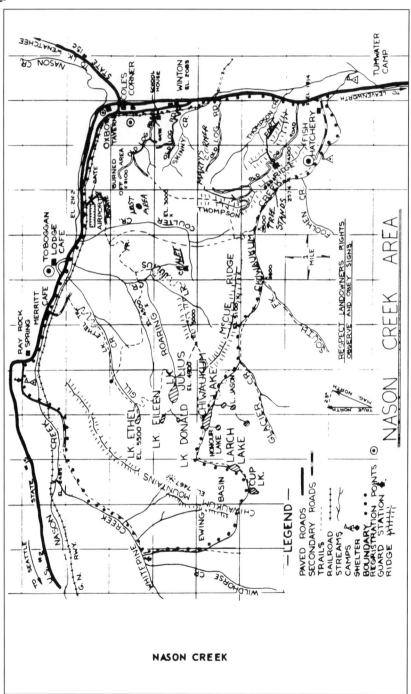

NASON CREEK

4

A WALK
IN THE WOODS

The usual hunting talk is beginning to subside — how they passed up shots — they're waiting for the big one. Hey, I've hunted with these guys for the last 30 years. Bob Kelly, Bill Jardine, Bob Arvine, they are my cronies — a man's gotta have cronies. *We're all trophy hunters . . . until something else comes along.* The chattering has stopped and, from the noise level that is beginning to rise, yes, they are asleep.

From the rattling of pans in the living quarters below, it is obvious that the resident field mice have taken over, all vying for the goodies left over from the table. That won't take long. Next they'll be back up here bouncing back and forth across our sleeping bags looking for a warm place to snuggle — occasionally inside.

This two story chalet, a crude cedar shake structure about 12 by 14 feet, is our hunting camp. Vintage 1952, it is completely hidden in dense timber and sits astride the best doggone migration route of mule deer coming from the far reaches of the Canadian border.

I am wide awake on my back, looking at the rafters above, brushing an occasional mouse off my chest. I am planning tomorrow's hunt. The sound of a bubbling creek outside is trying to put me to sleep. But no. I keep asking myself, where will those critters be? A light snow is falling, adding to the some four inches that are already out there. This is the first snow, the one that triggers the rut and tells the animals that it is time to get out of the high country and prepare for the winter. This first snowfall will disappear and allow time for the energies of the rutting animals to be restored before the real winter hits. If it's still snow-ing in the morning, I reason that I should look under the cedars. If it's wind and rain they'll be in the aspen and vine maple thickets. Sun and melting snow, the sunny slopes will be the place to look. Yes, if I were a deer, just where would I be? It's the answer I'm looking for. I'm ready. I have already checked off all the preliminaries. I've seen several deer. Lord only knows why I can never shoot the first one. I guess I just don't have my juices up. The clatter of the first underfoot grouse has scared the living daylights out of me. The first squirrel chattered away any shot that I might have had at a nice buck two days ago. Even a marmot has seen fit to give me a whistle — probably my plaid shirt. Yes, I've honed my senses to all the sights and sounds of the woods. It's time.

Long before daylight, I wake to the crackling of a wood fire in the black iron "Toad" below. Some of the aroma of fresh brewed coffee sifts through the cracks of the loft floor and if the snorts and blows of the other two still up here mean anything, that coffee aroma will soon be overpowered. As we peel down the ladder to the deck below, we are greeted by a cup and Kelly's favorite — bacon, eggs, and pancakes.

The sting of the ice cold water from the wash pan really sharpens one's appetite. The cakes are flipping and flapping. Bill's and Arvine's stomachs are very accommodating. A morning constitution later, I'm polishing off the last of the cakes. I am pouring syrup out of the chim-ney of a Log Cabin syrup can. Low and behold, out comes a long gray tail!

"E-gad! We've GOT to do something about these mice!"

"Yeah," Kelly remarks, "let me know when you figure out how to take care of ten million acres of them!"

"Let's keep the lid on that can, fellows," I plead. "I guess this little furry guy was sacrificed to get even for the rubber blunt thumping we've been giving them off the walls."

Kelly, having done his chores for the morning, with bow in hand, heads out the door. "I'm headed for Marty's corner. See ya."

Arvine, our so-called second cook is gathering up the dishes. The mice will clean up the scraps. Bill, never in a hurry, is contemplating over another cup of coffee. I'm gone.

"I'll be up at the saddle," I say as I go out the door. "Got a hunch, with this clearing sky, there'll be critters on the sunny south slopes close to the vine maples."

A thought — how would you readers like to go with me to the mountain? It's early and, if you have the time, I don't mind taking a little detour to a lookout about the 6,000-foot level. There you can get a pretty good handle on the whole Nason Creek Reserve. It's a climb — about 1,500 feet higher than the cabin — won't take long if we are not interrupted by a critter along the way. Bring your field glasses. You'll need a flashlight part of the way. It looks like there's about six inches of snow.

We'll head up along this open hillside parallel to the cedar flat where we got our shakes and material for the chalet. Beyond that is a spring feeding the creek that runs right by the cabin. The fresh snow deadens the sound of the crusty stuff underneath. Look out for the snow that will be falling from the willow branches as we plow through. The big buckbrush wall you see up ahead is the east side of the saddle that rises 25 or 30 yards above the slope that we are on. The flat of the saddle is where I generally start looking for the critters. It will be daylight about the time we reach the top.

Traversing that wall was not too bad. There is nothing in sight so let's proceed right on out to the Lake Julius switch-back trail. This is where I'll really begin the day's hunt. I'd like to get back here about the time that the sun ball breaks over the horizon and brings this flat awash. It will bring the deer out from under the snow-covered cedar trees that ring this area. We'll be gaining a little altitude and more snow, but the view will be worth it. See that rotten stump up ahead? I'll have to take a couple cracks at it. Got to get in tune with the environment. I don't like to take the first shot of the day at an animal.

Left-handed? Yes, shooting the bow is only thing I do left-handed. I switched about five years ago because of a problem. How did I cope with my right master eye? An instinctor doesn't worry about that — you shoot with both eyes open. Anything to the contrary is a myth. Fred Bear and many others are switch-shooters.

Let's go slow now, blow ourselves a little before we ease over that small rise. Got to be ready . . . you never know. O.K. All clear. Here's where it's at — where the ponderosa pines and clouds join. God's country. Look at the COLORS, even in this early light. It's THAT time of year. Julius and Eileen are the lakes nestled in the rock potholes below. Their waters are deep, cold, and harbor lots of fine trout. Many have felt the bend of the fly rod. Some even made it to the fry pan.

The furthest lake away is Eileen — the big rock on the far side. I leaned a bow against that chunk one day and, while scrounging firewood on the hillside beyond, I dislodged a boulder that rolled down

Looking over the day's work.

the hill and all but demolished my bow. Another string made it usable, but barely.

There's momma bear and a little guy down there on that snow line sucking up the last of the blueberries. Use your glasses. They are really fueling their winter gas tanks — I do mean literally. Lake Ethel lies on the other side of that ridge beyond Lake Eileen. You can't see it, but I know it's there. The tall rock pinnacles on the far side of Ethel are like a dam holding back the waters from spilling out the east side of the area. Those boulders along the horizon gather the sun's rays and, on occasion, harbor some nice bucks that like the warmth they find there.

From here, walking along the top of that wall looks easy, but don't you believe it! The trail is treacherous; you dislodge a pebble from the off side and it will wind up an avalanche 2,000 feet below.

That big mountain of rocks over there sits on the southwest corner, the highest point in the area, about 7,400 feet — not a blade of grass on the last 500 feet. I had to see what was on the other side one day. While nearing the top, a pint-sized pika rabbit ran down to greet me like he was going to eat me alive. Had me worried for a few seconds. There is nothing on the other side but more rocks which taper off into brushy slopes and benches that end 5,000 feet below, at Wild Horse Creek, the west boundary of the Reserve. Those were the days when I was known as "Ridgerunner George." I had to climb over everything just to see what was on the other side. I don't do that anymore. I know what's on the other side.

Back of us, off to our left, southeast — that big stand of ponderosa pine on the horizon — is Marty's corner. Kelly is going through it now like a fine-tooth comb. We've taken a few nice deer out of there and he knows where they hang out.

Well, that's about it — an hour into daylight. I have to get on with today's hunt. I'm sure you know your way back. Perhaps our paths will cross again some day. Stay here as long as you like. You'll really see the autumn colors when the sun reaches the hollow below. Drink in all the good stuff you can. You'll not find another place much closer to the Guy above.

The deer pasture that I'm going to doesn't need any witnesses. I want to be alone, if and when the once-in-a-lifetime comes along. Every time is a once-in-a-lifetime experience — all different.

Back down to the saddle, the sun is just breaking over the horizon. It will soon warm the nearby cedars. Deer should be hiding under their branches. As I traverse through this area, a slight breeze at my back isn't helping much, but I have no choice in getting to the wide dome ridge that will take me down to the lower slopes where all the deer seem to be headed. Tracks are everywhere. Now I have a quartering wind in my face and it will be a long haul to traverse from one side of the ridge to the other. Huge ponderosa pines dot the slopes, snow drifts piled at their base. There are a couple of deer, off to my left, just going out of sight. The sun is now beginning to wash this ridge. The deer seem to be feeding on a broad leaf plant that pops up through the melting snow. The pine branches are beginning to unload their covering of fresh fluff. There is still enough crunch left in the old snow to dictate that I stop once in a while, for 10 or 15 minutes, to allow time for a wandering critter to walk into me without hearing. From my perch now, I can see the stand of timber around the chalet off to my right about three quarters of a mile away. The sun is just getting to the slope above the chalet area where I took a nice heavy buck last year.

Yes, it appears that I am pushing the deer out ahead of me. It's about 10 a.m. I have reached the lower part of the ridge where it spreads out into a willow and vine maple flat about the size of a football field. The southeast side tapers off into the slope above the chalet. From the number of tracks going into this flat, things could get interesting. However, for now, it's time for a candy bar.

A nice big granite rock accommodates the seat of my pants as I anticipate the sweets. Gad, that wrapper makes a lot of noise! Sounds like someone stuffing a wastepaper basket. Next, an apple. Noisy, you bet. I have a feeling there's critters around. You probably know the feeling . . . like you're being watched . . . like something else might have heard the candy wrapper and crunch of apple. Foreign sounds competing with the falling chunks of snow. My head slowly pivots. Yes, my bow is ready, arrow nocked . . . it's always ready when I'm lookin,' listenin,' eatin,' and sittin.'

Did I see a glint off to my left on the edge of that flat? Yes, my field glasses confirm it. Horns! Fragile looking horns and the dark horseshoe above the eyes facing right at me. He not only heard, he sees. O.K. No use getting excited, don't make any fast moves or moves indicating I see him. Don't try to get out of sight. As long as he sees me and doesn't know I see him, there are possibilities.

Sounds complicated, doesn't it? Not really. A shot, there isn't. He's way too far. A close encounter perhaps, if he likes the area and I don't push him out. So, I'm sounding like a wishful thinker . . . anything but realistic. Surely, he'll spook any second now. O.K., but that's what it's all about — the unknown.

You start with the bare necessities. A loaded bow across your knees. You are sitting on a rock with a half-eaten apple in your lap and a pair of field glasses glued to your head, a deer standing, in snow, partly hidden by willows — out of range. Is this just a sighting or a possibility of a happening? It won't take long to find out. I stand up in full view, looking away, toss the apple aside, jostle my quiver of arrows back into place on my shoulder, stuff the arrow in and out, all as if I don't see, oblivious to anything unusual.

Trying to be nonchalant, I observe out of the corner of my eye, that he is still there, watching. He turns away like he's about to bolt, but no — seems like he's preoccupied with something else of more concern, perhaps another buck, a doe, whatever. Could be the rut. There is a well-used trail and a definite musk scent in the air. Possibly he has a set migration direction in mind and I'm in the way.

As we continue to watch each other, he nuzzles a willow sapling and starts walking diagonally, as if to go around. I counter by appearing to move away, but get behind some cover and sneak a little closer to what could be an ambush. However, conditions are still not right as he continues by. As he is about to go off the flat and down the slope, he looks back at me, makes a couple of bounds — probably winded me — and is gone. I tiptoe to the edge, only to be caught flat footed. There he is, squared away, looking right at me like he was expecting me. There we are eyeball to eyeball, neither making a move until I begin to cramp up. In such a situation, it is very difficult for me to look ho-hum. Difficult for both of us, because I know my own dog can tell when I'm thinking bath for him, even when he's not in the same room. I can only back off and give him lots of space. I wait in ambush with the remote possibility he will come back. Yes, 15 minutes or so later, he is slowly entering the flat — of course I am in the wrong place. Like my dog, this buck knows. He's looking and listening as he heads right back to where he was first sighted. Such behavior, the likes of which I have never encountered before!

Obviously, scent-sound-sight is not a factor. Well, this cat and mouse operation lasts for three or four more hours until a well-defined oval trail is worn in the snow. At times, I wonder who is following who. Rarely do I catch him broadside. I am either looking at his rear end or front end. The gap is closing, however. He is getting used to my presence . . . maybe he likes me! He certainly appears in no hurry to bring this episode to a head and I am beginning to wonder how much more of this fun I can stand. I'll have to figure out something. There has to be a way. Next time around, I'll try something different.

At the lower part of the loop, where the buck jumped down the slope, there is a little mound, sparsely covered with waist-high buckbrush. It is about 20 feet higher than the trail. If, in following the buck as he goes down the slope, I could cross over to that mound, I would be able to observe the lower trail and the buck coming back up the other side onto the flat. Surely, there would be enough cover, one way or another, for an ambush at very close range . . . I'll check this out.

I'm trailing him, but not too close, as he heads down the trail. I sneak over to the mound and get high enough so I can see where he will turn the corner below and, hopefully, head back up to the flat and past the mound. He occasionally looks back. I have scooped up some snow and toss it down the slope where I would most probably be. He looks back at the sound, and, yes, he is coming back up the slope toward my position. All the while, I am looking for the place a shot can be made. Not this time, I think — the next time, if there is a next time, if he doesn't figure out what I am up to. I'll let him go by and note the brush and the openings with possibilities. The shot will be downhill about four bow lengths, at most.

He appears to be stopping more often and listening. Perhaps he suspects because he is not hearing everything the same. I hold my position until he is clear out of sight. Meanwhile, I want to get behind again to assure him that I am still there. If all goes well and nothing changes, I have about 30 minutes to decide what to do.

Now it has become a question: if given the opportunity, do I really want to take my friend? He has given me a great hunt already — excitement, unknowns — one-on-one. Patience has allowed me to get his guard down, like moves in a chess game when you make moves anticipating the opponent's moves. I guess I'm just trying to justify what I am about to try to do. Yes, after all, this is what it's all about. Even if I don't make the shot, what happened today will never leave my mind (as even now, about 40 years later, I am emotionally writing it). No matter what, I assure myself, I'll never have regrets.

Why couldn't I have just jumped the critter, real close, shot and had it over with? The better part of the hunt is history. To culminate it is agonizing. Maybe this will make up for the doe I surprised in a brush patch earlier. I had just separated a small herd of deer from an aspen thicket. Something out of the corner of my eye got my attention and then I found my broadhead right on the nose of a doe which had hung back to care for her fawn that couldn't keep up. It was a very happy feeling to see her bound away with the little guy in tow.

Well, while the decision is still being made, the buck and I slowly head back to the ambush area. He goes over the end, down the trail. I gather up a snowball, crawl over to the mound, toss the snow down to where I should be. He's on the way back up and now I must pick the right patch of brush that he will be up against when he goes by. He stops, looks back, starts up — this is it! The bright coloring, where the arrow enters the snowbank beyond, tells me that it's over. There will be no need for another arrow. There will be no trailing, no lingering anguish and no beating of drums. I know why I wanted the Guy up there as my only witness. He knows my feelings and understands the contest between the hunted and the hunter. The buck has slid down the snowy slope into a little hollow. A beautiful animal — heavy — neck a little swollen, the rut could have dulled his sense of survival.

With the legs bunched up and tied together, the animal is ready for the slide down through the snow to the cabin. My bow is slung over my shoulder freeing my hands for the task of dragging the critter over logs, bumps and hollows. The camp robbers are already on the gut pile. As I make my way down the hill, I hear a raven sounding off across the slope. He knows and will be there shortly looking for his share.

It's 3 p.m. Where did the time go? Five hours! It was as if time stood still. A wisp of white smoke is threading its way out of the cabin area. Somebody's back catching up on the chores. Sure, I could go for help, but no, I need to spend more time reflecting on the day. Besides, there is a lot of daylight left. I need to unwind and be alone with my thoughts. I recall that I had two other such encounters where migrating-bent deer would not turn back, insist upon going through, but never have I had one go by and return. A "walk in the woods" . . . an animal . . . what a hunt! And you can be sure the story will be one day put to print.

It wasn't long before all the logs and brush patches had been negotiated and I found myself close enough to call for the guys.

What followed is a another real part of what it is all about. Whoops and hollers, a pat on the back, sharing with friends. With the critter secure under the cedar canopy, things finally quieted down. You knew we were back to normal when Kelly, cook extraordinaire, asked, "Where is the liver?" Yes, it will be liver and onions tonight.

With our dinner over and all the stories of the day told in detail — near encounters, four grouse that had fallen to their arrows — all in all, it was a great day with more to follow. The season isn't over yet.

"O.K. guys, ante up, it's jacks or better. Bill, will you please disturb that gray critter that's sitting on the window sill next to you? I can't concentrate with that piercing stare . . . Which reminds me, we'll have to open up another can of syrup in the morning."

The aging process begins.

5
WILD BILL

Another story that needs to be told happened in 1948 in Natapoc, one of Washington State's Bow Areas. The story is best told by "Wild Bill" Childs, a Californian who came with friends to participate on this hunt. Although, perhaps the word "activist" was not a household word in 1948, by today's definition "Wild Bill" was one of the most prominent activists for the sport of bowhunting in the state of California. This story is from the May/1949 <u>Archery</u> magazine.

YEAH – I GOT ONE, TOO

by *"Wild Bill" Childs*

The scenes, action and people depicted in this narrative are not fictional. Any semblance to persons now living or dead is purely intentional and if I slight some of my companions or pass over their deeds too lightly, please forgive my transgressions and remember that my best will be but the work of a clumsy pen and faulty memory.

I respectfully dedicate this poor narration to Tommy, Glenn, Margaret, Orlin and Biz, Louie and Helen, Herb and Maxine, Ed Ferru and the many archers of Washington who made our stay there so pleasant.

I know they at least will read it and forgive me . . .

*   *   *

I don't mind the flu — or the pneumonia, but when the doc tells me I have to spend the winter in Southern California under a sun lamp, I wonder if last year's deer hunt in Washington was worth it. I am fully recuperated by summer except for a wheeze and a slight halt in one leg where rheumatism has settled, and start building myself up to where I can shoot a thirty-five pound bow again. Then comes an invitation from Washington to enjoy the 1948 hunt at Natapoc. Now I know another month of the frozen north will be the end of me, but it is better to be dead than show the white feather at a time like this, so I start to work on some self-preservation.

I gather around me three of the most rugged individuals in California for a conference and explain my plight to them. We study Admiral Byrd's releases on his trip to the South Pole and wind up buying all the stuff he used and maybe some extra. We get a house trailer, insulated and guaranteed to float, and weather-proof it from stem to stern. Our bows, arrows and clothing are paraffine dipped and we shove off for Washington.

At Natapoc we borrow Orlin Lawson and his ten-ton potato truck and head for the nearest sawmill and buy eight cords of pine slabs or maybe a little more to keep the shelter fires warm.

We moor the house trailer to two pines, fore and aft and dig drainage ditches around our traveling ark and lay in a supply of gas for the furnace we have installed in it. We close our ears to the cat-calls we receive from our more sturdy northern companions, and smirk at each other because we remember how we laid in six inches of rain last year in our sleeping bags and know what they're in for this year because they're not prepared.

For the next thirty-one days we sizzle under a molten sun like a white hot poker dipped in a rum flip. We suffer from the heat with the mossback denizens of Washington and maybe Idaho, too. We bathe daily in the Wenatchee River, which should have been frozen over, and sleep at night beside our costly trailer house. They take pictures of us and our house and label them, "The California Boys Roughing It."

"Ridgerunner George," sometimes known as Glenn St. Charles, is very well qualified to give Roy Hoff lessons on deer missing. I'm not saying that Glenn couldn't hit a bull at three paces with a handful of bird-shot, but something is always happening so that George's big game kills are far and few between and sometimes worse than none at all.

Tom and I are sitting at the top of a rocky ravine watching two large does feeding three hundred yards below us, when we see Glenn

Glenn and Harvey Burnett sharpening 'em up for the occasion.

working his way up the ravine from the bottom. We get up and flush the two deer down the ravine right on top of Glenn. They set back on their haunches and slide to a stop nine yards this side of him and sit patiently side by side while he draws and shoots — twice.

We scramble down to Glenn and see him staring dismally at two broadheads buried an inch apart — exactly half way between the two sets of empty deer tracks. He says, "I couldn't make up my mind which deer I wanted so I guess I shot at the two of them."

His sad story touches our hearts so to show our sympathy we take him to the small bottom opening of a box canyon next morning and stand him where a weasel will have to wiggle between his feet to get past. Tommy and I work our way up and around and drop in the top of the canyon. We leave our bows on a ledge, separate ten feet apart, and at a sixty-mile-an-hour clip we cover the canyon from side to side as we work toward Glenn. We head everything in the canyon downhill — lizards, small birds, rabbits, grouse, coyotes, and lots of deer.

After our forty-sixth lap we stop for a breather and watch the avalanche of meat descend upon Glenn and wait for the massacre. The air is dark with escaping birds but the animals are all heading for Glenn, and leading the pack are six deer running nose to tail. We watch Glenn's bow arm come up, steady, and freeze. Slowly the nock comes back to the corner of his mouth. The big Ace head rides tight against the knuckle of his bow hand. He looses the screaming arrow into the face of the thundering herd and dives to one side as one by one they gracefully leap over his posterior. We pick Glenn up and dust the hoof marks off his back as he incoherently mumbles something about "thirty feet of solid meat — and I never touched a hair."

Now of all the people beside myself that I feel sorry for, the number one candidate is Ed Ferru — a sturdy little fellow and one of the best bowhunters I've ever seen. Ed is being seen around and about camp two days before season opens with a three-weeks vacation tucked in his back pocket and maybe a couple of extra days if he needs them. He is walking on air because he is going to hunt and hunt and live the life of Riley for three whole weeks before he has to go back to the old grind and start worrying about maybe a few bills and things that have been accumulating during his spree. I am going to tell you about the reason for Ed's sadness and his final melancholy departure from camp. The Washington season opens Sunday at dawn, so just as a mental hazard and maybe a handicap, the W.S.F.A.A holds its annual meeting in camp the night before. Now there is high goings-on during and before and after this meeting and maybe a party or two later. During this melee I must admit that I partook of a few sundry and different bottles and jugs of mixtures of a sort and sometimes a little camp food and also a few mugs of vicious coffee that was brewed for no reason whatsoever by Dave Hamlin and Louis Baldi. This coffee is not fit for a pig to drink because next morning I am so sick from drinking it that it ain't funny and I can stand for no light whatsoever to crash against my defenseless upturned eyeballs. The moral of this paragraph is that you should never drink lethal coffee if you plan on getting up early enough to catch the worm, or maybe a deer. Ed Furru and the HEARTY souls in camp break out at an unearthly hour to catch deer — minus me.

By nine o'clock in the a.m. Ed is back in camp with a numerous horned deer that is as big as a cow or maybe a small moose, and he is as happy as a lark because it is a beautiful deer indeed and he feels very fortunate to have bagged same. But by Monday or maybe Tuesday, Ed ain't feeling so happy because by now he has forgotten about his beautiful deer and time is hanging very heavy indeed on his poor hands and he has nothing much to do if any. He don't have much company because the rest of the camp denizens are very serious and bloodthirsty hunters for about eighteen hours a day and they have no time to waste sitting around gassing with Ed, who is forced to live the life of Riley because he kills his deer too soon.

Ed gives up his easy life about Wednesday and goes home to work in the garden or maybe sit around, and he cusses the buck that robs him of his beautiful three weeks vacation at Natapoc.

Maxine Phillips is the proud owner of some black curly hair, a pair of snappy blue eyes and a big forked horn deer that she bangs right in the ribs with her arrow while at Natapoc. She is also the owner of a husband named Herb who will be known from here on as Maxine's husband or Mr. Maxine Phillips. Herb is now enrolled in that legion of lost souls who are unfortunate enough to have a spouse who goes out and bags a buck deer. Maxine's wonderful deer and Herb's downfall happens about like this . . .

Herb comes into camp opening day dragging a big fat old deer by the ear. Now that is a lovely situation for Herb to be in because doe meat is just as good eating as buck meat and maybe a little bit better, and it takes more skill to kill a doe than a buck because a doe is a little smaller, more or less.

I can see that Herb is tampering with his luck right about now because he decides to linger in camp a few days and let the spouse try her luck. I can also see that Maxine is going about this hunting business in a very earnest manner indeed, so I call Herb to the side and suggest that maybe we should kink her arrows a little or something to slow her down a bit. He seems to think he has everything in hand because her bow don't shoot so straight and besides she just broke it. I needlessly remind Herb of the sad saga of Orlin Lawson who let his wife get serious with a bow and bring in a buck of large proportions, and also a few other cases I am acquainted with in which the wife became the hunter of the family. Herb goes, "Ha, Ha," a few times at these tales and says my idea is impossible in his case, so I back off and watch things proceed and start happening indeed.

Maxine's first stop is Biz Lawson's camp, which she departs carrying Biz's deer slaying bow, a dozen razor sharp needles and a whole noggin full of the finer points on the pursuit and dispatching of buck deer. Then she trucks off up Natapoc to the west slope where, in an unwise moment, I tell her about the big buggers I have my own eye on in this spot, but can't get within yodeling distance of.

Well, one of these big fellows pulls out in the open and strikes a pose and dares Maxine to shoot at him. Damn if she didn't let go with one of those little needles and smack him right in the ribs and the deer takes a hop, step and a jump and drops over on his ear — deader'n a mackerel. Then, to rub salt into the wounded pride of we poor males, she dresses the deer out while we sit on a stump nearby and sadly dream of the injustice of it all. One thing though, she can't lift the deer so she had to let us carry it in for her.

Some day I will finish this story of Natapoc and tell you all about how Orlin Lawson finally hit his big buck and how we trailed it next morning and came upon a big mess of bones the coyotes had cleaned. Hey, John Yount, do you pay off with the big game award on a bag of bones?

I would also like to tell you of the archer from Port Angeles who has the nerve to sit and tell us just how and where and when he is going to go out and get his buck the next day. Can you imagine that? But here's the pay off. He does it — and on schedule!

Yeah, I got a deer, too — damn if he ain't bigger'n three barrels of beer laid end to end.

1948 Bow and Arrow Reserve — Orlin Lawson, Tommy Loveland, "Wild Bill" Childs, and Glenn admire Bill's deer.

6

HUNTING THE OLYMPIC ELK

"So you want to go after the Olympic elk." This was the greeting from Lloyd Beebe. I had just pulled my car into the yard in front of his home near Sequim on the northeast perimeter of Washington's Olympic Peninsula. A cub black bear was swinging on a rickety front door screen. Another cub was asleep on the couch inside with all four feet in the air.

Lloyd and his wife, Catherine, were dairy farmers, loggers a close second. Cougar hunting during the winter months was one of Lloyd's main hobbies. And in their spare time, the Beebe's took in orphaned wildlife and trained them for starring roles in movies. Lloyd knew the vast Olympic Mountains so well that when anyone got lost in the coastal rain forest region, authorities asked him to search for them. He found many. Often he followed a trail of cast-aside clothes and abandoned gear; occasionally all he found were scattered bones. When asked, "Aren't you afraid you will get lost on one of your hunts or rescue missions?" Lloyd replied, "No, you don't get lost when you really aren't going anywhere."

This man was to be my guide, or maybe I should say companion, on the hunt. We had known each other as fellow bowhunters for years. Lloyd had lived in this elk country for much of his life. He knew elk

Roosevelt's elk country.

habits, he knew their "talk." He had taken many movies and still pictures of them in their native haunts. Obviously I was in good company.

Being late November, there would be little if any bugling. It was past the rut. It would be cold, foggy and wet — perhaps some snow. We planned to pack nine miles into the Bogachiel River corridor. The corridor reached like a bony finger — three miles wide by fifteen miles long — deep into the western edge of Olympic National Park. The backdrop, if you could see it through the ancient forest, would be 8,000-foot Mount Olympus, the dominant snow-covered peak overlooking the rugged Olympic Range. This is in the coastal rain forest of western Washington. Moss-shrouded trees form a canopy overhead, so thick in some places the sun reaches little of the ground cover. However, there are wide open areas throughout. There are alder bottoms, moss-covered ravines, each with its own little creek cascading through devil's club, ferns, boulders and rotting logs. You can unwittingly walk out on one of these huge fallen logs and suddenly find yourself 20 feet above the ground.

This fascinating country would be our hunting grounds for a week or as long as it took, chasing what the natives call Olympic elk. However, they are now known as Roosevelt's elk. These elk were named in honor of our 26th president, Teddy Roosevelt. Considerably larger than their Rocky Mountain cousins, they have dark, shaggy manes, tawny hides and blend in extremely well with the surrounding habitat.

The plan was for Lloyd, Bert Wallis, Hennie Cummings and me to pack in a ten-man life raft and all necessary food and gear. We would use the raft to float all of our gear and any animals we harvested down the Bogachiel River.

The trip began at the end of a park trail where the river crossed under Highway 101. The trail led through part of the Olympic National Park before it reached the corridor. At the park boundary, manned by a concerned Park Ranger, a sign made note of the fact that no firearms were allowed beyond this point unless sealed. Our bows and arrows did not violate this, so on we went through light snow deposited the day before. The trail stuck close to the river and at times forced us to criss-cross its frigid waters. It was a cold, wet and exhausting trip for this hunter whose body hadn't really prepared for such an outing. Lloyd and the others took it in stride. Elk sign was everywhere — this was not exactly a biological desert.

About a mile before we got to our intended destination, hypothermia was settling into my bones. Lloyd mustered a fire out of the damp

Bert Wallis preparing to head out from the Bogachiel elk camp.

woods and Bert and Hennie quickly had a nice warm tent in place. A cup of hot soup found its way into my hands. Later, after a dinner of stew and hot coffee, it was off to bed.

Daylight the next morning found us heading upstream again. Fog hung over the river. A short time later we set up our permanent camp in a little meadow, beside the cold clear Bogachiel. There was still time to do some scouting. Bert and Hennie chose to scout the north bank, Lloyd and I the camp side. The sign that we were seeking showed up in a big alder bottom about a mile from our camp and you could bet we would be back there the next morning. Bert and Hennie came in with glowing reports of what they had found on the opposite bank. They had watched a sizeable herd cross the river and would be headed for the ridgetop in the morning. The rest of the evening we spent preparing our equipment by lantern light, sharpening our Ace express broadheads mounted on Sweetland's forgewood shafts. Our bows were my baleen-backed self yew wood bows with 60- to 62-pound pulls.

The next morning, we headed for the alder bottom where we had seen fresh sign the day before. This bottom was typical — a ground cover of alder leaves, rotten moss-covered logs, sword ferns, and dense patches of four to five feet tall blueberry bushes. A low-lying fog slowly drifted through the area. It would be reasonable to assume that when we sighted elk, we would be very close.

Moving along a game trail through the area, we soon found ourselves in the muddy tracks of a sizeable herd. The pungent smell of elk hung in the air. Lloyd cautioned that we could jump them at any moment. After 50 yards or so of one-step-at-a-time, Lloyd suddenly pulled up short and pointed to some alder tops ahead. A thick cloud of mist filtered up through them. He motioned for us to back off. Fifteen yards back along the trail, he whispered, "That's vapor coming off the warm hides of the herd." Oh boy! We had found them!

We immediately got out of the noisy mud and circled to our left away from the herd to find a place where we could observe without being seen by all those wary eyes. We found an old uprooted tree whose root mass had been washed free of all the dirt and debris creating a perfect screen. We sneaked up behind it and peered at an incredible sight! More than 60 critters lounged before us, some looking almost like the moss-covered logs they were laying beside, others casually browsing. There were bulls of every size, cows, calves. Yes, a herd, the likes of which every elk hunter dreams.

This was not a good situation for a stalk. On the way to any one of them you could spook another and blow the whole operation. They were spread out all over the flat, 30 or 40 yards away. Surely I could launch an arrow from where I was standing. But no. Lloyd and I would wait them out and look for a better intercept somewhere else. Sooner or later, all would be up browsing and moving.

Feeling that they could not scent our outpost, we decided to have an early lunch. One of the browsing calves wandered our way ten minutes later, spotted us and hurried back toward the herd.

"Now, watch what happens," Lloyd whispered to me. "The calf will sound alarm, but since he's just a 'kid,' they won't pay any attention." Sure enough, the calf barked — a gruff, coughing sound. Nothing stirred. The calf continued to look our way with apprehension, uttering an occasional alarm. We kept watching and nibbling on our sandwiches.

After half an hour or so, others in the herd got up and started to browse. One cow finally was in a position to get a clear view of us. She stared us down for awhile. Then, deciding we were something to be alarmed about, she barked. This really got the attention of the rest of the herd, and away they went, popping up out of the brush and ferns from every direction. Naturally, I was disappointed about not having taken a shot.

"Not to worry," Lloyd assured me. "They will leave a very obvious trail and won't go far. We'll give them time to settle down. Let's go down a bench or two toward the river, finish our lunch, and take a few practice shots."

After about an hour of embedding arrows in rotten stumps and logs, we resharpened the heads and moved in the direction the elk had taken until we found their trail again. Small trees had been bowled over, mud splatterings everywhere, and they had plowed deep furrows in the ground. After about a half a mile of slow easy climbing from one bench to another, it appeared that the hill was topping out. It was then that we began to hear what sounded like magpies chirping. We could also hear an occasional stomp and a bull began bellering, topping off the utterances with a series of low, guttural grunts, not really a bugle. The herd was just over the rise, deep in "talk!"

We eased up over the edge and what we saw was quite startling. They were feeding in a huge blueberry patch, bulls scattered here and there. One huge rack stood out above all the others, a cluster of points gnarled off the royals on each side. He was on an upper bench swinging his head and nosing the ground, while looking over his flock as if in defiance of any interference from some of the smaller interlopers . . . shades of the rut! Moss hung in curtains from the lush trees and sun rays streaming through the steamy vegetation added a surreal touch to this whole eery scene.

Cautious as it was, our approach did not go unnoticed. There were just too many eyes watching from all directions. One cow, especially, seemed very concerned. Although there was very little movement in the air, our scent must have wafted in their direction, because they all suddenly quit feeding and looked around. They started milling slowly as if they were looking for direction from the herd boss — generally a wise old cow. The bulls slowly worked to the perimeters of the herd.

I loaded for action and prepared to move to intercept one of the less wary bulls; but no, Lloyd's wisdom prevailed. My broadheads were destined to rust a little more. The sights and sounds from the milling elk were incredible. They finally headed down a creek bed toward the river, barking and brushing aside trees.

"Now we will get some shooting!" exclaimed Lloyd. We waited till the main herd got over the side and out of sight. Then we were pinned down for the next few minutes by a cow — evidently the lookout. Only when the rest of the herd was off the bench and down the hill did she follow them. We raced away, circling around to the left, then paralleling the elk down a small ridge about a 100 yards or so from the creek bed they had gone down. We dashed pell mell through the jungle thickets, over moss-covered rocks, and under huge deadfalls. Lloyd reasoned that they would be going much slower than we were. After a quarter mile of this, we set our sights on intercepting the herd. Sure enough, after going into several gulleys and over a number of small ridges, we could hear them sloshing down the creek. They were still quite a ways uphill from us, and, as we crept up to the last little ridge overlooking the drainage that we figured they were coming down, the noise became louder and louder.

We stationed ourselves where we could see them as they approached. They were jostling and talking to each other as they moseyed along. A shot directly below us would be about seven or eight yards. The noise they were making along with the bubbling creek would certainly drown any sound from above. Several cows and calves led the procession, followed by some small bulls. Excitement soared as I saw a huge rack hove into sight. Boy, was he ever old and gaunt, a bag of bones — but he had the horns!

I got set for a shot at the old monarch. In no hurry, Lloyd was relishing the experience, a wide grin on his face. As I drew, I felt a "WHAP," a chop to my bow arm. My bow and arrow lay on the ground! "Don't shoot that old critter," Lloyd said. "You wouldn't be able to put a fork in the gravy! Take one of those nice fat cows."

Oh no, I thought! Lloyd was strictly a meat hunter. Putting good meat on the table was his priority. I had no choice. We dispatched two nice cows with quick clean hits. The big monstrous rack bull and all the rest of the herd slowly walked by without a clue as to our presence. I couldn't help thinking about what might have been, but I was happy.

We quickly quartered the cows, leaving the hide on, and stacked the quarters on piles of brush to keep them off the damp ground. It was about a quarter of a mile to the river where we would bring the life raft the next day to float the meat to our camp. With heart, livers and back-straps in our packs, we headed for our canvas haven downstream. There would be fresh meat for dinner that night, and much rejoicing with Bert and Hennie. Hopefully they, too, would have some interesting experiences to share around the fire.

Hunting the Olympic elk is truly an unforgettable experience and hunting with Lloyd Beebe added a whole new dimension!

A Return To The Bogachiel

It's November, 1951. The day before opening of the bulls-only gun season for the Olympic elk, I am headed back to the area of the Bogachiel River corridor where I hunted successfully last year. This time it's with John Wolz and Wayne Hathaway, a taxidermist, both from Port Angeles, Washington. The week before, we had taken in most of our gear and set up our camp beside the river, about the same place as last year. Today, John and I packed in food and extra gear while Wayne carried the eight-man life raft to float us out at the end of the hunt.

The hike in was the usual tough grind so we are dog tired when arriving late in the afternoon. We get a few chores taken care of and are gathering a wood supply when three gun hunters hove into camp! Surprise? You bet! The coffee pot is on and we feel it proper to share it with them. They are new to the area and look to us for a little help. All we can think of at the moment is for them to locate a quarter mile upstream and suggest that they hunt the timber on the other side of the river. At that campsite they will find a big log where they can cross the fast-flowing stream. The gun hunters were soon on their way.

We continue preparation for the morrow, securing more dry wood and fire-starting pitch shards. Lunches are prepared and quiver packs loaded with necessary gear. We coordinate our plans. We will split up to cover as much ground as possible, and locate the herd or herds, or at least, find where they have been feeding. Most likely, like last year, the elk will be found in one of the alder bottoms along the river, or on one of the blueberry and fern benches that rise in a series toward the ridgetops.

We are up before daylight. A short breakfast later, we are on the move. John and Wayne head upstream through the alder bottoms. I will start directly away from the river and cover the benches back of the camp for about a half mile or so, then swing in the direction of my other two companions upriver. Somewhere along the line, one of us will certainly find some fresh sign! There is a light fog hanging over the area. It is cold, cold enough to see one's breath.

As I slowly make my way up the benches, I cross several well-used trails, old tracks in mud. At one point, I reach a bench with an almost unpenetrable growth of vines and brush, and course the perimeter until coming to a tunnel-like opening I can crawl through. It opens into a small meadow-like area — a carpet of finger-like fungi, short grass, and moss. At the far end, about 30 feet away, is a backdrop of several big logs suspended about three feet off the ground. It is dark in there. While still on my knees, my eyes come into focus and I find myself looking eyeball to eyeball with an elk that is lying down just beyond a huge moss-covered log about ten yards away. The log has the usual tiny evergreens and salal growing out of it and is covering the elk's head, horns and any other positive sign that it is a bull for the taking. About ten feet to my left is a chipmunk, chattering up a storm, looking upon me as an intruder.

The elk does not move. I'm afraid to stare for fear of giving it some reason to leave. Perhaps it doesn't sense that I am aware of it. This happens with animals. All kinds of thoughts raced through my mind. Regardless, if anything good to come of this, I must get my bow through the crawl space and get in a shooting position on one knee. While trying to appear as nonchalant as possible, I slowly drag the bow on through and get into position. With arrow nocked, I am now ready. My only shot would be at the base of the neck. The dark shaggy mane hair gives me a clue, but that's not enough. I have to be sure that it's a bull. It occurs to me that, if and when the elk does stand up, its head will be above the log and I'll know if it sports a rack. Oh no! At the same time, his entire body will be covered by the log. Such a dilemma! Chances are it's a no-win situation, but I must hope. Perhaps the noisy chipmunk will be the play-maker?

After seven or eight minutes of this standoff, I'm beginning to feel a muscle cramp coming on. It will be difficult to stand up without moving forward because of the brush hanging on my backside. To do any moving would mean stretching my luck in keeping the elk where it is. Finally, the chipmunk makes a move — a beeline toward the elk. My quarry jumps up and pauses long enough for me to see that it has a full-blown rack! It slowly walks out of its bed, leaving between the logs. A shot? Legs — head — horns do not call for loosing an arrow. By the time I stand up, get my wits about me, crawl under the log and get out into the open, the elk has long gone. I feel drained. I have to sit and unwind a minute or two before picking up the trail again.

The tracks lead me to a muddy trail where it heads to the upper reaches. I continue to follow. As I climb I find a sifting of snow on the ground. Apparently the bull had settled down. I see where he has stood in one place long enough to snatch a bit of browse. About 50 yards fur-

The boss rests.

ther on where the slope levels off is a man track following the bull. Surely, it is either Wayne or John.

As I continue along the way, I come to a huge area that is loaded with blueberry bushes. The smell of elk is in the air so now I start looking and listening for telltale signs, like rising vapor — chirps. Yes, there is a faint sound of "elk talk." Now, my ears pick up a distinct "whop" — the sweet sound of a loosed bowstring meaning that an arrow is in flight! I don't hear the "chunk" of a hit, but the sound of crashing trees is unmistakable! Scrambling bodies! Then another whop! I hurriedly make my way along the trail toward the sounds and there is Wayne polishing off a spike bull! Wayne is happy to see me. Congratulations are in order! I am just a little too late to get in on the action. Now there is work to be done. There will be another day!

Wayne thought about 30 or 40 elk were in the herd, several bulls. He had slowly trailed the bull I was following for about a quarter of a mile when he spotted the herd feeding along a swath of blueberry bushes. He backed off, circled around, and entered the blueberry bushes 100 yards or so ahead of the elk and let them feed in to him. The spike bull was the first one to come into his bow range broadside, at 15 yards. The spike was a beautiful animal, huge in keeping with the fact that a mature Roosevelt's bull can weigh 200 pounds more than a mature Yellowstone elk.

Wayne made short work dressing out the critter, and since we weren't equipped to carry out much meat, we stacked it on some branches and small downed logs so the air could circulate. It was one o'clock as we prepared to stow the heart and liver in our quiver packs and discovered our forgotten lunches. We made short work of the sandwiches and headed for camp, planning to be back tomorrow with necessary meat-packing gear and more manpower. Perhaps John and I will get in some hunting. That herd won't be far removed from this area.

We headed down through the benches going abruptly to the river. As we approached the gun hunters' camp, we observed one of the hunters hovering over a lively fire and a pot of coffee. He wanted to share it with us. We told him of the kill but were careful not to say where. He had found some old tracks on the other side of the river. We suggested that we could use another pack if there was one they could spare. It was agreed and Wayne would pick it up in the morning on his way back to the meat pile.

John was in camp and starting to prepare supper. Some liver was added to the fare. It was a happy threesome that went through the details of the day. John had gone upriver beyond where Wayne had cut off. He had seen lots of tracks — jumped one elk. Couldn't tell if it was a bull or a cow. We conjectured it was probably one of the lone bulls that hung close to a herd. The rut is supposed to be over. We were not hearing any bugling. However, the loners were still hovering nearby.

Before hitting the sack that night, we made plans for the next morning. John and I would retrace my steps from this morning and join up with Wayne at the kill site about noon. We would be hunting all the way in. Early morning found us making our way over the clutter of downed logs, through ferns, and across creeks lined with devil's club, stopping briefly at the place where I encountered the bull and the chipmunk.

A short while later, we hit the main muddy trail. One fresh track loomed out at us as we made our way up the benches. This time, we combed the area slowly on each side of the trail, peering over every little ridge and hollow. As we approached the top of the slope, we stopped to wind ourselves and then cautiously peered over the top. There before us, not 15 yards away, was a many-horned critter feeding, head down, with his rump facing us. It looked good to me as I drew my already nocked arrow and let fly, hitting the bull inside of the left ham. As the bull jumped, he presented a shot broadside to us. John's arrow was now on the way, striking high in the center of the back. My arrow appeared to have penetrated to the bright yellow feathers. The bull in headlong flight could be heard for some time, crashing through the brush and trees.

Now it was time to wait and conjecture. Either arrow could be fatal if there was enough penetration. I really don't know what equipment John was shooting, but I had shot a 660 grain wood arrow out of a 62-pound static recurve Bear Grizzly. After a long 30 minutes, we proceeded to check out the encounter area. There was no problem tracking — like following a bulldozer.

We found the bull a short time later. Wayne was sitting beside it! He had spotted the fresh track in the light snow on his way in to the meat pile. He followed it a short way to where he saw the bull lay down and then roll over into a mud hole created by the rootball of a big tree. One of the antlers was buried in the mud clear to the socket! It was a five by five — not the crown head that I had seen the day before.

Glenn with hunters about to head down the Bogachiel.

Now we really had our work cut out for us. This critter could weigh 1000 pounds. Getting the antler out proved to be a real problem, taking us about 20 minutes to move the elk in a position to extract the horn from the mud. Dressing the critter out, it was determined John's arrow had not penetrated the heavy back bone into the spinal cord. My arrow had brought it down. It is difficult to describe one's feeling when you see a magnificent animal of the rain forest fall to the ancient weapon. While there is a sense of accomplishment, I am always torn — my level of emotion has always been pretty high. I elected to take out most of the hide to assure I'd have a good shoulder mount. The weather was cold and clear, assuring a quick cool-down with little chance of souring.

A rifle shot in the river valley reminded us that there were gun hunters about. A barrage of shots indicated that they must be practicing or sighting in their rifles. Not a good situation if we choose to do more hunting. Oh well, there was plenty of meat for all of us. Wayne then told us that when he picked up the pack at the gun camp and headed upstream, he stopped once to get a drink at riverside. When he looked up, he noticed that he was being followed at a distance by the

The 5-point fits nicely on the fireplace wall.

gun hunters. So, instead of heading directly to the meat, he kept going upstream and back-tracked to throw them off the track.

Now we had the meat of two bulls to pack out. We checked out Wayne's stack of meat. There he and John each loaded their packs with hams. I strapped my elk rack, the hide, the heart and liver to my pack board and we headed down to the river. There we built another crib and a shelter of boughs to store the meat until we were ready to raft it out. We kept out part of the backstrap and shoulder to give the gun hunters on the way in to our camp. When the gun hunters found that we now had two animals down, they were concerned. They hadn't seen much of anything. That soon changed as we made trip after trip with the loaded meat packs for the next two days. We decided that we'd had enough. Competing with the gun hunters would be a little difficult and awkward.

One bright morning, we loaded up the raft with all of our gear and meat and headed downriver. We tied our bows and valuable gear to the raft with rope, which proved to be a lucky thing. The river was low. It was so shallow in some places and our raft so deep in the water, there were times we had to get out to bump it through while pulling with ropes from the bank of the river. About halfway through the nine mile trip, we got hung up on a log, and the raft overturned, dumping us and all of our meat and equipment that wasn't tied down. After a mad scramble for a quarter mile, we were able to gather everything and continue on to a happy landing where our truck was parked by the highway.

A great trip? You bet! The water-logged meat turned out to be the best ever!

Lost In The Rain Forest

November, 1952. Lloyd Beebe and his friend Del Ray, with a string of pack horses, set up a camp in the middle of the Bogachiel elk hunting corridor. It consisted of a cedar shake cook shack complete with a cook and a huge army tent that would house 10 to 12 hunters.

This was prime Olympic elk country as attested to by the successes we'd had in the last two years. With the word out about our two previous years, this camp was full of eager hunters. Besides furnishing all the meals, the camp put up all the lunches and the rules. When you checked out in the morning you would give general directions as to where you were going from a big map which hung on the cook shack wall.

Come opening morning, Keith Gunnar and I had paired up and headed out through the alder flats in back of camp and would climb the benches beyond, and if nothing showed by the time we got to the top we would take one of the ridges downriver in a westerly direction.

We hunted hard and wound up getting lost. Getting lost in the Olympic Rain Forest can be quite an ordeal and this was no exception. Keep in mind that the country was covered with ancient trees, cedars 10 to 15 feet at the butt, huge spruce, and firs. Steep hillsides with ravines, like fingers, from the top clear to the bottom drained the area. Devil's club, little waterfalls, and rock slabs covered with slippery wet moss made for hazardous walking. There were alder bottoms lined with thickets. Some places, visibility was near impossible. There was fog, snow in patches and it was WET. Clouds rolling in from the Pacific Ocean dump 200 inches of rain on this area every year.

This day, we were quite lucky. It wasn't raining but we were lost. Lost in the sense that the ridge we followed downstream sheltered a

Elk hunters Lloyd Beebe, Chuck Edwards, and Irl Stamps.

Cook shack.

pretty good-sized creek on its south side. We started out with the creek close by. As the ridge topped out and we started down the other side, it was far below us. We didn't notice where we could no longer hear the creek and apparently didn't notice a fork in the ridge, but did notice when we got to the bottom and into an alder flat that the creek we decided to sit by for lunch was flowing in the opposite direction than when we started out! Our compasses verified this and we immediately lost our appetite and decided that determination of our location was a PRIORITY!

After five hours trying to retrace our steps on slopes unrecognizable, since we hadn't paid much attention to them when we came through in the morning, it was time to take stock of our situation and prepare for spending the night out. We sought the highest prominence in the area, one that overlooked most of the countryside east and north of our position. Although there was still quite a bit of daylight left and a long twilight, the gray sky and deep timber would soon eat up that light. We felt our way out would probably be northeast but weren't sure.

As evening wore on, we managed with our belt axes to cut enough fir boughs for a shelter. We gathered what little dry wood and pitch shards could be found from the underside of toppled snags to get a fire going, all the while keeping our eyes peeled for smoke, any clue as to the whereabouts of the cook shack. While gathering firewood from the ground, out of the corner of my eye I thought I saw a speck of light to the east. Couldn't confirm it with a repeat glimpse. I marked the spot and called Keith over to help with a possible detection. We crawled around that spot, raising and lowering at different eye levels trying to pick up the elusive sign. Keith finally spotted it and was able to hold it in view. It had to be a Coleman lantern hung on the side of the cook shack like the ones there the evening before.

We had to make a decision. Was there enough twilight to get us off that mountain safely and into the bottom? Could we intercept the main Bogachiel trail which would take us to that light? It was far out — just a pinpoint of light. But should we take the chance? Anyone in his right mind would have waited till morning to head down. Then we thought how the others would be concerned. It would be disruptive to the hunt and we had best try to make it!

We snuffed out the fire, gathered up our gear, stuffed it in the little sacks on the backs of our quivers, unstrung our bows, pocketed the bowstrings, and peeled over the side of the mountain and down a steep

Looking over the map.

In cook shack after a tough day in the rain forest.

Bill Jardine's truck camp with elk hunters preparing to head out for the Olympics.

ravine. The ravine was dry when we started down, but a couple hundred yards later, we found ourselves sloshing in water — runoff from the hillside. In all, it was a mad scramble! Flashlights were not yet necessary. Hopefully we could at least make it to the bottom with the light we had. Bows in hand, we only had the other arm and hand to help in our descent. We had put on rain gear to protect us from the elements, mainly the devil's club, and when we finally made it to the bottom, we were wet, cold and our rain gear was pretty well ripped up.

A short rest and a couple candy bars later, we struck out by compass in a northeasterly direction hoping to intercept the main Bogachiel trail. After traversing several alder bottoms, and crossing creeks on slippery logs, with barely enough light, we intercepted what looked to be the main trail . . . horse tracks . . . the trail we were looking for!

An hour or so later, as darkness settled in, we hove into camp. A couple of bedraggled looking characters, tired, but nothing that a hot meal and a cup of coffee wouldn't cure. There had been some concern for us but it had not yet turned to alarm.

So much for the '52 hunt. As I remember, three elk were taken. 1953 saw the camp in operation once again, but that was to be the last of the hunts in that area. After the 1953 hunt, on January 6, 1953, by proclamation of President Harry Truman, the Bogachiel corridor and other small parcels that had been overlooked before, became part of the Olympic National Park.

ELK CAMPS

My favorite animal to hunt has to be the great Olympic elk. Between the '50s and '70s, we spent time in many camps throughout the area. We hunted National Forest lands outside the National Park. On the coastal slopes there are very many short rivers draining the mountains into the ocean. They support some of the best steelhead runs in the world. Their drainages are also great elk habitat. Most of the rivers have Indian names such as Dosewallips, Humptulips, Hoh, Quinault, Queets, Bogachiel, and Calawah.

A big gravel pit alongside Matheny Creek, tributary of the Queets River, was one of our best so-called "hot spots." Year after year we put up a tent city complete with generator for lights and a fir-lined privy. Bill Jardine's big-bodied truck served as the kitchen and contained several bunks. Come fall, seven or eight of us called the gravel pit home . . . the likes of Mal Malinoski, Warren Berg, Jesse Rust, Bob and

Olympic elk camp at Matheny Creek.

Wayne Buck, and those mentioned in this story. From there, we had access over old logging roads to many creek drainages, deep canyons, ridges that spread out like fingers of your hand, and a patchwork of clearcuts and timber — BIG timber.

Matheny Ridge was where Bill Brown stalked a lone bull for hours and finally brought him down as he edged out from behind a big spruce. The royal fourth point was broken off the right antler and still scored enough to be the first Pope and Young world record. Bob Beebe shot a three-point one afternoon. It immediately jumped into a vast patch of salal bushes six feet tall, elk trails all through it. We knew it was down. We could SMELL it! We hunted all night with lanterns and finally found it at 3 a.m. next morning, 50 yards from where it had been shot! While glassing for elk from a high vantage point, I watched Chuck Kroll, on a nearby hillside, patiently try to set up a shot at a two-point bull feeding back and forth through a blueberry patch. Two hours later, he came away empty-handed without having loosed an arrow. He

Lloyd Beebe, right, and Del Ray, center, bringing the raft into the landing.

had come all the way from Grayling, Michigan to hunt with us in the Washington rain forest and loved every minute of it!

Feeling adventurous, Bob Kelly, Arvine, Jardine and I hauled an eight-man life raft to the headwaters of Matheny Creek with the idea of floating back down to scout its perimeter for elk. We started in fairly flat water. That was soon to change. Deep narrows through rock boulders with fast, rough water terrorized us much of the way. And finally near the end of the trip, we hit a sharp splinter sticking out of the bank which penetrated one of our main tubes. Half the raft collapsed, dumping most of our bows, quivers, arrows, and other gear into the water while we hung on to the other half for dear life. We finally beached the raft about a quarter mile from the camp. One of the Kodiaks was later found where it had lodged in a pile of brambles in the middle of the river. Bow collectors might do well looking for three others, a Bear Kodiak and two of my Thunderbirds, along the banks of Matheny Creek!

Early one morning, the wife of one of our elk hunters came to pick him up. For some good reason he was wanted at home or at work. On the way out he was doing the driving down the dirt outlet road. His wife, sitting in the passenger seat, glanced out her side window at one of the many logging roads. "Oh," she remarked, "someone has a bunch of pack horses down there." A quarter mile later he came to his senses, stopped the car and exclaimed to his wife, "What did you say?" "Nothing," she replied. "No," he shot back. "Not now — back there aways." "Oh, that," she remarked. "Somebody has a string of horses on that side road." "Pack horses, my eye!" he exclaimed. "Nobody is fool enough to bring pack horses into this big timber where there are no pack trails." Almost before he could finish the remark the car was headed back to the gravel pit. He literally tore up the road on the way back, and glanced at the questioned side road — sure enough an elk herd!

The gravel pit gang still in camp gathered up their equipment and headed out for the attack. Yes, the herd was still there feeding through a clearcut just off the road. There were enough of us to literally surround them. I headed for the big timber nearby guessing that they would head in that direction when they left the area. As I got into position, the herd had spooked and was headed right for me! I hid behind a huge fallen log between me and them — surely the log would turn them and I would have a ringside position to loose an arrow as they turned away from the log. But no. They were on the run! The next thing I know I am staring at the hoofs of many jumping elk! I ducked

Bert Wallis at elk camp shelter in Olympic Mountains.

the first one and hastily found a place to lie under the curve of the log as the others, about 30 of them, sailed on over. All I got was a good view of their bellies. So much for THAT day!

In 1964, Margaret and I bought some ocean property on the Quinault Indian Reservation near the village of Queets. Access to it was the Cape Elizabeth Road, put there during World War II. The road's purpose was to access the U.S. Military, in case the Japanese invaded the coastline. Interestingly enough, aircraft spotter shacks were still in place on all the prominent cliffs overlooking the ocean, with Japanese aircraft silhouette posters still nailed to the walls.

We built a 20 by 24-foot shack on a shelf of land 40 feet above the ocean high tide mark. The framework was from salvaged lumber off the beach. We covered the outside with 6-foot cedar shakes cut from fallen cedar logs on our property. Each fall it became a hunting headquarters for elk hunters — 15 minutes from prime elk country. George Moerlein, from Alaska, hunted one season out of it with me in the early '70s and remarked that this was the only cabin where you could tell which way the wind was blowing *outside*, by the way the clothes drying on the line *inside* were moving.

In the winter of 1994, the cabin disappeared off the shelf. The winter storms had eaten away the bench and it simply toppled into the ocean. Since then, I have been looking toward Hawaii, China, Japan, or anywhere west for someone I can collect some cabin rent from.

Yes! Every season, two or three elk were taken from these camps. It was camaraderie at its best!

The Pacific Ocean elk cabin.

7

TWEEDSMUIR PARK,
BRITISH COLUMBIA – 1954

The scenes of some of my most memorable experiences were in Tweedsmuir Park in west central British Columbia, Canada. It is a huge island park surrounded entirely by a chain of beautiful lakes. At this point in time, these lakes were gradually being engulfed by a flooding of the surrounding terrain as a backwater of the Kitimat Dam. This hydroelectric plant was to generate electricity from the flow of waters that surged through a tunnel in the coastal range and exited on the Pacific Ocean side.

Tweedsmuir Park was not open to settlement of any kind. The only access to this pristine wilderness was either by boat or float plane which could land on its many lakes. The coastal range, with its many jagged peaks, served as a backdrop for this land of tundra meadows, wildflowers, crystal clear streams, and thickets of tag alder, aspen, jack pine, and larch. Truly, this was a hunter's and fisherman's paradise. Moose, caribou, goats, grizzly and black bears were in abundance. Marmots chorused through the high country. Porcupines and wolverines waddled and loped aimlessly about in their search for food. It was not uncommon for a hunter on a campout to be awakened at night by the howl of a wolf so close you could hear the foot pads on the trail as they raced by. Every stream and lake was alive with hungry trout.

I spent three different seasons hunting there with a bow and arrow, beginning in 1954. My host and guide was pipe-smoking Wes Loback, who called Seattle, Washington, his business home. He and his

"Loback Spread" with Lake Ootsa and Tweedsmuir Park in the background.

brothers operated a very popular meat market at Seattle's famous Pike Place Market. His hunting and fishing lodge, located about 50 miles south of Burns Lake, and just across Lake Ootsa from the northeast side of Tweedsmuir Park, at Marilla, British Columbia, was now our headquarters.

Loback's "work horses" consisted of two aircraft, two big outboard motor boats, and a canoe. The Cessna 190 wheel plane ferried him and his hunters back and forth from Prince George, British Columbia, and Seattle. A 1,000-foot landing strip stretched out beside the lodge. A 180 Cessna float plane was used for scouting and getting him and his hunters in and out of the park. Nate Metcalf, of Seattle, was his partner and camp roustabout — a very pleasant and personable addition to the crew.

Our native guide was Charlie Michel, a 40-year-old Stick Indian. A deeply-etched face made him appear very much older and he did have the savvy of a man twice his age. Charlie was also the winter caretaker for the Loback spread. Although better quarters were available, his choice for a year-round home was a 24 by 30-foot dirt floor log

Loback's trophy room.

"Work Horses." Note lake debris in background.

cabin. This he shared with his wife and two small youngsters, a boy and a girl. His needs were meager and, as most natives of the country, they lived off the land and government subsidies. Staple foods he bought at the country store, about 30 miles distant. There he also bought the ammunition for his old reliable Model 94 30-30 Winchester carbine. Speaking little English, he would simply flourish his weathered trigger finger in the form of a "W" to get the right ammo. This carbine was certainly not a potent weapon by modern standards, but it was all Charlie needed. You would never see him without it and he really was an incredible shot with this old beat-up machine.

Wes Loback, although being a very capable and affable fellow, was prone to being absent-minded — the kind of absent-mindedness that could cause a horrible accident. It kept us on edge much of the time just wondering when it would happen. He had to be reminded constantly to check the oil in his engines, pump the water out of the pontoons, etc.

August, 1954. I am here upon the invitation of my very good friend Bryan Stangle, a part-time bowhunter. He had successfully rifle hunted from this lodge with Wes Loback several years before for bear, goat, and moose. Bryan knew that I was always looking for a good bowhunting area and thought that I should check this one out. We had just been driving for a grueling two days from Seattle over the most God-forsaken trail-like road. A highway is being built from the Canadian/U.S. border through the Frazier River Canyon to Prince George, then west to Burns Lake. There, we turned south, ferried across Francois Lake and overland to our destination, the lodge on Lake Ootsa. It was a welcome sight, and a beautiful place. The interior was quite modern, with a combination lounge and trophy room overlooking the lake and facing Tweedsmuir Park. This lodge and the camps nearby were to be our headquarters for the next two weeks.

This day, we will call DAY ONE. There was much activity outside the lodge and at the dock. Two lake boats were being relieved of what looked to be a ton of moose meat and lake trout. In addition there were four hunters and two Indian guides. They had just returned from a moose and bear camp, 35 miles down the lake chain at the junction of Chelaslie and Euchu Lakes. The four hunters would be heading home to California in the morning.

DAY TWO. It was evident, with the departure of the hunters, that Loback and his crew needed to unwind for a day or so and regroup before finalizing the plans for our hunt. Bryan and I also needed that day. We unlimbered our gear, and when the bows were strung and arrows began to fly, yes, we had an audience. You could have hung a hat on Indian Charlie's eyeballs. He had to tug at the bows, run his gnarled fingers over the broadheads, all the while his head shaking in disbelief. Wes and Nate had known we were bowhunters, but to Charlie this was a surprise!

For this trip, I had made Bryan three Thunderbird bows, 50, 60, and 70 pounds at 27 inches. His idea was that he would start with the 50-pound bow and gradually work through the 60-pound bow and hunt with the 70-pounder. He would try to take a black bear with that bow. While Loback and his crew were catching up, Bryan and I went plinking around the perimeter of the area. We even managed to bring in a couple of hapless grouse, which brought from Charlie a very toothy grin.

DAY THREE has now arrived. The guides are not quite ready to commit to our hunting trip. About 10 a.m., things were looking up and Nate offered to take us fishing that afternoon. Bryan was ready, but I opted to help Charlie do a few more home chores. After lunch, Wes took off for Prince George in the 190 to pick up a grizzly bear hunter from Seattle. They returned about 2 p.m.

After the unloading of the hunting gear and all formalities were taken care of, the good weather and anxiety of the new hunter prompted Wes to suggest that they take a quickie scouting trip over the park in the float plane. I was invited along, and as I never go anywhere in hunting country without my hunting equipment, I promptly loaded it in the back of the plane. I then flopped myself down on the apple box seat in the rear. A sleeping bag and a sack of survival food were beside me. The barrel end of a rifle was sticking out the top. As the plane engine warmed up, Wes loaded up his pipe.

There were wisps of vapor rising from the lake, as we taxied out and lifted off the water. A few white clouds hung over the park — in other words, a beautiful day for scouting. Wes proceeded to make a wide circle to encompass as much of the park as possible. Along the way we sighted several horned animals and a black bear or two. It is a generally accepted fact that where there are black bears, there are no grizzlies — blacks avoid them like the plague.

We had been out about 45 minutes and were on a course that would take us to a landing at the lodge. We flew out over the lake and were hanging close to a long, sloping sidehill covered with patches of low-lying brush. There, to our left, almost at eye level, was a grizzly sow with two large cubs. They were feeding among some tag alders along a stream that cascaded down the hillside. Wes swung around and went in close to get a better look. The cubs stood their ground and the old lady greeted us by standing and flailing at us, not a friendly gesture to say the least. We were close enough to see that she was really mouthing at us — yes, an awesome sight. Wes guessed her weight at about 500 pounds and cubs at about 300 pounds apiece.

Our bear hunter was fit to be tied and started shouting, "There's my bear!" He wanted a crack at it RIGHT NOW! Wes reasoned the cubs were certainly big enough to take care of themselves, the noise of a creek, tag alders, a perfect setup for a stalk, so why not? To be sure, the level of excitement now rose along with the extra smoke from Loback's pipe. I was apprehensive and, while Wes swooped in for a landing about a half a mile away, I was thinking that, in all respect for common sense, I did not want any part of this impulsive bear hunt. Wes taxied into a little cove and jumped out on a rock to tie up. The hunter grabbed the survival rifle — a 30-06, and was out the door right behind him. He headed up the bank.

From my apple box, I hadn't made a move. Wes noticed, motioned and exclaimed, "Aren't you coming?" "No!" I said as I put my head out the door. "The way I look at it, this is a gross example of how not to hunt a grizzly. The bears have all the advantage. You've literally stirred up a hornets nest up there. Did you notice the cubs didn't run for cover? They are big mature cubs. Wes, there are at least 1,000 pounds of angry critters up there spoiling for a fight. Your hunter has never shot that gun. The calibre could be a little on the light side to do the job. You don't have a backup gun. If your hunter doesn't bring that big bear down with his first shot, or if he wounds any of them, we could be in big trouble. They would be on us in seconds. I'm no Art Young or Howard Hill. Try to imagine how quickly I would abandon my bow and arrows in the face of a charge. My only thought would be how to outrun both of you. No, Wes, I didn't come up here to commit suicide! Count me out! However, before you go, would you mind giving me a one-minute check-out on how I could start this machine so I could taxi out of here to the lodge, just in case?!"

That did it! Wes pondered what I had said. A couple more puffs on the pipe and he yelled at the hunter: "Come on, let's get the hell out of here!" Off we sailed to the lodge and a fine dinner of fish the other fellows had brought in. The bear hunter was, of course, quite glum. Later that night, Wes took me aside and said: "Thanks, he's a lousy

Beached craft at junction of Chelaslie and Euchu lakes.

shot, even with his own gun. I'll find him another bear that doesn't have any helpers with it. It's hard enough to deal with one grizzly, let alone three."

CHARLIE BECOMES A BELIEVER

Early on DAY FOUR, Nate, Charlie, Bryan and I, in two boats, were on our way to the moose pasture at the junction of Chelaslie and Euchu Lakes, from where the four gun hunters from the States had just returned. It was sad to see all of the drowned trees around the edge of lake. The 35 miles through the flood debris took us about three hours. Wes was to take care of the bear hunter and would join us later. Our anticipation was pretty high.

The gut piles of the moose taken by the gun hunters before us should now be getting pretty ripe and a gathering place for foraging bears. The remainder of the moose residents had not heard rifle shots for three days and should be pretty well calmed down. Our camp was located on a flat finger that jutted out into the lake. After about an hour of settling in and getting oriented, Nate prepared a lunch. Bryan and I limbered our so-called muscles by stringing and drawing our bows. We plunked a few arrows here and there and noticed that Indian Charlie was watching. Yes, he was still leery about how potent these weapons were. Bryan was now shooting the 70-pound bow. As usual, he was only using about 50 pounds of it. I didn't have the heart to tell him that, with every shot, about six inches of the arrow was still out in front. Oh well, he wanted to try for a bear, and he'd only be shooting about ten yards at the most. Whatever the quarry, there would be a backup gun. Before any of us got to sneak around too far out in the brush, Nate and Charlie thought it best to check out the four moose gut piles. They wanted to know if the bears had found them yet, and if so, which bears, blacks or grizzlies. This would determine how we would be hunting.

Meanwhile, Wes Loback showed up in the float plane with the bear hunter. They wanted to know if any grizzlies had been sighted on the gut piles in the area. It seemed that only black bears had hit the piles. Wes soon took off with the grizzly bear hunter for parts unknown.

Nate was teamed up with Bryan to hunt bear or whatever they happened to run into and I was to hunt with Charlie. In British Columbia, at that time, each hunter must have his own guide. Indian Charlie was skeptical of my bow and arrows. Why shouldn't he be? His limited knowledge of what the outside world was doing could not relate to a weapon that was obviously less far reaching than his old Winchester. I felt that he was gradually cracking, however. He was curious. Surely the time would come when he would be curious enough to wonder what I really could do with this primitive weapon. Somewhere back in time his ancestors probably used similar tools for survival. Perhaps he was a little bit shy of taking me out with the bow. Perhaps he needed more time. Maybe we should get better acquainted with each other. So on this first day of action I suggested that we limit today's activity to fly-fishing, which I was itching to do anyhow. So, while Charlie carried my bow and quiver, I caught a nice batch of trout in a nearby stream. Bryan and Nate had stumbled on to a black bear feeding on one of the gut piles. Bryan attempted a stalk, but the bear got wind of them and took off. With time to spare, Charlie and I climbed a knob nearby to glass the surrounding area. We spotted several moose on a flat across the flooded lake. They might have to be dealt with at a later date.

That evening, while we were gathered around the camp fire, it happened. Charlie sidled up beside me and said, "Me, you, get moose." Early the next morning I was ready. I noticed Charlie, for the first time, was wearing soft clothes. He must be serious — he was READY. We boated down the lake very slowly, as close as possible to the flooded shoreline. We scanned the low sloping hills and flats for any sign of movement. Charlie must have had some preconceived idea as to where

A typical catch at nearby creek.

we were going. He shut down the noisy motor and took to paddling. I found that, while I was looking for moose, Charlie was looking for other sign. The boat suddenly slowed and turned into the bank. Charlie's eyes were on a grassy shallow ravine with a little creek trickling through it. Moose tracks were evident. Charlie scrutinized the area with a knowing eye — the bent grass, each track — and looked up the gradually-rising creek bed, which appeared to end in an aspen thicket about 200 yards distant. He checked the sun's position, sniffed the slight crosswind and proceeded to draw a picture in a nearby patch of mud. "Moose here," he said. His sign language and crude map indicated to me that a bull moose had been here a short while ago. It was now probably lying on the little bench on our side of the thicket trying to soak up what little sunshine it could find.

The plan was for me to go up the left side of the creek, very slowly, straight toward the bench and be ready to shoot at any time. Most likely the shot would come as I topped the slope. Charlie would circle around the right side and get into the thicket in back to keep the moose from going into this patch of aspens and possibly head the moose my way. I was, to say the least, skeptical. We hadn't seen anything yet but tracks. Did he really know moose habits that well? My answer was to come soon.

The big one!

Charlie followed the moose tracks up the slope. He was in sight some of the time. Once, he straightened up and looked my way. He sniffed the air and held his hands at his head like, "Yeh, big moose," and pointed toward the bench. I was nearing the top of the slope but worked very slowly, wanting Charlie to get around to the other side of the moose and into the thicket before I reached the top. Now Charlie was nowhere in sight. It was then I became a believer. All kinds of confusing things were going through my mind as I topped the rise. Slowly, a huge dark shape got up off the ground almost exactly where Charlie had said it would be. The moose was looking away from me and toward the thicket which hid Charlie.

To shoot now would be way too far — could I hit the side of a barn at that distance? Could I possibly get closer? How long would this critter ponder its position without lumbering off? While I was calm as anyone could be under the circumstances, I could not take such a long shot. I must get closer and did, through a swath of tall wildflowers — about another 30 steps! The moose then slowly turned and walked broadside to me. It was now or never! I mustered all of the instinctive powers I could to draw that 62-pound bow and, concentrating on a

Glenn congratulates Charlie.

patch of hair behind the front shoulder, let go. Yes, the arrow thumped into him and off he charged! Charlie had heard the hit. He came charging out of the aspens yelling, "You hit 'um! You hit 'um!!" Not knowing about the waiting period we bowhunters normally endure, Charlie was right after him!

Well, to make a long story shorter, Charlie found the moose on its side about 60 yards away. The big broadhead had put him down, but I proceeded to polish him off with more arrows. Charlie was all smiles. He was one proud fellow and it is well he should be. His incredible savvy had made it all possible. I, too, was most happy to have had that adventure with Indian Charlie. We had made "believers" out of each other!

The Canada moose rack scored out a respectable 164-1/8. The mount now hangs in my trophy room as a reminder of that memorable hunt.

BUYING THE FARM

At some time or another hunters who do a lot of hunting find themselves in a predicament they will remember forever — something that really makes your whole past flash by in a matter of minutes because your future at the moment doesn't look too bright. For me, it happened this way . . .

On this particular day, Nate and I were to bowhunt for goats on Michel Peak — one of the taller granite lumps on the northwest perimeter of the park. The plan was for Wes to fly the pontoon plane in as close as possible to the base by landing on one of the many small lakes near the foot of it. Wes sorted through a few, trying to find one deep enough to land on. His gauge for safe landing and take-off was how high the reed grass stood up in the water. If it bent over, it was too shallow; straight up — it was O.K. The one he picked was fairly round and looked to be about six or seven acres. He landed and put us ashore on the peak side. The lake, not big enough for a straight-of-way take-off, dictated that he go around and around to get up enough speed. That was standard procedure in these small ponds. We watched Wes disappear over the trees on the way back to the lodge. He was to pick us up an hour or so before sundown.

The goats were there on the mountain, all right, but we couldn't get to them. We tried every trick in the book to get above for a better overlook — no way. They kept out of reach of my arrows in their climb to the top and then went over the other side. It was too late to go on. We ate lunch about one o'clock and started down. The sun went over the coastal mountains about the time we reached the bottom. Immediately, it started getting quite cold. We made a small fire and waited for Wes. He was late and shadows were lengthening rapidly. We were attracted to a tinkling sound as the water lapped the shore — ice! The edge of the lake was starting to freeze. There was the drone of an approaching aircraft. Soon, Wes, with the floats, suddenly appeared over the trees. He dipped toward the lake, landed, and we hastily got aboard, noting to him the icing on the shoreline. Wes revved up the engine and proceeded to go around and around the lake for a take-off. No matter how much steam he got up, the plane would not lift off that pond! We now noticed that the spray off the back of the pontoons appeared to be freezing. Our main problem was, however, that the floats were, as usual, half full of water and were riding very low and heavy. This was perhaps a moot problem. Was there time to pump them out?!

A quick decision made by Wes. One of us would have to get off to lighten the load. Nate elected to do just that. Wes would take me to the big lake a half mile away, drop me off and come back for Nate. Wes tossed Nate a box of crackers and suggested he build a fire just in case. Away Wes and I went, around and around until finally we made it, barely missing the surrounding trees! We glided in to the big lake and taxied, not to shore, but to a big rock right in the middle of that lake!! There I was deposited and before I realized what was really happening, Wes took off to get Nate. While I watched that lunatic disappear over the trees, it occurred to me that he just might have "sold me the farm!!"

A survey of my 20-foot absolutely bare boulder produced nothing but a very bleak outlook — not a very pleasant place to spend the last hours of one's life! It was at least a good bow shot to the nearest shore. Even if I did make it, how would I fare with no clothes and no matches in the freezing cold. Swimming in that icy water was unthinkable! My only hope was in the drama occurring back at the small lake.

The top of that pond would be starting to freeze over and the chances of Wes getting off with Nate were lessening by the minute. Would they now have to abandon the take-off with Nate? Would Wes, alone, be able to get the plane off at all? It was very possible they would be forced to give up and spend the night there. Could I last out the night? This chain of thoughts passing through my mind was broken only by the distant roar of that plane revving up and down and flapping like a wounded duck around that little pond. This went on for about ten minutes, perhaps the longest ten minutes I have ever experienced.

Then there was a complete shutdown. My imagination ran rampant. What was going on over there? All was quiet! At a time like this, a whole life can pass before you. Could they be taking out a seat? Were they pumping out the pontoons. Boy, oh boy, my options on the rock were certainly limited — drown in the lake trying to reach shore or possibly freeze to death on the rock. I had matches. However, there wasn't a sliver of wood on this boulder. Five minutes — ten minutes

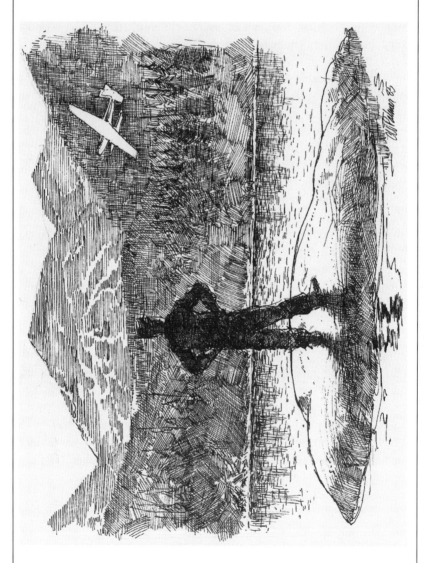

My rock haven?   Drawing by C.W. Palmer

went by. I thought I heard a motor cough — then again — and again. Now the motor was going full bore. He was trying once again — by the off and on again fades in sound from him circling the pond, he was frantically making a run for it. Then a tremendous roar as he poured the gas on for takeoff. He made it! In seconds, I could see the plane in the fading twilight barely clear the trees and head my way. Without experiencing this, you can't know the feeling!

As a pontoon slid beside the rock, I quickly got aboard. Nate was not with him! We took off the long way down the lake and circled back over the pond to see if Nate was alright. A small fire and a figure hovering over it. Nate waved. He had crackers, cheese, some dried apples and a 30-06. All of this would give him some comfort during the long night. In the morning he would have to walk his way about a half mile to the big lake along the rock-strewn base of the cliffs that the goats called home. It was an untried route. Hopefully it could be done.

Wes was pipeless — first time! He described the scene I had strained my ears for earlier. He had tried to get off the pond with Nate. It was no go. The water was just too heavy with the freeze. He unloaded Nate once again and to be sure he could get off at all, the two of them wrestled the caps off of the floats, grabbed the pump and took time to pump some water out of them. It worked — just barely! The next morning I went with Wes to check out the scene and hopefully pick up Nate at the big lake. As we approached the end of the big lake and my rock haven, Wes noted it and shook his head apparently in disbelief, while I conjectured as to how that rock MIGHT have looked.

Nate was there, alright, on the big lake shore hovering over another small fire and seemed none the worse for wear. However, he was very happy to get aboard and go back to the lodge for the hot meal awaiting him. We circled the little pond that almost did us in. A thin sheet of ice covered about half of it.

Such a harrowing ordeal all of us will long remember. I'll always wonder just how close I was to "buying the farm!" Meanwhile, all must have been normal for Wes, his pipe was once again fired up and spewing up a "storm."

This was bowhunting pioneering, something necessary to get bowhunting off the ground for future hunters. There were many outfitters needing to learn — untried guides. Bowhunters would learn from this mix in the wilds of British Columbia. This was a hunt and pioneering concept Fred Bear would relate to. Since I would be going back next year, I would most certainly invite Fred to come with me.

8

FRED BEAR JOINS GLENN ON
TWEEDSMUIR PARK HUNT – 1955

Fred and Henrietta Bear drove to Seattle the latter part of August, 1955. They visited friends and scenic places along the way. On the afternoon of the 24th they arrived at our home where they would stay until Fred flew north in Loback's Cessna 190. Henrietta had planned to visit friends in Oregon and Washington while Fred was on the hunt. She was not comfortable with flying in small planes and was not ready to change.

The next evening, Jane and Wes Loback hosted a dinner for all of us at their home. While there, Henrietta was persuaded to make the trip with Nate and me since we would be driving a station wagon, loaded with supplies, to the hunting lodge.

Early the morning of the 26th, Fred and I met photographer Don Redinger's incoming flight from Pennsylvania, and drove to a small field north of Seattle where the Loback's were waiting with their Cessna 190. Fred and Don hopped aboard with some of their gear and were off to the hunting lodge on Lake Ootsa just outside Tweedsmuir Park. It is an exciting and beautiful three hour flight through Canada's Fraser River Canyon, some of the most spectacular mountainous country in this part of the world. They would pretty much follow the highway to Prince George where they would pick up permits and licenses before going to the lodge.

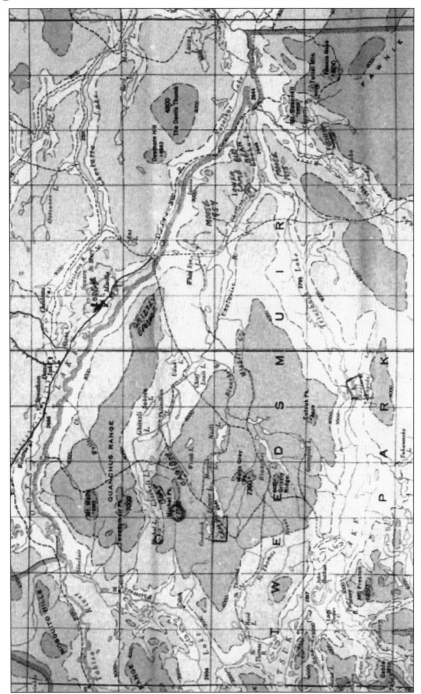

Tweedsmuir Park, B.C., Canada, scene of the action.

While Henrietta and Margaret ran some errands and did a little sightseeing, Nate and I spent the rest of the day preparing the station wagon for the trip north. We left Seattle at daylight the 27th of August.

It was a terrifying trip for Henrietta. The many curves around cliffs and the seemingly bottomless canyons we passed by on our way through the Frazer River Canyon were disconcerting to all of us. A night's stopover at Williams Lake was very welcome therapy. The rest of the way through Prince George and points west we coped with dusty dirt roads. From Burns Lake, we headed south, made the short ferry crossing of Lake Francoise, and on to the lodge, arriving at 5 p.m. on the 28th.

We found Fred, Redinger and the Lobacks "cooling their heels" in the lounge over a nice frosty brew. Fred's greeting: "What took you so long?" For the last two days they had been living the "life of Riley," scouting the area by plane and fly-fishing for trout at Redfern Rapids. We would be having some of their catch for dinner. Henrietta was delighted to find such a interesting place to read and write — a very comfortable setting, with bear rugs and all the other trimmings of a hunter's lodge.

What was happening around this triangular-shaped park at this time was quite spectacular. The entire area of flooding was now engulfed in different shades of red and brown as live trees were inundated and the dying process began. The lakes, rivers, and rapids that had not yet felt the full impact of the flooding provided excellent fishing — big hungry trout.

Loback found that the quarter mile stretch of lake between the lodge and the park was very deceiving when landing a float plane. When the water was calm, the unnatural shoreline of dying trees sticking out of the water seemed to create an illusion that the level of the water was not where it appeared to be. Sometimes he would have to make several passes to properly gauge the water line. On one such landing, I was sitting on an apple box in the back section. We hit the water so hard I went right through the box, crushing it to the floor!

Fred, Wes, and the two Stick Indians guides hadn't been idle while the rest of us were on the way overland from Seattle. Horses were barged across the lake on a raft and trekked to the prepared campground at the west end of four mile long Fenton Lake. The lake is situated in the northcentral part of Tweedsmuir Park — elevation 4,500 feet. Our campsite, from which we would be hunting, was in the middle of a 25 mile by 30 mile plateau, from which several 7,000-foot

Hunting camp at Lake Fenton.

peaks protruded. The north side of this plateau was nothing but cliffs which dropped off into a wide valley of lakes and marshes connected by creeks and rivers.

These cliffs are mountain goat country. Hunters access this by a series of deep rocky canyons that nature has cut from top to bottom. We would access the area by going overland from the camp or being dropped off by plane on one of the many lakes at the bottom of the cliffs — elevation about 3,500 feet. The west and south sides had rolling foothills reaching to mountains elevating from 7,000 to about 8,000 feet. East of this area the land mass dropped off into a flat region from which basic civilization was gradually creeping.

The ground cover of tundra, wildflowers and thickets of aspen were beginning to take on their fall colors, a sight one never forgets. This was the stomping grounds of the mountain caribou, moose, wolf, wolverine, bear and many smaller animals.

We would be going in to camp the next morning. Loback, wanting to use the twilight hours left in the day, elected to crank up the float plane and take a load of supplies to the Fenton campground. Meantime, supper was being prepared and we road travelers would attempt to clean up and get our feet back on the ground. The two Indian guides, Charlie and Don, were already at the Lake Fenton camp caring for the horses and preparing for the hunt. Nate was our cook and general camp manager. Weather and time permitting, we might get in some hunting tomorrow.

Wes was back within the hour. The main course of lake trout was quickly dispatched after which we prepared for a much needed night's rest. As I dozed off I contemplated tomorrow. Wes, Nate and Charlie had bowhunting experience with me from the hunt of the year before, but the new younger guide, Don, was untried.

Morning found us anxious to get going. There was much activity. After a sumptuous breakfast of sausage and eggs, the Cessna 180 float plane was fired up again and the process of ferrying more supplies and the hunters began. Two trips would be necessary. Wes would not be staying for the beginning. He had some maintenance to do and would come back later in the week.

Mountain Caribou

It was about lunch time when the campsite was secured and ready for business. Nate had prepared sandwiches and coffee. The weather not too bad — a little overcast and a light wind, but not enough to discourage the vicious black flies. Fred and I would do some scouting with the guides not too far out toward Michel Peak, orient ourselves, and really prepare to do business the next day. We collected a few ptarmigan which we would eat later. The scouting indicated that there were caribou on the low-lying ridges of mountain spruce southeast of Michel Peak. Most certainly that's where we would be going tomorrow.

A moose pot roast with all the trimmings was prepared for dinner. Later, we all sat around a campfire with stories of past hunts and what the program would be tomorrow. It was off to bed and soon it was morning . . . the kind that made you want to hold your coffee cup with both hands . . . cold enough to keep the black flies and no-see-ums down.

With the horses and guides readied, we headed for the hills we had scouted yesterday. Ptarmigan were plentiful. They were continual-

Ready to hit the trail.

ly being flushed out from under the horses hooves. Fred and I both had blunt arrows at ready in sidesaddle quivers, arrows we could shoot and forget if it was a miss — there were many misses. Before getting too far out, we decided to split up so we could cover more ground. Fred, Redinger, and the older guide, Charlie, went northwest toward Michel Peak. I would be with Don, the inexperienced guide, and go southeast to get into the lower reaches of Well's Gray Peak.

Shortly after Don and I split with Fred's party, we moved to where we could glass the surrounding hills. There were many fingers, and small ridges of spruce thickets, flats cluttered with huge colored boulders, and packed snow fields on most open slopes shaded from afternoon sun. The weather was meant for hunting — cool and a high thin cloud cover. The sun would be shining through somewhere.

We spotted a band of about ten caribou, feeding as they threaded their way through scrub spruce down one of the many ridges coming off Well's Gray Peak. The situation appeared to lend itself to a good ambush, provided we could get ahead of them. They were moving at a pretty good clip. We ran our horses for about a quarter mile, ditched them and made a run for it, hoping that the wind would be right and we would have enough cover.

I was apprehensive over the fact that when Don got off his mount he levered a cartridge into the chamber of his carbine! What did that mean? A small bull was bringing up the rear of the column. We would have to let the entire band go by to get him. A patch of mountain spruce just under the ridge afforded us cover. Hopefully they would zig instead of zag so as to not catch us flatfooted while I was noisily trying to catch my breath. Sure enough, a cow looked down our way. She paused briefly, but continued on. The rest fed aimlessly by and finally the bull presented himself for a good shot! He was moving — about 15 yards. The arrow on its way — a good hit! Don had his carbine levelled at it! I was close enough to lay my arm across the barrel — confrontation! He was concerned the animal didn't drop in its tracks. Now I am begging him to give me a few more seconds to put this animal down! The animal obliged by taking a few steps and collapsing. We would have a talk back at the camp.

Resident wolves and wolverines dictated we would be taking our kill in with us. The sun was just beginning to go over the snow-clad peaks to the west when we arrived in camp. Fred and his crew were already there. Fred also had a caribou. We had stories to tell. Both of our racks were in the velvet. Fred's had more points. Over a cup of coffee, I told my story and of the confrontation I'd had with Don.

Fred told this story: He, too, was to find out about the coastal Indian way on their hunt. They ran into a small herd of caribou skylined on a ridge about 200 yards away. One was more respectable than all the rest. Fred declined to make a stalk. The animals were aware and had lots of places to run and hide. First day — let's just look them and the country over. Charlie felt otherwise. He wanted a kill. He brought his old 30-30 into play and knocked down one of the largest of the bulls! Fred and cameraman Redinger were a little non-plussed. They all walked up to it, Charlie kicked it and walked on, apparently with no thought of taking it in — not a good start!

They walked across the fairly flat ridgetop they were on and looking down the opposite slope, they spotted, about a quarter mile away, another band of caribou standing in the middle of a huge sloping snow field, apparently seeking relief from the pesky flies. This was a much better opportunity for an interesting stalk. The snow field was surrounded by mountain spruce which made for good stalking. It would

Glenn and guide Don with mountain caribou.

Fred Bear with caribou.

only be a matter of getting into the brush patch with the right wind. The shot would not be any more than 15 or 20 yards. About a half hour later, Fred settled into a thicket and waited for his chance. Like "people watching," the animals entertained by dancing up and down, wandering here and there, occasionally tossing their heads, completely unaware that danger lurked nearby. All the while Charlie was watching, Redinger was filming with the long lens. In due time, a good bull presented his right side, quartering away from Fred. When the bull went down, he slid to the bottom of the snow field. Fred punctuated his story with a handshake and a big smile.

And so it was, first day — two nice mountain caribou. Nate's supper of delicious stew made from leftover moose meat cooled our concerns considerably about our guides' behavior and later a campfire under a three-quarter moon polished off the tension.

Fred and I decided not to make any big deal out of what we thought was the odd behavior of our guides. They undoubtedly had deep-seated ideas about hunting. We would wait and perhaps discuss it with Wes Loback. Weather permitting, he would be in at sun-up the day after tomorrow. Meanwhile, we temporarily solved the situation by switching guides — Fred would have a short chat with Don before going out. Charlie and I had worked well together the year before.

Time to hit the sack and contemplate tomorrow. It is getting colder. Far off, wolves' serenading indicated that they had found the gut piles. During the night, foot pads on the trails nearby and the yapping of pups, probably haggling over a morsel or two, reminded me that I was certainly not in downtown Seattle. Sleep came while I was wondering what to do about guide Don and his desire to "help" us almost before we could get an arrow away. In the morning I expressed my concern to Nate and suggested that maybe we could persuade Don to leave his rifle in camp. Nate reminded me the law dictated that there be a rifle and guide with each hunter — there were grizzlies in the area.

MOUNTAIN GOATS

Morning found us looking at a near cloudless sky, quite nippy — again cold enough to keep the black flies at bay. This was the day Fred would hunt the mountain goats on the cliffs, on the northern perimeter of this plateau about six miles distant. The area overlooks lakes and meadows 1,000 or so feet below. Charlie and I would head for the northwest perimeter cliffs overlooking Michel Lake. Nate and I had hunted this the year before, but from the bottom up. I was always one to want to know what was over the next hill, around the next corner — kind of like prospecting, you never know what you'll find. Our caribou tags were filled. Goats would now be in for a lot of trouble!

Glassing along the way was quite entertaining. Far off a wolverine was dragging something. Marmots were out in force expressing concern over every little movement. A black wolf with four pups watched us from a distant ridge, pacing nervously. Charlie and I passed on the west side of Michel Peak about 10 a.m. The ground started to fall off toward the lakes. We were able to traverse with our horses down the rocky slopes for about half a mile, glassing the cliffs northeast of us at all levels. Fred and the two Dons would be there somewhere east of us about five miles.

A pretty good wind was beginning to blow. Some places, we had to dismount and lead our horses by the more treacherous spots. There were goats, all pretty spooky . . . to be expected in wolf country, even though wolves are not prone to taking on animals in rocky heights. The boulders now are in different shades of green. We did try a stalk on a billy or two but always they would disappear around a cliff we could not get to. Charlie was tempted to shoot one off of a ledge — what for, who knows? Glassing a meadow by a lake directly below produced a cow moose feeding on the edge of a pond. Far off to our right in the same valley we spotted a fine bull moose with a set of horns in the velvet, way out of our reach for the day.

At this point we decided to see what Nate had packed for lunch. Baloney sandwiches. Boy, oh boy, the aroma had better be long gone before we attempt any more stalks!

We finally pulled out of the area and I'm thinking once again about hunting these cliffs from the bottom up. For now we decided to head east to see if we could by chance hook up with Fred and Don. A half hour of picking our way through the rock-strewn tops of these cliffs, we heard a rifle shot. Soon after, we spotted Fred, Redinger and Don coming out of a rock canyon. It appeared that they were about to partake of lunch. We caught up with them about 20 minutes later. Comparing notes, they had just had an encounter with a billy on a steep hillside. Wind was blowing up a storm. Fred had suggested to Don that he could do better sneaking on it alone. The goat was about 100 yards out — not aware. Fred ran out of cover at about 50 yards. The wind and distance did not allow for a shot. He wanted to wait it out but when the goat started to feed away he decided to abandon the encounter.

It was then that Don, who had sneaked up behind him, started yelling: "Shoot — shoot!" A startled Fred yelled back, "I can't hit that goat at this distance in this wind." Don, for whatever reason, put it down with his carbine! It promptly rolled off a nearby cliff, to a landing perhaps at least 1,000 feet below.

With their lunch over, we decided to split up again and comb the cliffs for a couple more hours. The wind was unrelenting and prone to blow us off some of the ledges. So much for goat hunting on that day. This is where the goats are. They were seen there before and it would appear it was just a question of time before we would get one. Something would have to be done about Don's trigger-happy behavior.

About 3 p.m. we all headed back to camp, taking time out to glass. On the way we collected five more ptarmigan and lost several arrows. Darn — it was pretty out there. It felt GOOD just BEING THERE! Again we found especially active and noisy marmots. We wondered to our guides if they knew why; was it the weather or did it have something to do with what was coming? From them, all we got was a shrug. We discussed what the morrow would bring. Wes Loback would be in early. He would have some ideas.

Arriving at camp about 6 p.m., we found Nate preparing supper. The guides took care of the horses' needs. Fred, Redinger and I took a much needed dip in the lake. COLD — you bet! After a supper of caribou, Fred took Nate and me aside and told us the rest of the story about their goat encounter today. As Don shot the goat, he yelled at Fred, "If you want a goat, get yourself a rifle!"

FRED HEADS FOR MOOSE CAMP

Next morning, the drone of the 180 was our wakeup call. Wes put the floats on the water with barely a ripple. He brought more supplies from the lodge. Plans were jelled for the day. Fred, Wes and Charlie would fly to the camp in the southern part of Tweedsmuir Park at the junction of Chelaslie and Euchu Lakes, the camp I had hunted out of the year before. There would be excellent fly-fishing, a moose pasture nearby, and a chance for a bear.

Wes was not too surprised at our young guide's behavior. Wes faulted himself. He had not coached the guide as to why we were hunting with the silent stick, a weapon that he had no knowledge of even though his ancestors had perhaps used it long ago. The solution for now would be that the guide would carry the gun and I would carry the cartridges!

Wes would check back here in a day or two. He would now fly the guide, Don, me and the photographer to Michel Lake below the goat cliffs. Fred needed goat pictures more than he needed a goat. He had taken a nice one the year before in the Yukon Territory. We would be walking the entire distance from the lower lake back to camp, a distance of about 10 to 12 miles — quite a day planned.

With all of the goat hunting crew's gear and lunch loaded in the plane, we were soon airborne and heading northwest to the edge of the plateau, and then slowly dipping into the valley, 1,000 feet below. We flew by Michel Lake and on to the little lake that almost iced us in the year before, just to look it over — remembering the near disastrous episode last year. This time, he put us down on Michel Lake which he would not have to circle for a take-off.

After watching Wes easily lift the floats off the water, we prepared ourselves for the difficult hunt ahead and glassed for goats. There were a few, alright. Whether they were approachable or not remained to be seen. Our unpredictable Indian guide was carrying his gun again. I had the cartridges. As we headed up, Redinger took pictures. It didn't take long to figure out we were in for the same scenario as last year. The goats simply stayed ahead of us and occasionally appeared over the ledges, then disappeared.

Today we went clear to the top of the cliffs and beyond. The goats continued right on up Michel Peak from the top of the cliffs and eventually we found ourselves at about the 7,500-foot elevation. There were at least three nice animals ahead of us. They never made one mistake. We last saw them heading down the other side in an easterly direction.

It was about that time that I found myself standing on an outcropping of blue-green rocks; not just colored ones — solid blue-green. My chemistry learning from school indicated to me that these were not just ordinary colored rocks, but copper ore; a very interesting happening, to say the least! I stuffed an apple-sized chunk in my pocket. The goats were long gone. Redinger and the guide, about a quarter mile away, were already contemplating a beeline for camp. They were glassing for landmarks. Apparently, we had lost track of time. It was now 1:30 p.m. and surely time for lunch and a rest. Our chase had taken us from an elevation of 4,000 feet to 7,500 feet.

Getting back to camp meant travel over bare rocks to the plateau floor about 3,000 feet below and the six or seven mile hike in to camp. With the lunch devoured, I made a note of the whereabouts of the copper outcropping. We headed down the jarring, rocky terrain, chomp, chomp, chomp, ever downward. This about did us in. Our knee joints wanted to bend the opposite way. Reaching fairly level ground never felt better. A rest and the energy from a big chocolate candy bar can do wonders. Three very tired characters finally straggled into the comfort of our wilderness camp. If there was ever a time for a sip of good old bourbon, it was now . . . a sip that you could feel clear to your toes.

We did get pictures of goats and my blue-green rock did make for interesting conversation. Nate had caribou tenderloins prepared. Boy, oh boy, were they ever tasty!

Before hitting the sack, we discussed the prospects for the morrow. By no means, was I ready to give up. Hey, there's white critters out there and we gotta go after 'em! It was simply a matter of being in the right place when one of them makes a mistake. We would try again tomorrow.

By 6 a.m. the next morning we were at breakfast. Twenty minutes later, Redinger, Don and I mounted up. The horses, idle yesterday, seemed to welcome some activity, and, given their head, seemed to know which way to go. Don had his silenced rifle and I'm still carrying the ammo. Two hours later, we are scouring the cliff area again. Every once in a while you'll see a flash of white as they appear around ledges. We would sneak up on the sighting to find nothing. As Don and I pick our way along the rocky prominence, Redinger stops to film some of the valley below.

Don is sitting down to glass the area as I continue to mosey along. I've gone about a hundred yards beyond where the two fellows are and climb on top of a huge boulder. I am about 15 feet off the ground. As I look back toward the guide, he is wildly waving and pointing at something below me. I don't see anything in the cliff area in front of me and am confused as he seems to be pointing right at my rock!

I quietly get off the boulder and circle around the left side. There is a goat directly under my boulder lying in an opening facing the cliff area! It is looking out over the valley — appears to be completely oblivious to my presence. It's amazing how one's body can change instantly from passively looking to animal-red-alert! While I can clearly see the goat, there are some sparse brush stalks growing along the side — places to put an arrow through, but barely. The critter is lying with its left side toward me. The vitals would be more accessible if he were standing.

Now it's a case of how much time do I have to worry about the options. A scramble of 30 feet would put him over a cliff. If I whistled, would he launch himself or would he stand? No more pondering. I crouch almost to my knees — find the hole — let out a sharp whistle. The goat jumps up — looks — all in an instant — anything else is too late. The arrow is on the way! A lunge of about 15 feet is all he can muster and he's down for good. He's a beautiful animal, not too big. At last I have my prize. There is some remorse. Too bad he had to pay the price. After all the hide and seek Fred and I had been playing with these critters, surprising how much better a hunter can feel after a quest has been accomplished.

Glenn with mountain goat.

Guide glasses as photographer Don Redinger watches.

Horses will carry goat and riders back to camp.

Don made short work of getting my prize prepared and loaded on the horses. And so it was. We headed for our canvas "barn." There would be a celebration tonight, simply because it would be a fitting climax for the day.

By the way, Don has his cartridges back. The wide grin on his weathered face told me without words that he understood. He now felt the challenge. As for my goat, it would need to be caped and the skull plate with horns removed. Perhaps I could get that done tomorrow. Nate would undoubtedly want to pare off some of the good meat for a dinner.

An Indian And A Bow

We made no plans for the next day. Perhaps it would be a day to reflect, rest and generally go into neutral. We figured we might see Fred and his crew some time today. A cold spell was felt to be in the making. Could snow be far off? Nate's breakfast was one for hungry men. While I sat by the fire preparing the hide and head for transportation, I noticed Don eyeing my bow — running a weathered finger across the broadheads. I offered to show him how, but no. I detected a shyness and the fact that he was not ready to concede that these things were for real.

Since I might be leaving later that day, I activated my extra Kodiak, a 55-pounder. With a few blunts stuck in my back pocket, I proceeded to do a little tundra shooting. Don followed along. Once again I suggested he give it a try. This time, a nod of the head indicated he was ready. Sure, he fumbled at first, but as with most outdoor folk, he soon got the hang of it. The bow was a little heavy, but even at half draw he did put the arrows out there. Gleefully he was picking up arrows and moaning over some reduced to bits and pieces. There were no lost ones — he knew right where each had gone. I finally sat by and watched while he continued, like the proverbial kid in a candy store!

Nate wanted to take a moose home to Seattle for a winter's meat supply. He looked to check out an area of swamps, ponds and small lakes about three to four miles west of our camp. Wes Loback generally checked into his camps before noon — Nate would wait till then. Unless Wes had a better idea, I might go with Nate. We might be able to scare up a critter I could get close enough to for my arrows to take.

Wes and Fred showed up about 10:30 a.m. from an overnight stay at the lodge. Before anything else, we had to exchange stories, and while looking over my goat, congratulations were in order, with a whack on the back by Fred's big hand. My copper ore was cause for a lot of conjecture; and what to do about it? Get it assayed in Seattle!

The last couple of days, Fred and Wes got in much fishing from the lower camp — they left a lot of their scent in a nearby moose pasture and spent most of yesterday trying to coax an exceptional velvet head out of the marsh area. They had seen it several times. For now, they were letting the pasture cool down a bit under the watchful eye of Charlie.

Meanwhile, since my goat was in hand, I should throw my gear aboard and we could do some sight seeing and fishing for a day or two. This would also leave Nate and Don time to exercise the horses, unlimber their rifles and look for a moose out there somewhere. I left the Kodiak bow in camp for Don to monkey with, also blunts and six broadheads. It didn't matter if I ever saw the outfit again. It was for a good cause, leaving a possible convert to plant the seeds of the old ways among the local tribe — gad, I hope he can get that thing unstrung and strung without getting clobbered.

While I am getting my gear together, Fred is pumping water out of the pontoons. All is at ready. The extra heavy load dictates a long take-off westerly over the camp and we continue on a few miles to see what chances Nate and Don would have on a moose. The moose were there all right, a couple of heads feeding in the middle of a pond. Our first stop would be at the lodge to unload my goat hide and horns. A bit of a ripple on the water made the landing routine.

THE HORNS DISAPPEAR!

We tied up at Loback's float walkway, which consisted of logs about 50 feet long and 4-foot boards across them. The whole walkway was parked up against the tundra-covered bank. I unloaded the goat hide, gingerly removed the goat horns attached to the skull plate, carried them the length of the walkway, set them down and went back for more stuff. Meanwhile Fred and Wes were walking to the lodge. When I got back to the end of the walkway the goat horns were gone! Fred and Wes had left the area even before I laid the horns down.

The search was on! The Loback's had a little cocker spaniel who was always at hand during any activity. He was there during the unloading. He, of course, was a likely suspect, but managed to look pretty innocent. Needless to say, as the search went on the dog was constantly under surveillance. We even searched the lake bottom under the dock — all to no avail. The only other thing we could think of was that perhaps another animal had carried them off — an otter? Who knows? The horns were never found!

To get on with the story, the ladies, Jane and Henrietta, had prepared lunch. The four of us got out of there about 1:30 p.m. and headed north. Wes wanted to show us just how remote this country was by taking us over the nearby town of Marilla. The town consisted of a general store with gas pump and a few outer shacks, the bare necessities of the local Indians, guides, and a few hunting lodges. About five miles out of Marilla, Wes landed on a small three or four acre lake which seemed to be on the fringes of what little civilization there was. No roads whatsoever, a few trails through solid scrub spruce poles. The lake barely afforded a landing for the plane. He shut down the engine and drifted, got out on the pontoon, and threw some edible objects into the water which literally erupted. It was full of hungry fish.

This lake and many others were within the land mass, hundreds of miles in every direction, which was open to homesteading. Canada needed settlers to bring money and life to the land. U.S. Nationals were welcome. A section of land one mile by one mile could be had by simply filing a claim. The claim would be kept alive by simply working it to the tune of $100 a year. Government section maps were available with each section numbered. You simply picked the section you wanted and made out an application to the Government Office at Prince George. Even the lake we were on was available within a section.

From there, we headed south toward the lower camp about 45 miles away. As we cruised over the flooded area, it was WOW! What a difference a year had made! Where there had been lakes with connecting streams, most of the streams were gone and it was becoming all one lake. Even the Redfern Rapids, which had been our best fishing hole, was impacted. Wes assured us that there was no need to worry, there were plenty of good fishing holes outside of the flood area. We flew over the camp. Charlie could be seen waving to us. He had a nice campfire going and was happy to see us. That afternoon he had garnered enough frying-size trout for dinner. The camp simply consisted of a cook tent and two other white sidewalls large enough for two or three hunters in each. Two 16-foot wood skiffs were hauled up on the shore nearby. There was a lot of debris, downed trees, logs, etc., which made mooring a little difficult.

Pan Fries And Moose

Morning found us in cloud cover; pleasant fishing weather. Wes proved to be as good a cook as you would expect of one who had to be a jack of all trades. It's about 9 a.m. With bows and fly rods in hand, Charlie and I are piling into the Cessna. Wes is taking us just out of the flooding area to a little lake about the 4,000-foot level, out of which there is a 20-foot wide stream, complete with rapids and shallow crossings. It empties into the flooded area below. He then headed back to pick up Fred and Redinger. They were to check out the moose pasture about five miles away where they had sighted the nice velvet-horned critter a couple of days before.

Well, the fish were there in the rapids for us to take. It soon became a case of catch and release. When we weren't casting, the black flies were biting. There were fish ducks. I've never seen so many Mergansers in my life. Flock after flock sailed by, low over the water. It was, at times, like clouds going by and as if something had made them aware that there was a hatch taking place somewhere west from there — perhaps fish fry for the taking. These colorful fish ducks were well-equipped with the tools. A long beak with teeth-like notches to grab and hold. They are considered a nuisance and undoubtedly impact the

Redfern Rapids

Fred pumping gas into float plane.

Charlie and Nate with catch.

fish. However, one has to assume it is nature's way of keeping everything in balance. Charlie never let my bow and arrow be very far away just in case. In one huge spruce thicket we found a bevy of ptarmigan. We gathered in enough for a good meal, skinned them and readied them for the skillet.

FRED BEAR TAKES A MOOSE

Loback appeared for the pickup about 4:30 p.m. As we loaded the mess of pan fries, he commented that they would make fine dinner fare. Wes had little to say, other than that he and Fred had a good day. In a matter of minutes, we had swooped into the moorage at camp. Fred greeted us with the kind of grin that goes with a good day. The cause was propped up against a tree at the top of the bank — a fine velvet moose rack, unique in that it was of variegated color. They had coaxed it out of the brush with a lot of snorting, blowing, and grunting on a makeshift birch bark horn. The critter was not too eager to come out, since the rut was still a week or so off. The story over a plate of fish and spuds was quite credible and convincing. The rack was more colorful than any other I have ever seen. Yes! They had a GOOD DAY!

Fred and Wes with Fred's moose.

Wes with lake trout.

THE HUNT WINDS DOWN

We would leave the camp in the morning. Charlie and Redinger would bring the moose and most of our hunting gear to the lodge in one of the outboard powered boats — a good three-hour trip. The rest of us would fly to the lodge and then check out the Fenton Lake camp. While Charlie loaded the boat, we prepared the float plane. Fred again busied himself pumping out the floats. He was concerned about the load we would have. This camp was simply to be buttoned up and left for others who were due to hunt out of here in the weeks to follow. This was moose and bear country. Gut piles would attract bears — grizzlies. While they don't mix, an occasional black bear will claim a kill site until a grizzly runs him off.

Charlie and Redinger left camp about 9 a.m. They were already well on their way. We were ready to go about 11 a.m. After taxiing slowly beyond the flood debris, Wes lifted the floats off the water. We headed out over Fred's moose kill area. Yes, there was a pair of wolverines feasting on the remains. It occurred to us that they would most certainly "mark" the kill so that nothing else would feed on it. Such is the way of nature.

It was time to think about winding down this hunt. We had two animals apiece. They had to be prepared for transport — and if Nate had a moose at the other camp, much more to do. We were soon unloading at the lodge. Loback would look in on the Fenton camp by himself, leaving necessary room in the plane for meat or whatever. As Loback lifted away from the dock, my lost goat horns came to mind. No one had seen them — the dog, still looking innocent, but still the prime suspect. Loback was back in about two hours. They had a moose in camp all boned out, ready to go. Don, the young guide, was to stay at Lake Fenton to tend the camp and horses. Gun hunters were due in next week.

Henrietta anguished a bit with Nate and me over the frightening road trip back to Seattle. Fred, Redinger, and Loback would not be flying out till the day after we left so we would all be arriving in Seattle about the same day. Meanwhile, Wes would take Nate's moose to a meat processor in Prince George for a later trip home to Seattle. Jane Loback would also go with Wes to Prince George, where she would stay while he was away. The big Cessna 190 with four people and a station wagon with three people would hopefully carry most of our take, all boned out — a moose, two caribou and a goat. For all story purposes, the hunt was over.

TWEEDSMUIR PARK HUNT – 1955 UPSHOT

The blue-green ore was assayed in Seattle.

My hunter friend Bob Arvine and I went back to Loback's lodge with a miner's permit in hand in 1956. The two of us walked from Fenton Lake to the top of Michel Peak. The outcropping of ore was covered by a snow field! We were too early. We could have staked the whole mountain — but didn't. We later found that Anaconda Copper Company explored the area with electronic devices from helicopters. I do not know the results.

Lab certificate.

The goat horns: Two years later, Loback brought me a set of horns from a winter kill. The dog remained noncommittal.

Don, the guide we had problems with, was last seen loading the Kodiak bow and what few arrows he had left into an old pickup truck and heading for home. During the time between our hunt and the later hunts, both Don and Charlie had a lot of fun with that gear.

As for the guides, and their behavior: Natives, with little or no contact with bowhunters and bowhunting, cannot be faulted. They are there to help the hunter get an animal. Until you show them otherwise, they are doing their job. We are all learning.

Hindsight: Oh how I wish I had gone to the trouble of staking out a claim on one of those beautiful sections of land. I did try half-heartedly, though. The sections I picked were not available and I lost interest at that time.

9
TRAP CREEK

November, 1954 my hunting partner, Clint Diessner, and I took up temporary residence in the Willapa Hills of southwestern Washington. This is part of the Olympic Peninsula, rain forest country, the home of the elusive Olympic elk. We were bowhunting during the elk rifle season. The area we wanted to hunt was so far from the road that few if any rifle hunters would be seen. A week earlier, we had scouted the area and set up a 10 by 12 by 3-foot sidewall tent complete with cooking fly. In this country, which gets about 150 inches of rain a year, you need all the cover that you can get. Trap Creek, a sizable stream, flowed alongside. To get there from our station wagon, we had to go through the roughest country you could imagine. It did cross our minds that it would be very difficult to get a critter out if we did get one. Personally, I never worry too much about that until a critter is down. We have always managed.

These hills, like the rest of the Olympic Peninsula, have a canopy of huge evergreen trees reaching far into the sky, diameters at the base six to ten feet. Moss hangs from their branches and covers part of their trunks. The canopy above is so complete that much of the ground cover never feels the direct rays of the sun. Many trees, ravaged by time, have fallen and lie like match sticks throughout. Some have splintered, with shards of wood protruding like porcupine quills. Some of the fallen

Sun shining through the rain forest.

trees have huge root growths filled with dirt and clay. The ground cover is of ferns of all kinds, patches of blueberry, vine maple, and rotten logs, with new trees, fungus and mushrooms growing out of them.

This forest is alive with chipmunks, squirrels, and field mice. Spotted owls, eagles, and ravens prey upon them. Most every creek is lined with colorful vine maples and devil's club, with spines that reach into you like porcupine quills. There are many open areas we call arenas that allow you to see quite far while looking for the elk that blend into the environment. There are alder bottoms along the larger creeks which attract and harbor the animals that we are looking for. These bottoms and the blueberry patches along the ridges are the feeding areas where the elk are most apt to be found.

This particular day, there was a light fog and it was cold enough to show one's breath. This in itself is quite a help to the hunter. Many times a herd can be spotted by the vapor drifting up through the trees as it rises from the warm hides of the elk. This can be detected for quite a distance. In other words, this was a good day for hunting. We were up before daylight, wolfed down a meager breakfast and stuffed a sandwich in our backpacks. Arrows were in quivers lashed to our packs. We had to take everything with us: extra arrows, a meat-carrying pack and all the equipment necessary for the possibility of a forced stay in the deep woods away from our camp.

For starters, we headed up a nearby ridge, sparsely shrouded in fog; a ridge that sloped out of an alder bottom along Trap Creek. There were tracks and the pungent smell of elk was in the air. Not a leaf was stirring. We moved very slowly, arrows nocked, stopping once in a while to listen for telltale chirps coming from the elk or an occasional stomping of a hoof. A half hour of this passed and the ridge split. I proceeded to cover the right ridge that came out of the alder bottom, Clint coursed along the other. He was soon out of sight. The only noise came from the squeaking of trees rubbing against each other and the sounds of water coursing in the myriads of rivulets. An occasional rifle shot was heard coming from the direction of civilization a long way off. At one point, the ridge offered a fine observation knob where I could cover a lot of real estate with my binoculars. There had to be elk around somewhere close.

Not long into this waiting and watching game, in the vicinity of where Clint had disappeared, I heard the distinct crashing of bodies knocking down small trees. This brought me to my feet. Something had spooked a herd. Clint, no doubt, but I could only watch, listen and wait. No telling which way the herd was headed. I tried to visualize what was happening. The crashing subsided rather abruptly and one would have to assume that the elk had gone over into a depression somewhere out of hearing. Could be that they had come out of a gully to my left. Clint may have jumped them and they may have gone over the other side of the ridge.

While contemplating my next move, I scanned the entire area like my head was on a swivel. My observation post overlooked a clear-cut area to the alder bottom and a strip of vine maple behind me stretched all the way down to the alder patch. Then I thought I saw movement in the alders below me — a movement of some branches. While focusing on that, from out of them popped the head of a spike bull elk! He was about 200 yards away — appeared to be headed right toward me or very close. If he were to continue, I would have to move into some kind of cover and the only cover was the vine maples behind me. It would

Elk in the alder bottom.

have to be done right now before I would be visible and he could hear. I slowly crawled through the maples and took another stand where I shed my pack. I then watched the spike slowly feeding up the hillside. He would grab a mouthful of ground cover, whatever it was, stomp a foot occasionally and slowly make his way toward me.

At this point, I decided that I'd best back up a few yards and go down the slope aways to be sure my scent didn't somehow get to him. I had to prepare an ambush. I am about five or six yards from the vine maple patch looking for holes to shoot through. If the elk continued in this direction it would be a 20-yard shot, since he would be about 15 yards beyond.

A patch of fog had moved in, obscuring my vision. He was barely visible, but I could hear him stomp with each step. I moved behind a little knoll where I could peek once in awhile. There were several holes in the vine maple large enough to shoot through. They were about the right height, but I would not be able to pick the right one until the elk got to where the shot was right. There was concern as to whether or not my arrows would straighten out soon enough to get through the hole. I shoot with a rhythm sequence of look, draw, and release. It all would probably come down to a matter of split-second timing. I cannot hit anything by holding my bow at full draw and aim.

Yes, I was excited, my heart thumping, arrow at ready! I'm trying to cover all the angles. This bull is in no hurry and doesn't have a clue that he is about to be ambushed. He is getting closer and now all I am seeing is a patch of tawny hide here and there. I can hear him ripping the fodder out of the ground. His head is going up and down with each bite and all the while I am looking for the crease behind the front leg. Seemingly the moment of truth is at hand but until the right picture appears in one of these holes, I don't dare fire. I'm determined not to blow this opportunity. Then it happens! The crease! The arrow is on its way. It sounded good, but I have no idea of where it hit as the elk charged on up over the hill and down the other side, crashing through brambles and trees into the gully depths below. I scrambled after him up to the top of the ridge to see and hear better. This crashing continued for a minute or two. I don't know whether the silence occurred at the bottom of the gully or when he'd gone over Clint's ridge and down over the other side. At any rate, there was silence once again.

I went over the shot again, looked for my arrow and any telltale signs of a hit other than tracks of a stampeding elk. It was now obvious that the bull had been feeding in the tracks of a sizable herd. A straggler, no doubt. This is what immature bulls do — hang out away from the main herd. Now, it was wait and listen.

While contemplating my next move, I glass the dark shadows below. There are small trees like hair on a dog's back. I could see the trail my elk had made through them for about 50 yards. After a half hour of this second guessing, I slowly made my way down into the gully below. Still no sign, arrow, or anything except a trail of downed saplings. Now the bottom has come and gone. I am going up the other side. Suddenly the tracks show that he has leveled his charge by veering off to the right. Another ten yards, he's headed down. And finally, there he is — piled up at the very bottom! A beautiful animal, and, while I did feel a sense of accomplishment, there was no need to celebrate the death of this young bull. There was need, however, to get this carcass cooled out before the high humidity of the surrounding air began the souring process. The hams and shoulders, with the hide removed, would have to be hung from one of the nearby fallen trees.

Clearing a little work space got the attention of my partner Clint who was barely visible about 150 yards away, atop the ridge that he had been hunting. I invited him to join me as I was certainly going to need some help. As he closed the distance, I noticed that he too would need help. He was was carrying an elk rack, tied on top of a quarter of meat. Yes, there were going to be several long days of work. Clint had jumped the herd as they crested his ridge. As they streamed by, he'd put an arrow into a nice 4 by 4.

Well, as a result of all this, we spent the next two days making a trail from these carcasses to our campsite, and getting the meat secured and readied to go on to our parked car a mile beyond. We did encounter a few rifle hunters closer to civilization and they stood in wonder at our success.

UPSHOT

Our bows were 1953 55-pound Thunderbirds, some of the first working recurves on the market. Our arrows were 600 grain brown glass with 160 grain two blade Ace heads. Although the Olympic Peninsula does get a good amount of rain, we didn't have any on this hunt. And for those of you who hunt in the midwest and along the eastern seaboard, the Olympic Peninsula is an area free of poisonous snakes, chiggers and ticks — how about that!

TRAP CREEK – 1955

1955, the very next year, my three Nason Creek cronies, Bob Kelly, Bill Jardine, and Bob Arvine decided they'd like to try a Roosevelt's elk hunt at Trap Creek where Clint Diessner and I had been successful.

As the season approached, Bob Kelly and I were elected to go to the area and set up a tent camp to be ready for the opening. The day we went was downright miserable; rain that could only be compatible to web-footed frogs and the like. We drove to the area, looked the situation over from inside the car, and decided that there was no way we were going to haul in a tent through brush, over logs, and ford the creeks that ran through bottomless canyons. There had to be a better deal or perhaps another day.

We drove back to the nearest town of Raymond, about four miles distant. There we anguished over a cup of hot coffee at a local coffee shop. Just outside the shop window, a sign was blinking at us like it was trying to literally convey a message. It did! It was a motel sign and we were in the motel's coffee shop. Kelly and I both jumped to our feet. The thought came to us simultaneously. A half cup of coffee was forgotten and we found ourselves at the motel office. We reserved a room for the week of the hunting season!

Back in Seattle at a meeting of the gruesome Nason Creek foursome, Kelly and I assured the other two that we had taken care of everything. The camp was all set up, complete with firewood — the works. All we had to do was pack in the Coleman lanterns, stove and sleeping bags, and what groceries we would require. We would shop for the groceries at Raymond.

Came the time. Again, it was one of those rain forest type days. All was quiet in the station wagon as we headed for the area. Arvine and Bill were not talking. Undoubtedly, the miserable half mile hike into the camp was on their minds. The weather outside looked like 50 feet would be too far. Kelly and I joked and acted like it would be a breeze. Who cares if we get soaking wet? We are hunters. That's just part of the game. No big deal!

We got to Raymond about 2:00 in the afternoon. Kelly suggested that before we shop for groceries and hit the trail, we should have a cup of coffee. Sure enough, right before our eyes was the cafe. We parked right near the motel office — our room was just across the parking lot. In the middle of the coffee break, Kelly got up and went out as if to get something from the car. The others didn't pay much attention to what he was up to. Assuming that he was ready to take off for the hunting area, we all went outside. We found him unloading his gear into a motel room! Arvine and Jardine were of course shocked, but their relief was impossible to hide! It couldn't be any better than that! Somebody produced a deck of cards. Even at 2:30 in the afternoon, that sounded like a good idea.

Well, you can guess the rest. As to the hunt? We hunted hard, got wet, saw little, got nothing. However, it was the most comfortable elk camp we ever had! — Now I didn't say the best!

10
PIONEERING IN 1957 –
FIRST LITTLE DELTA HUNT

THE DREAM

Yes, I'll bet many of you have dreamed about the day you might set foot on the vast tundra of the far north, Alaska, the last frontier, and try your hand at bowhunting where there are many different animal types and lots of them. Well, I did just that. I dreamed and finally made it happen. If you have any curiosity at all, you will sit back and just "listen."

Here's how I did it in 1957. To the stateside bowhunter, the Alaska varmints appear to be as safe as if they were in church, that it takes vast amounts money, guides, and endless red tape to get through to the far north hunting. I really got serious about going in the spring of 1957 when I found out that the U.S. Fish and Wildlife Service, which administered the hunting in the territory of Alaska, had abandoned the age-old Alaska guide law. This meant, simply, a guide was not legally necessary any more. Or, in more down-to-earth terms, $75 to $100 a day was lopped off of the hunting bill. Now, all one had to do was find a place to hunt, plan it like you would any other hunt in the lower 48 and go.

Until now, hunting in Alaska had been done mostly with rifles. Bowhunting, everywhere, was under scrutiny. The bow was not thought of as a viable tool for hunting big game. It needed testing. We needed a visible track record and Alaska certainly would be a good proving ground. Gun hunters, with their long range weapons, were doing the hunting and writing the stories, mostly in terms of skittish animals, especially the great dall sheep. Stories told about how the hunter would crawl on his belly for hours through snow, sleet, fog, and rain, up and down cliffs just to get within shooting range from 300 to 500 yards, to touch off a shot with a 30-06. When I would read that, as a bowhunter, I always wondered, were the animals really that difficult to stalk? Did the guides really try to get the gun hunters closer?

I wanted a sheep and I wanted the answers. To get these answers, I had to get to Alaska. Many hunters I questioned all but laughed at my chances of getting close enough to the great white sheep.

Transportation to Alaska was a factor in terms of money, a big factor when you add all the other expenses in. The whole idea was very thought-provoking.

Sometimes, sleepless nights turn out to be great thought-producing times and can possibly change your life considerably. It happened this way with me. This particular night I was half asleep, but my head was operating — thinking. All of a sudden, I sat upright in bed. "That's it! That's it!" I exclaimed out loud. Now my wife Margaret may be a sound sleeper, but not that sound. "What are you talking about?" she said. "I'm going to Alaska!" was my reply. "Good bye and good luck," she retorted, "and if you're still here in the morning, tell me about it?" (funny lady) "O.K., it can wait, but I'm sure it can work!"

The rest of the night, I laid there and worked out some of the details. My latest out-of-state hunts to Tweedsmuir Park, British Columbia, were good, but seemed just like a practice run for what an Alaskan hunt would be like. Dall sheep, moose, caribou, bear — a bowhunter's paradise.

That morning, over coffee, I outlined my plan to Margaret. Here it was: Alaska Airlines, a young, locally-based company could surely use some publicity in the form of a bowhunting film in Alaska, and could show the way to open up a whole new concept of hunting in that great territory. Gun hunters have had it all to themselves. Now it was time to share it with the bow. I would contact Alaska Airlines advertising agency, get an appointment, arm myself with all the stories, pictures, etc., of my previous hunts — yes, lots of pictures! I wasted no time. It was spring, and if all went well I could be on my way north by early fall!

After two or three days of preparation, I called Burke Advertising Agency, the Alaska Airlines public relations people. Yes, they would talk to me. When I walked through that door, a young good-looking chap took me in tow. We exchanged greetings and the whys and wherefores of my visit, and he showed me to a seat. About 15 minutes later, I was ushered into a back room. My eyes focused upon a red-haired gentleman in his early '60s and it was like old home week! He jumped out of his chair with the words: "Glenn, I haven't seen you in — well let's talk about it over lunch!" This was Rusty Burke, my old scoutmaster from the '20s! What a surprise and a pleasant one in more ways than one!

After much reminiscing, we got down to business. He agreed my plan had lots of merit. Alaska Air could use some promotion. They would furnish all of the transportation to Alaska and return, plus all of the bush plane travel in and out of the hunting areas. Also 4,500 feet of 16mm film would be available. I would furnish the rest — food, lodging, and any help that was needed to carry out this assignment. If I came up with a good story and suitable pictures, there would be other considerations and compensation.

Fair enough. I would work out all of the details and bring them to Rusty for review.

It was difficult to believe my luck and I "sailed" home on a real high. Finally, with my feet back on the ground, I started figuring the needs for such a trip. It would take, at best, two working companions with some know-how, preferably bowhunters. I was already equipped with a Bolex movie camera and a lot of other camera gear, so on with the search for these other fellows.

An Alaskan friend, Jesse Rust, working out of Fairbanks for Pan American Airlines, suggested Keith "Clem" Clemmons, a master sergeant survival expert, out of Ladd Air Force Base in Fairbanks. He would know what was needed and could perhaps outfit such a trip. On May 9, 1957, a letter went to Keith and he replied on May 20th (letters on next page).

Yes, it appeared I had our needed outfitter and he was a bowhunter to boot! As for a professional photographer, this was easier than I had expected. A call to Dick Bolding, the official photographer for the Washington State Game Department, brought another bowhunter into the fold. Dick, the adventurous type, agreed it was the chance of a lifetime. Keith already had most of the equipment necessary, could easily get the rest, and will come into the picture just for the chance to help pioneer such a bowhunting expedition.

Dick "Mac" McIntyre, of Frontier Flying Service in Fairbanks, would take care of the air transportation. He and Keith decided that the Brooks Range would be the place to go for the sheep — less competition from the Air Force personnel.

May 9, 1957

M/S Keith R. Clemmons
Hq. Sqdn. Sec. 5001st AB Gp.
A.P.O. 731
Seattle, Washington

Dear Keith:

Jess Rust has given me your name as someone who might be interested in lining up a hunt for a sheep this coming fall. I am mainly interested in sheep as it is one of the trophies that I do not yet have. I would like to concentrate on this animal but, of course, if something else should happen to stumble in our path!!!

Would you give me an idea as to how we could go about a trip like this. I would like to know such things as how we get to where the sheep are, the camping equipment necessary and the cost of everything pertaining to such a trip from Fairbanks.

To me, moving pictures of the whole trip will be very important and Jess tells me that you also have quite a camera set up. I have a 16mm Bolex that I would like to have in action quite a bit of the time.

Jess recommends you very highly and I'm sure that we could have a fine time together if and when the trip could be organized. Please let me know as soon as possible.

Best regards,

Glenn St. Charles

Glenn St. Charles

GS:rr

Glenn's May 9, 1957 letter to Keith Clemmons.

Armed with all this information and preparation, I went back to Rusty Burke. He agreed our plan looked good and gave a stamp of approval for the first phase. So we were off and running!

ALASKA — THE LAST FRONTIER

All of this preparation had taken till midnight of August 11th, when Dick Bolding and I boarded an Alaska Airline DC-4 for Fairbanks. While it was black when we left Seattle, the sky brightened considerably as we approached the far north.

20 May 1957

Dear Glenn,

Dick Cooper told me that you were going to write about a sheep
hunt so was very happy to find your letter. I have been down
to Kodiak Island in quest of the wily brown bear. We didn't
do any good but had a good time.

As to the sheep hunt. I talked to Dick McIntyre (owner Frontier
Airways and beginning archer) and he feels that the best place for
a hunt such as you want would be Loon Lake in the Brooks Range. This
area has hardly felt the pressure of hunting. I'm sure Jess knows
of the area that I'm talking about. Tell him the lake is located
at the head of the big valley coming in from the left just before
you get to Anatuvick Pass. It is some of the wildest most remote
and beautiful country in Alaska.

Dick feels that he could fly three people into and return for
about $200.00 per person. This would include a trip into Bettles
for extra baggage or supplies and one trip to bring the meat out
to Bettles. To get baggage in and out of Bettles you could ship
it via Wien Airlines. He can haul three people and about 50 lbs
going in and out. (50 per person)

How many will you have in your party?   I have plenty of leave time
coming but am not financially fixed to go on a hunt like this but
will be glad to make arrangements for you.

These prices are only approximent and might vary with more or less than
three. If a fourth was included he suggested for him to go to Bettles
and he could pick him up there.

Wien also has a bush service out of Bettles but Dick's estimate
is quite abit cheaper than flying to Bettles and then bush plane
from there.

There are quite a few Barren Ground Grizzlies, Caibou, and Dall Sheep
in this area but only Caribou and Sheep open on the 15th of August.
I might say now that anyone hunting in the Brooks Range after 1 Sept.
is taking a chance of having to walk out. The lakes freeze early
and safe landing areas other than lakes are few and far between.

I am not in the movie taking business any more and have sold all
of my movie equipment but I still know how. I also had a Bolex
Supreme.

(continued on next page)

Clem's May 20, 1957 letter to Glenn.

The two pilots were very casual and informative — open door
cockpit, the whole bit, until we approached and hopped over the Alaska Range and started our descent down into Fairbanks. The cockpit
door was then shut; regulations, I assumed. We started down too
quickly. Most of us passengers experienced a very painful descent into
the heavy air with earaching cries. Did the pilot shut the doors so as not

(continued from previous page)

As to equipment I have plenty of gear for three or four people.
I have a ultra light tent that could be set up in the high country
and possibly can get another one for a base camp on the lake.
Plenty of cooking gear and gas stoves.

About all you would need is your sleeping bag, hunting equipment,
and personal gear.

It rains quite abit and is very cold in the Brooks at that time of
the year.   .

Food, dehydrated or regular can be purchased here. I have plenty of
storage space and an extra bedroom in my quarters. Also my wife can
cook a pretty good meal if she isn't hurried.
                                              OTHERS
Loon Lake isn't the only place to hunt and a great many can be reached
at less expence but every one and his brother is hunting sheep now
so any place that is easy to get to is heavily populated with gun
hunters.

The chances of getting a record head out of the Brooks are pretty
slim but the heads are large and very beautiful.

I hope all of the above drible will be of help to you and am looking
forward to helping you in any way that I can.

                         Your servant,

                         Clem

Clem's May 20, 1957 letter to Glenn.

to hear the pain? The DC-4 was not the most modern machine — no
pressurized cabin. So much for the trip.

Keith "Clem" Clemmons met the plane which hit the dirt at 5 a.m.
Welcome to Fairbanks — the last frontier — and that was soon to be
very evident!

After a settling cup of coffee and get-acquainted bull session with
Clem, Dick and I believed that we indeed had the right man. Easy-
going, experienced, and glad to be aboard. Our gear was then loaded in
Clem's truck and we headed for the Nordale Hotel — the best in town
— the only one! We were to stay there Monday night only and head for
the mountain the next morning, the 13th.

While Clem and Dick unloaded our bags, I registered with the
clerk who explained, "We don't rent the rooms here — just space. You
might find someone else in the other beds by morning." "Oh," I
exclaimed. "I have a partner for the other bed. He will be here in a

4 July 1957

Dear Glenn,

I am sorry that I haven't written you sooner but it seems that
the summer is really our busy time up here. I have been guiding
and trying to get our archery club in shape.

I talked to Dick Mc Intyre about the sheep area again and he says
that if he can't get us in there that there are a great many other
areas that he can set us down. As to an alternate it will have to
be in the Brooks Range if we are to hunt on the 15th of August. I
know of several other places that could be hunted after the 20th but
none compare to Loon Lake and area.

As to equipment I have tents, gas stoves, cooking equipment,eating
utensils and if you want sleeping bags. I don't have any cots or
air matteresses. About all you will need is your hunting gear, warm
clothes, rain clothes, skinning knives, personnal gear, and I
suggest shoepacs for foot gear but many people don't like towear
them. I have worn them all over the territory and find that they
are the best for all around hunting and hiking that I can find.

Food. I can get anything and everthing that we need up here.
Regular and dehydrates are available so we have no problem there.

I will be more than happy to act as your photographer if you
think that I am capable. As I told you before I don't have the
Bolex any more.

The new gamelaws haven't been published as yet but I will send a
copy as soon as they are. One thing I have heard is that grizzly
has been pushed up to the first of November. In other words they
have practicaly closed it.

Moose, caribou, and sheep will be open where we will be hunting.

I can't think of any thing else at present. If I think of any thing
else I'll let you know.

                              Your servant,

                              Keith H. Clemmons

Clem's July 4, 1957 letter to Glenn.

minute." "The room you have has three beds," he replied. A single drop
light lit up the "space," with three iron beds and three chairs. A common bath was down the hall. Yes, this, after all, was a frontier town and
boasted 10,050 inhabitants. We parked our bags and headed for downtown Fairbanks where the three of us shuttled all over town getting
licenses, tags, and odds and ends we thought we needed. Occasionally,

Fairbanks, Alaska in 1957 – 10,500 population.

we would check in with McIntyre at Frontier Sporting Goods whose plane was to be our wings for the flight north.

Mac was in the middle of a bonanza, selling the new 44 Magnum pistols that had just arrived from the lower 48. The buyers were lined up for half a block around his store. This situation, sooner or later, was bound to produce some physical evidence that could only happen in this "last frontier."

Late that afternoon, while I was crossing an intersection on the outskirts of town, a really odd thing happened. Four people, including myself, were about to cross the street with the light. An impatient truck owner was revving up his engine — vroom, vroom — and appeared about to run us all down before the change of the light. Ahead of me was a tall, pioneer type — floppy hat, old suitcoat — who apparently didn't cotton to that truck. He solved the problem his way. He simply whipped out a huge magnum from his belt, put it up to the radiator and let it roar! Hot water and steam flew everywhere! A few engine parts dribbled down to the pavement. The fellow put away the pistol, and all those nearby flicked a little hot water off themselves and continued on across the street like nothing happened.

After gathering our wits, some of us stood around waiting for the police who would surely show up any minute. The guy with the pistol

Mac's Frontier Sporting Goods, Fairbanks, 1957.

walked on with no apparent concern. The truck driver, of course, was in shock. Several bystanders helped push the truck off to the side of the road. Finally, we all realized that nothing was going to happen and went about our business — indeed the last frontier!

Back in our hotel room that evening, Dick and I expressed our opinion that Fairbanks was certainly different — with hamburgers $1.50 each, milkshakes 75 cents, and beds $12 a night, we agreed it was a good thing we were going to the mountain. Who could afford to stay in town and be bled like that? And, sure enough, next morning there was a stranger in the other bed! When we checked out of the hotel, a white-haired old fellow ahead of us was dribbling gold dust onto a scale out of an old leather pouch. Noticing our surprise, the clerk obliged us by saying that they had several prospector-type residents who paid their rent with dust and nuggets.

BETTLES – INDIAN COUNTRY

Very soon we found ourselves out at the float pond, loading gear under the supervision of Andy Anderson, one of Mac's bush pilots. He was to take us out. We three, with 200 pounds of baggage, were all the winged pontoons could handle. The rest of our supplies, groceries, tents, etc., had been shipped north to Bettles on Friday by Wein Airlines. When the floats broke the plane of the water and we were airborne, Andy announced that we may not get all the way to Loon Lake, our destination. The weather was a bit messy in the region of Bettles, where we would probably hole up for the night. Our flight took us directly toward Bettles, 180 miles northwest of Fairbanks.

As the myriad of lakes and tundra slipped by below, I mused, *at last it was happening — like prospecting!* What would we find in that desolate far north? Patches of clouds obscured some of the view below. However, about 100 miles out, the great Yukon River snaked its way through the tundra. Rampart was on our left, and then Stevens Village on the right. Tiny Indian villages dotted the river bank. About 75 miles further on, the Koyukuk River loomed up, and Andy circled for a landing at a little Indian village about two miles below Bettles. Beyond, up the John River 80 miles to Loon Lake, our ultimate destination was really socked in so the village was to be our home for the night. This turned out to be one of the more interesting stays of our trip.

We landed upstream on a fairly smooth surface and taxied ashore to be greeted by Sam and Ludy Hope, Koyukon Indians. They grabbed the tie-up rope and promptly secured it to a gnarled old root sunk in the stream bank. It was fishing season. They were busy cooking dog salmon for their sled dogs and putting up the winter supply of salmon fillets, which covered the racks next to their shack. They took time to show us around, before leading us to one of the shacks which was to be our place of lodging for the night. Only two or three Indians and a white prospector were staying there at the time.

Empty gasoline cans were lying about everywhere. Gasoline at $1 per gallon was shipped in five gallon cans by air freight or barged, when possible, up the Yukon and the Koyukuk tributary to Bettles. The native's shacks were covered with flattened-out gas cans. Their wood boats were 16-footers and all of them seemed to be powered with Evinrude engines.

A local store carried most everything that you could find in Fairbanks and at the same prices as Fairbanks. The store's back room had many beautiful wolf hides hanging from the rafters, all color variations, and most at $20 per hide. Outside the store building was an open shed which housed the remains of a DeHaviland Beaver float plane that had more or less cracked up in a rough river landing on one of the smaller tributaries of the Koyukuk. The store owner had lots of time on his hands and somehow managed to get this wreck onto a raft and float it down to his store where he was gradually restoring it. Claiming it as salvage could someday pay him some pretty good dividends.

Float pond, Fairbanks, 1957. Note medals on Clem's quiver.

Loading Cessna for trip to Brooks Range.

We gave the Hope's sled dogs a wide berth. While they seemed docile, they looked at you like they were sizing you up for a meal. For instance, your arm — clear to the elbow. We took many pictures of the area, and I bought a small grizzly bear hide from one of the natives. He was no amateur bargainer and apparently sensed that I wanted the hide real bad. It cost me 20 bucks! Along the river bank, we found pieces of fossil mastodon ivory sticking out of the gravel. Most of it would disintegrate when brought to air. It was beautiful stuff.

Late that afternoon, we took two boats to Bettles to pick up the 300 pounds of gear that we had shipped from Fairbanks by Wein Alaska Airlines. It was to be left at the Indian village from where Andy would ferry it on up to Loon Lake after depositing us there. What was really interesting on the trip to Bettles was that the operators of our boats stopped at Koyukon Indian encampments along the way to pick up their shopping lists. We went ashore at several of these stops to see how these natives lived. We stopped again on the way back to drop off their needs. At one encampment, our boatman simply laid a pound of butter on a rock as we went by. There are no other words to call this whole experience other than it was "a lesson on living in the raw." Healthy and happy they were, without all the frills we city folks are used to.

That evening around the campfire, we swapped yarns with the natives. Sam Hope demonstrated how he repaired snowshoes with a crude ivory drill. He held an ivory socket in his mouth for the back end of the drill to revolve in. He used a string and bow contraption which he sawed back and forth to turn the drill — a very ingenious rig.

Yukon River

Bettles Village on Koyukuk River.

Ludy and Sam Hope on front porch.

Dog salmon drying.

Main Street, Bettles Indian Village.

Bettles residents, Sam Hope's sled dogs.

Ernie, right, storekeeper at Bettles with friend.

Ludy Hope preparing a pelt for curing.

Sam Hope drilling snowshoe.

Waiting out the weather at Bettles.

Up The John River

Weather that night seemed to be clearing a bit. Morning would come soon and we would be off early if everything was right. After saying our goodbyes to our native hosts, it was off to bed. Morning found us loading our gear into the floats, and soon we were off into scattered clouds and on to Loon Lake, flying low up the John River — just keeping barely under those clouds.

Animals seemed to be fairly scarce although an occasional lone caribou was sighted. About 60 miles from Bettles and 20 miles from our destination, we began following the Hunt Fork of the John River. The last vintage of trees was left behind. We had crossed the North American tree line. We were getting some sun breaks now, and near our landing site at the bottom of a high cliff, Andy pointed out a crashed plane. It was the remainder of a previous trip to this area which did not wait for flyable weather. Barren hills and mountains lined both sides of the valley. Streams of all sizes poured from the surrounding canyons. Lakes dotted the area. Finally Loon Lake, a long narrow body of blue water, appeared in the middle of a big flat. A four-posted trapper cache stood at the lower end. We barely cleared this structure for the perfect landing, and taxied ashore to what was to be our home for a week or two, depending upon availability of animals.

While we set up camp, Andy headed out to get the rest of our gear back at the Bettles Indian village. We no more than got the coffee pot going when a Federal Wildlife Agent in a Supercub swooped down upon us almost as if he had smelled the coffee. He was there to check our licenses and give us some words of sound advice. We shared an early lunch with him and he was off. Andy soon came in, unloaded the rest of our gear, and headed south for Fairbanks. He would be back to check on us in a week.

Now we were on our own. Clem wasted no time in showing us the perfect refrigeration system of the far north, the permafrost — anywhere from one to three feet under the mossy tundra. The ground is frozen solid and the melting from the top supplies the moisture for the tundra. He explained further that only roads that are absolutely necessary are built over this, and at great cost. The constant contraction and expansion due to many freezings and thawings causes eruptions in the roadbed. Overnight a smooth highway can become a mass of ruts.

Even building on the permafrost is a problem. Heat from the buildings melts the foundations out, thus causing them to sink in the mire. Only in recent years have engineers figured out that, rather than fight this permafrost, it is better to join it. Thus the idea of refrigeration was introduced in the floors of buildings so that foundations are kept frozen. So much for civilization.

Now how does all this affect the hunters? Well, walking on this spongy grass over long distances is very difficult for a human being. It is similar to walking on sand. You don't seem to get anywhere and your feet are constantly twisting and turning to conform to clods that rise on what is an otherwise smooth surface. Thus the caribou and moose are born with exceptionally large hooves, which help them in their wanderings in this moving land. In this great far north country, most travel to hunting grounds is done by horse, boat, airplane, or swamp buggy. Some outfitters use the swamp buggy, a four-wheel drive contraption, which enables them to go over most any type of terrain — swamps, creeks, and potholes. The hunters make sorties out of established camps. We here at Loon Lake are in the middle of this type of terrain and will encounter it every day.

The surrounding bare peaks stand like sentinels waiting for our next move. Any wildlife in the area will have perfect lookout positions and, quite naturally, we feel like we are being watched, although nothing is in sight. We spend a couple hours consolidating our camp and equipment which leaves us little time in the rest of the day to look around. We get four ptarmigan which we will have for dinner. Far off, we think we see a lean-looking wolf with three cubs. Further observation indicates they are coyotes. They are as curious about us as we are of them — they keep their distance. A den must be nearby. The cache at the other end of the lake arouses our curiosity and of course we have to go take a look at it. It has been tampered with — probably by wolverines — claw marks on the poles. Anticipation for the next day is high when we hit the sack.

The following week is quite routine. Up early each day, climb to the top of a peak, glass for critters. We encounter lots of fog, some rain, spot many small sheep. One legal ram, we begin to call "Sam." He eludes every move we make to reach him. Every day he is in the same spot, but in no way is he to be had. Only one lone caribou is sighted by Dick — too far for a shot. Our only real accomplishment in the whole week is lots of pictures of far off small rams, a wolf or two. We have many hearty meals of ptarmigan, and that's all.

When the float plane hits the watery deck on the return flight to check on us, the pilot this time is Marc Stella! He is greeted by three

Loon Lake Camp

Abandoned four-post cache, Loon Lake.

dejected characters. He decides to move us about 65 miles east in the vicinity of Mount Doonerak, the highest mountain in the area at 8,000 feet. Much of our gear, we find, is not necessary. He takes us and only the gear that we absolutely need to the new site, leaving the rest of the gear at Loon Lake. He will pick it up on his return to Fairbanks.

On our way to the new site, we did witness an interesting "nature in the raw" episode that was developing. A bull moose was standing in the middle of a small pond which had four or five wolves circling it. We could not wait around for the ending of that episode, but I can imagine it was quite startling. Our flight continued. We landed on a small lake which was harboring many ducks and geese. We quickly unloaded the plane and watched it fade in the distance — would Marc remember WHERE he left us??

There were grayling in the clear waters, and it wouldn't be long before we would be applying a rod and hook to them. The weather was almost like down-state summers — butterflies, flowers. We were equipped like we were about to take on some ice flows! To better avail ourselves of the animals that might be in the higher elevations, we set up a spike camp, in the hills nearby, about three miles from our fly-in lake. We got the same picture as before — small ewes and lambs and no caribou. A grizzly invited himself for breakfast one morning while we were holding coffee cups instead of bows! It gave us quite a start until Dick got on the movie camera. The "whirr" startled the bear away. We got movies of him ambling over a small rise and out of sight. The only time you think of guns is when something like this happens. We had none.

We were back down at the base camp after six days of this biological desert, all set for Marc's return. The plane was a very welcome sight — he had remembered! We very quickly loaded our gear in the Cessna 180 and headed back to Fairbanks, and unless some miracle was out there, our dream hunt was over.

Clem opening a hole in the frozen tundra for our ice box.

Clem and Dick sampling our supper.

Glenn and Clem scouting Loon Lake.

Back in tent at Loon Lake.

Our camp near Mount Doonerack.

High spike camp.

Marc Stella, center, wishes us well at Doonerack Camp.

Marc coming in for pick up at lake near Mount Doonerack.

An Incredible Flight And Discovery

I wasn't about to give up. Sure, we had lots of background pictures, but had not loosed a shaft at a big game animal in two weeks. I had a commitment with Alaska Airlines to do a job, and as long as there was time, I would try to carry out the assignment. We had eight more days to work with. McIntyre recognized that he also had some responsibility for my concerns. He suggested I take a scouting trip with Marc southeast of Fairbanks into the Alaska Range. That evening, the three of us got together with Marc and McIntyre as to what they had in mind.

Marc was one of those "fly by the seat of your pants" pilots. He had been over most of the country with a Supercub ferrying prospectors and hunters. Much of the area around had been hunted heavily by personnel from Ladd Air Force base. That's why McIntyre hadn't sent us out there in the beginning. Now, the Alaska Range was our only hope.

The detailed plan was to check out some of the glacial drainages coming out of the Yanert and Gilliam Glaciers at the foot of Mounts Deborah, Hess, and Hayes, all 12,000- to 13,000-foot peaks.

It is 8 a.m., Wednesday, August 28, 1957. I'm in a Supercub in the seat directly behind Marc Stella. His lap is covered with contour maps of the area we are going to scout. In my lap is a fully loaded 16mm Bolex movie camera. The Tanana River is off to our left. We are flying very low, looking over the fall-tinted terrain for animals. We are reaching for the snow-capped mountains, clearly in view, though they are about 90 miles away. Huge white clouds billow over them, obscuring our view from time to time. Willows, tag alders, and scrub spruce dot the landscape. An occasional tall spruce seems to reach for us and we find ourselves looping over it.

At times, I show my concern by yelling like a back seat driver at Marc. Yelling is the only way you could communicate over the noise of this flying machine. It would appear that this would be an exciting trip, but little did I know that this was to be the most incredible and exciting experience ever. Now and then a moose would appear, sometimes two or three feeding together. Small bands of caribou, feeding on the lush cover below, only paused long enough to wonder at the strange noisy bird above.

The lower ridges we flew over were intermingled with small streams. In the valleys were lots of ponds and little lakes, each with a few white swans — beautiful contrast to the otherwise blue-gray water. The hills rose toward the elevation of the peaks ahead. Far off to the south, we see the Nenana River, which is soon lost as we fly higher, putting us into patchy clouds. Dodging them could become a problem.

About 50 miles out, Marc points to a good-sized stream below, creeks entering it from all sides. "The Wood River!," he yells, "Good hunting!" We dive into the main valley. There are sheep in all the higher elevations — caribou on the valley floor. There is also smoke, what appears to be campfires or cabins, indicating perhaps hunting activity. The cloud cover now is lowering to most of the ridgetops — quite worrisome. Marc spots a little airstrip below and decides to wait out the cloud cover. As the wheels touch the ground, I get my wits about me and exclaim: "The Wood River! The head waters of this valley is where Art Young shot a Dall sheep in 1923!" Marc looked at me questioningly, but before I could go into a long explanation, some hunters from a camp nearby saved the day. I would tell him about Art Young later.

The gun hunters had just landed and set up camp. They were also waiting for the weather to clear before scouting the ridges afoot for sheep. We exchanged questions and pleasantries until Marc, noting a break in the clouds, called for a takeoff. He elected to follow the Wood River on out toward the glacier area. Soon, more sheep are seen on the ridges — could be some offspring of Art's nice ram. All this conjecture was soon lost as we were enveloped by scattered clouds, above and below. Occasionally, through breaks in the clouds, we can see Mounts Deborah and Hess ahead and off to our right. The valley has swung left. We are now headed east and approaching the blue ice of the Yanert Glacier. Marc would like to get over the ridges on his left and head more northwest away from this inaccessible country. He is trying to get over into the next valley. We are dodging and turning, up and down, trying to find the right opening and get out of this mess. It is getting to me! My guts and head are telling me something. I find it difficult, with the queasy feeling, to keep my mind on what we are out here for!

We are now entering what appears to be a big box canyon. A cloud bank closed behind us, huge rock cliffs on three sides, and all we can do now is circle 'round and 'round, and wait for an opening up through the clouds. I thank God this Supercub is no ordinary one. It is powered by a souped-up Lycoming engine — a real mountain climber. The cloud cover above does not look too promising — always shifting. Mounts Deborah and Hess should be on our right. Hayes should be far ahead, but a little off to our right. For now, we could do nothing but circle and wait. Suddenly, a hole begins to develop above — blue sky. Marc nosed up the Cub and headed for it. The hole grows larger and we

Supercub heading for grubstake area.

are through it. Again, we must circle and wait until we can see the ground below. We continue to climb, to get well above the enveloping mountains and clouds. My head is reeling — sign of vertigo. My thought was, would we ever get out of this? Marc seemed unconcerned, even though the clouds again enveloped us. We couldn't turn back, and actually, in this situation, where was back? I am really into vertigo now. Marc yells some encouragement and points to a hole developing in a cloud, exposing a thin stream in a valley below. The question is: what valley? Are we back over the Wood River? Down we went. The camera almost left my lap, and as we leveled out about 500 feet above the valley floor, I thought I would go through the seat. Now Marc is intermittently glancing at his map and the terrain, trying to match them up for our whereabouts. Sheep are on all of the ridges and moraines next to the glacier ice on our right. We now head north, downstream. Other little streams here and there are entering the main valley. All of these are clues on Marc's contour map. We continue on down the valley. It widens out. Willow patches, scrub spruce, tag alders, small bands of caribou are appearing on the lush hillsides — moose in the meadows, sheep dot the ridges.

On down the valley we go, until Marc spots a big stream coming in from the right, another on the left, which are the keys to his map and he exclaims, "Could be the Little Delta!" To be sure, we need more clues. Another one was not long in coming. Through an opening in the cloud cover off to our right, a big snow-capped peak appears. "Mount Hayes!" exclaimes Marc, as he peers at his map. "The West Fork of the Little Delta"! We continue on downriver. So far, there is no evidence of hunters. Plenty of animals.

Marc points to a black ridge where about 30 or 40 sheep are trailing along the hillside. He motions for me to ready my camera and yells to anchor everything down. He crams his packet of maps into a crevice. I stuff our sandwiches and coffee thermos under my seat. All this in preparation for him to open the side window, better for me to take pictures. I am ready, he opens the window, and literally points the right wing at the sheep, dropping vertically toward them. Everything that wasn't tied down was literally floating around the cockpit and Lord only knows what went out. The rush of wind was simply overwhelming, but I did get some spectacular footage. This is indeed a beautiful valley!

The question now is, where is the nearest landing strip, how far will we have to hike, and exactly, where are we in this valley? The answers could only come by continuing on down the valley. Marc looked at the map and exclaimed, "There is a survey landing strip at Portage Creek." It will be off to our left and down the valley a ways. A grizzly bear digging for something on the river bank, loomed up ahead and dove into the brush as he heard the plane. As we passed over, he stood up in defiance — an awesome sight! The valley is now widening out — lower rolling hills — animals circling.

"Look, Marc — off the right wing. What is that against the hillside?" Something black stands out in a patch of scrub spruce. A half a mile from the river, that black object turns out to be an old run-down cabin with a few outbuildings. There is a wholesome growth of brush growing out of the roof! A small stream flows nearby which eventually enters the main stream a half mile below.

Several passes over this site indicate it certainly has possibilities for a campsite. The semblance of a door lays flat out in front. A band of caribou are feeding on a little flat nearby. This could be it!

We head for the main stream to look for a gravel bar to build a landing strip. We most certainly will need something from which to land and takeoff, with any critters that we might get. Marc points out two possible areas, either one suitable. They are both near where the small cabin stream enters the main river. Both will require the clearing of willows and the moving of some boulders. Prospects look better by the minute. Now we head downstream to find the Portage Creek landing strip. I set my watch.

Sure enough, we soon sight what we are looking for off the left wing. It is time for a break to consolidate our findings and go over our options. We decide to land at Portage Creek.

The landing is a dog leg, uphill — a 10 to 15 degree incline. This was the strip used by survey crews in the early '50s. A miscalculated downhill takeoff would put you into a marsh. As we eat an early lunch — it is only about 9:30 a.m. — we take time to check over the maps. According to my watch setting, the cabin appears to be about 8 or 9 miles away. Mac's Tri-Pacer could land us and all of our gear here at this Portage Creek strip. Clem, Dick and I would hike in to the cabin at an appointed time and signal an airdrop by Marc in the Supercub, ferrying our gear from the big strip. Axes, machetes and other tools would be dropped on one of the potential airstrips. Parachutes would have to be used to get some of the fragile stuff down. While conjecturing all this, we are being watched by caribou as they continue their migration down the valley.

We climb aboard our wings once again and head back up the valley for another low-level look at our cabin find. Eight to ten miles in a Supercub doesn't take long. This time, I note there are quite a few sun-bleached moose horns and sheep skulls lying about — another plus. Yes, there are more caribou feeding on the lush blueberry patch in front of the cabin. This is the only band we see that isn't feeding at a fast walk down the valley. This time we also note there is a small, posted cache near the cabin. Age has probably destroyed most of what is stored there. Everything else — the possible airstrips and river crossings are all adding up to very encouraging possibilities. This IS it!

Now back to Fairbanks to see what my cohorts think about it. I note the terrain we will be hiking over between the cabin and the Portage Creek strip. It appears that the best route will be to follow the river; probably will have to make some crossings. The first half mile from Portage will be marshy — lots of tundra knobs. Rubber shoe pacs covering the ankle will be necessary. Glacial river levels will be low in the morning since there will be little glacier melt during the cold night. Regardless, in some places the water level will be over our shoe tops. Wet feet mean sore feet. Wool socks will be a help. All this is going through my head.

Looking upstream, Little Delta River valley from the Supercub.

GO FOR IT!

In about 45 minutes, we land and find Clem and Dick cooling their heels at Mac's Frontier Sporting Goods. We had been gone about 3 hours. A brief outline of what we had found is in order. Almost before I can finish my story, they are excitedly saying in unison: "Let's go!" The details of the "hairy" flight Marc and I had gone through can be told later.

Parachutes had to be made — different sizes. Groceries had to be bought, packaging planned for the chute drops — everything, hard stuff, fragile, including our precious arrows. All would be tossed out of the side of Marc's slow, low-flying Supercub. There were only six days left to prepare, build an airstrip and hunt — no small task.

The morning of August 31st we loaded Mac's Tri-Pacer with all of our gear. The three of us plus Marc headed for Portage Creek. Weather was a little bit iffy, but Marc seemed to think we would have no problem. We flew low southeast up the Tanana River valley, then southwest up the Little Delta valley to where it branches off onto the West Fork. We were about 45 minutes out of Fairbanks. We found ourselves flying the last ten miles up the West Fork valley where we had located the cabin. The

Portage Creek strip where we were to unload the Tri-Pacer was off to our right. We kept on to give Keith and Dick a bird's eye view of the terrain we would be hunting over and to look for the best route for our hike to the cabin from Portage Creek. During the two or three low-level circles we made, two moose and a grizzly bear were sighted. The excitement was building; no wonder with the animals, the snow-clad mountains, glaciers, and colorful terrain. It just couldn't be any better!

We were ready to get on with the program, so headed back to Portage Creek, landed, unloaded, and saw Marc off to Fairbanks where he was to pick up the loaded Supercub. He would be back for the first airdrop at the cabin about 3 p.m. We would have to hurry if we were going to get there at the appointed time. With only the clothes on our backs, light packs with some survival equipment, a few rations, cameras, bows, and fiberglass arrows tipped with Bear razorheads, we were gambling that a successful airdrop would provide the rest of the necessities.

Negotiating the first half mile of marsh was, as suspected, quite tiring and tricky. Tag alder thickets along the river bank had to be avoided as much as possible. About two miles out, we thought it best to make a river crossing to avoid a cliff area on our side. As we approached the river bank, I saw something that made me exclaim, "Hold everything! It looks like we may have a welcoming party on the other side." The back of a big blond grizzly was just barely visible above the brush. The river noise had apparently kept our presence from it. To us, it was quite a startling sight!

Three or four caribou on the slope beyond the bear had noticed us and were poised to bolt. We decided to abandon the crossing and make the best of the side we were on. The caribou took off and in turn alerted the bear. It stood up, swiveled its head, spotted us, took a couple jumps up the slope, and then REALLY looked us over! Then it glanced to the river bank, and out of the brush, two fair-sized cubs nearby headed for Ma bear. By this time, we were making a hasty retreat. We were not in the mood and had no time to argue with their firepower. Apparently the critters were in agreement for they simply ambled off about their business. When they were out of sight we thought it might now be safe to cross the river.

From there on, the going was not too bad. We crossed and recrossed the river about three times. There were several spots with brush tearing at our clothes. Our back quivers hung up occasionally. Clem's quiver was loaded with shiny medals that he had won in field tournaments. We had been questioning that medal-bedecked quiver, even in the Brooks Range. "I just want the critters to know I'm coming," he would retort — a true conservationist!

En route we saw several bands of caribou and several moose which we dared not attempt to shoot because we had no way to take care of them or get them out. There was simply no time for hunting since we must get to the cabin by 3 p.m. The closer we got to the cabin, the more lush the terrain. Colored lichens, vines of red Kinnikinnick berries clung to the ground and covered the sloping hillsides.

It seemed we were never out of sight of at least one or two caribou at all times. So far we had seen no big heads. Some were still in the velvet, but most were shedding and had bits and pieces of velvet hanging from their tines. Some were clean as a whistle and colored brown. We witnessed two of them do a little sparing, but nothing potent. We marvelled at some of the big sun-bleached moose antlers along the way.

All of this reflecting activity in the area was quite heartening. Spirits were high. About six miles out we approached a huge muddy flat just above the river. A big black mountain was the backdrop. From a distance it appeared like the flat was moving. With field glasses, we could see that it was full of caribou. Apparently they were working over a mineral lick. The patches of scrub spruce and willows adjoining this flat would make wonderful cover for a hunter. We were hoping it would be close enough to the cabin for a hunt some time in the future.

On we went, our feet by now very wet and beginning to feel blistery. Yes, they hurt! The hills ahead now were beginning to look like the country we had noted on the earlier flight over the cabin. We figured we must be within a mile or so, and it was 2:30. A little farther on, we saw Marc in the Supercub fly right over our heads and head for the cabin. He circled around and we could see him starting the airdrop. All the non-fragile goods, we hoped, sleeping bags, etc. We finished the hike in a flourish, blisters and all.

Keith set off a flare in an open flat about a hundred yards from the cabin where we wanted the bulk of the drop. The flare would indicate the wind direction for the parachute drop. When the drop was really on, Dick and I recorded it all on movie camera. The chutes drifted as planned with us trying to keep up with their location. It was a beautiful sight. You could tell Marc was relishing his role in this as he made pass after pass.

The arrow boxes were saved for the last. He held one out the window indicating he was about to make the box drop as we had planned. This was to be at a very low level to avoid all possible damage to our arrows. One at a time and sure enough, they came out like they had been programmed. The boxes stayed intact with arrows snug inside. With this done, Marc headed for the river where we had planned to build the strip. There he was to drop the tools. We watched the Cub circle a spot, and out came the sack. We marked the spot in our mind's eye by our position and the mountain backdrop across the river. A bunch of caribou swooped out of the river bottom as he headed back to Portage Creek for the final load.

We had yet to look at this strange cabin with brush growing out of its roof. With a few pieces of the dropped gear and loaded bows, we slowly approached, almost as if we were afraid of what we might find inside.

LITTLE DELTA CABIN

A well-traveled game trail led us right to the doorway. Astride the trail, about 30 feet from the entrance, were several small spruce trees which practically loomed out at us, in that there were claw marks much higher than any of us could reach — black and blond hair everywhere. Rather disconcerting to say the least! The black entrance-way of the cabin yawned out at us like a mouth in awe over the demolished door which lay in disarray on the ground before it.

Surely the commotion of the plane and airdrop would have put all varmints, inside and out, to rout. We slowly entered. Yes, it was empty of critters. The first glance showed us that certainly it was what we had hoped for. Enough light came through two small screened windows to see that there was an overturned table, two chairs, bunks, cupboards and shelves in disarray. A dog sled lay across the bunks in the rear of the cabin. There was a sheet metal stove with cast iron top. A chimney, still in place, was partly hidden by a roof covered entirely by willow shoots. Bears, wolverines, and parka squirrels had apparently sorted through everything — truly a mess. But, with a little cleanup, it would be home sweet home.

"Nobody will believe this!" I exclaimed. "We've found it! For now, we must gather the rest of the gear before we forget where it is."

The chutes were widely scattered. As we headed out for the pick-up, I noticed several small hutches, probably dog kennels, and a root cellar type storage building, all pretty much in shambles. All part of a story, no doubt. A small platform cache built between two trees stood off to the side. Old rusty fruit cans were scattered below.

We soon gathered in the chutes and their precious cargos — Coleman lanterns, fuel, and canned goods, etc. All were temporarily put under the overhang in front of the cabin.

We could now hear Marc on the way back with the rest of the drop. He circled and then started shoving stuff out the door. Sleeping bags, extra clothes were strung out on the ground for a couple hundred yards. With this done, Marc dipped his wing and headed back to Fairbanks. He'd be back in the morning of the 7th day to pick us up from the airstrip we had yet to build. We were now alone for 6 days of hunting in what looked like an animal paradise, and no guides yet! It was now 5 p.m. The drop had taken about two hours.

Cleanup was next on the program. The door must be patched up some way before dark. From the sign around, it was very apparent that this place was a grizzly hangout or at least on a main bear thoroughfare. Yes, fix the door! Clem set to work on that. Besides the tools, nails, etc. we had brought in, there were basic tools hanging in the cabin. Dick and I took on the job of cleaning and straightening up the inside. All the while, we were itching to glass the hillsides. That would have to come later.

A rusty old can was removed from the chimney top, wood was cut, fire started, and water from a pristine creek nearby was soon boiling for more cleaning and washing. Shelves were put back up. A few pots and pans that were scattered about were washed and set in place. An hour or so of this and we began to feel in good shape with our home. Our gear was then unpacked and stored, and lanterns were readied for the night. Clem had straightened the bent hinges and had a semblance of a door in place, complete with a rope latch.

Twilight would soon set in, so a short glassing of the hills seemed appropriate. Yes, they were there alright. Caribou feeding through a flat below us, two moose in a grassy meadow about a mile downstream. A pretty good sized band of white sheep on a big black mountain downriver caught my eye. They were gradually feeding down toward the valley floor. Now all we needed was a little luck. No lack of excitement, for sure!

While gathering our gear we took notice of a patch of blueberries outside the cabin. Sooner or later, we would be into those. During all this initial excitement, we had all but forgotten our water-soaked, blistered feet. They would certainly have to be tended to before morning. Twilight had now set in, but because of the cloudless sky there was still lots of light. It was now time to rest and gather our wits. Dick and Clem would soon prepare a supper of stew. I grabbed my bow, glasses, and with sore feet and all, head for a lofty site above the cabin. There I will assess our surroundings so as to have a better understanding of how to proceed, in the few days left, to build an airstrip and hunt. "Stuff some greenery into the stove just before the soup is ready. The smoke will tip me off and I'll head down."

As I wound my way toward the hill, I could not help but notice the colorful ground cover, tundra, lichens, Kinnikinnick vines, willows, and scrub spruce. I could only reflect in awe as the utmost beauty and solitude enveloped me. I finally reached a perch about 400 feet higher than the cabin. The sun had long gone down over the western ridge across the river. High, snow-capped mountains far up the valley still reflected the sun's rays and glints of glacier ice showed through, all per-haps 10 to 15 miles away, but looking like very close and frigid neigh-bors. From this spot, with my field glasses, I just knew nothing out there could hide from me. Everything was so clear.

The sheep on the black mountain were out of sight. A big bull caribou, feeding furiously near the river below, seemed not yet aware of a few cows that foraged ahead of him. Across the river from me, a big black grizzly was headed upstream, stopping occasionally to rip out a luscious alder root or sniff around granite boulder piles, apparently savoring the scent of many terrorized parka squirrels living under-ground. Four or five ewes and lambs were on a low white cliff area on the river bank, apparently licking at the tasty minerals encased in the clay. Something was moving pretty good-sized willow branches in a big patch about a mile upstream. Further glassing showed an occasional glint of cream-colored antlers. No doubt a moose haven. I wondered if the grizzly that was headed that way and the moose were aware of how close they were to each other, or even if they cared.

I could see part of the gravel bar where we were to make the airstrip — tomorrow's project. To my left and on the same hillside I was on, a big bull caribou hove into view. Could I intercept him and put fresh meat on the table? He was in a fast walk, feeding as he went, shak-ing his head occasionally to rid himself of the velvet he was shedding. My blistered feet told me no; even if I was in good shape, it would be a difficult intercept. I was tired and hungry. The animals would be there tomorrow and, time permitting after our work on the strip, perhaps then. A curl of near white smoke poured from the cabin below. I head-ed back slowly. A happy hour, consisting of a short drink of bourbon and water was in progress. The beef stew was great.

We next nursed our feet and prepared for the morrow. The two movie cameras were reloaded and made ready. Lunches were prepared, as daylight would come early and we would not want to waste it. Even the excitement of this day did not keep us from sleeping very soundly. Yes, Clem made blueberry pancakes in the morning. He could not resist gathering some the night before.

About 6 a.m. we were on our way toward the airstrip site, a half mile away down a slight slope through low ground cover, streaked with a few little creeks. In the middle of a big gravel bar beside the river, we found the sack of tools. Evidently, this was Marc's choice of the landing strip. Clem, experienced about such things, immediately paced off a hundred by thirty yard section of this gravel bar. With machetes, the willow patches dotted here and there were soon made short work of. Boulders were rolled aside. After about two hours of this, the strip began to take shape. A break was in order. We gathered up our cameras and bows and headed upstream on a scouting sortie.

Pristine country, the glacial stream was low, not over our boot tops. Glaciers do not melt during the frigid night. We'd gone about a mile to where a big glacial tributary entered from our left. The huge valley opened up and exposed a backdrop of the magnificent snow-capped peaks of Mount Hayes, Hess, and Deborah — all about 13,000-footers. The weather was clear. I could never get over the fact that objects very far away looked so close. A country where you could see forever and so quiet you could hear a pin drop. Far up against lower hills, caribou were feeding, too far, but looking very close. We had not yet seen the right one in the right place.

While glassing, I suddenly caught a movement out of the corner of the glasses and was startled practically out of my wits to find that right in front of us, a big "hairy" head loomed up, not twenty yards away. It was sticking right out of the top of a big patch of willows. Not wanting to make a sound, I banged the arms of Clem and Dick and pointed. We instinctively readied our bows and stood there transfixed. The bear looked right at us, then looked upstream, as two smaller heads popped up. Hey, was this the trio we had seen downstream near Portage?

I don't know how we looked to the bears, but I know that these three critters looked pretty awesome to us. Cameras should have been rolling. I've seen a few grizzlies in my travels, but obviously I have never been confronted by a real hungry one. These were no exception. With a low woof and a bound, Mama bear herded her offspring away from us. With a sigh of relief, we climbed the hill behind us to get a bet-

Downstream look at Little Delta River valley from hillside above cabin. Black mountain in the background.

ter overview. The bears soon settled down as if nothing unusual had happened, only to give an occasional glance. Yes, we were still on their minds.

Our ridgetop vantage point again accentuated the tremendous mountain peaks behind the big valley. Caribou were still there. There was no sign of the moose we had seen the day before in the big willow patch now below us. The band of sheep I'd seen yesterday was now feeding up the black mountain. Yes, tomorrow I would head for them. Wherever we went, it seemed there was always something in sight. With the work at the airstrip in mind and our sore feet, none of us were in the mood to really try for anything today. Tomorrow would be the day of reckoning.

We ate our lunch and headed back to the strip to finish our job. By the end of the day we felt our work was done and we would be ready for the Supercub when it came in to pick us up. It was our job to make some kills. It seemed strange, but we had seen no birds, no grouse or ptarmigan. We had shot no arrows. After a short rest we did a little practicing with blunts. Now it was back to the cabin, tired but enthusiastic about our lot.

We are ready to look over the surrounding cabin area for clues to the story behind this unique setting. The root cellar type building is partially underground, probably to make use of the refrigerator temperatures found in the tundra — too dilapidated for any use now, however. There are seven or eight almost demolished dog kennels. We surmise that the several rusty cans of food that lay under the tree cache had probably been pitched from above by ravaging wolverines. It was too high for a bear, but teeth and claw marks indicated that bears were involved. Several sheep skulls lie here and there. The last human inhabitants here also knew of the tasty sheep meat. A pile of gnawed and deteriorating bones nearby attested to a life of living off of the land — probably long before hunting laws were in existence in the Territory of Alaska.

The cabin, about 14 by 20-feet, has a fairly smooth wood floor. There are circular saw marks still evident. 2 by 2-foot glass windows are covered by wire mesh on the inside with spruce bars nailed on the outside. All of this semi-finished lumber and glass must have been brought in by dog sled from the nearest town, where the Little Delta joined the Tanana River and the Richardson Highway, 50 miles away. The sled, 2 by 10-feet, is still in good shape. Its frame of spruce poles is held together with rawhide. It has 3/4-inch wide polished steel runners.

A big spruce ridgepole about 12-inch average diameter runs from end to end and out over the front to hold up an 8-foot overhang. The rafters, half-round spruce poles, show marks of whipsawing. They are set in a slight peak and hold up a birch bark roof covered with sod and gravel. This sod is the life support for a spectacular growth of willows growing out of the top of the roof. The cabin perimeter logs are 8- to 9-inch in diameter, adz smooth on the inside and tightly chinked with moss on both sides against the hard winters that no doubt prevail in this area.

The cupboard and shelf lumber also show saw marks. A trap door in the floor covers a box type area holding a few odds and ends of old rotten canvas, rope and rawhide. There are claw marks on this door — bears have been curious. Wolf and wolverine traps hang inside and out under the overhang. Two 6-foot crosscut saws hang on rusty nails on the outside wall. Two wood planes, an axe, and a couple of hammers are hanging here and there — all part of the past. We wonder . . . trappers, of course; prospectors, perhaps? Somebody knows. We will try to find out when we get back to Fairbanks.

Twilight has again set in and it is now close to chow time. We are having moose steaks tonight from Clem's freezer. Tomorrow we should have fresh meat. Hopefully, we will have our moment of truth that we have been looking for these past three weeks. We prepare our hunting gear for the morrow, nurse our feet, and head for our bunks. Our heads are doing a lot of conjecturing. Will that band of sheep on the black mountain be where I want it to be? Are they as wild as hunting stories say? Will the big moose be in the willow patch and caribou be heading downstream from all directions? All thoughts — perhaps well into the night. As of now we are ready. The flames in the Coleman lanterns fan our fancies and polarize our thoughts for tomorrow. The aurora borealis is in full bloom. We wonder what the folks are doing back home.

THIS IS THE DAY WE HUNT – DAY ONE

The northern lights were awesome last night. Lights flickering in our tiny windows got us out of bed. Wave after wave of ribbons swept the sky — ever-changing. A sense of reverence sweeps over you. Something up there really is in charge, and brings one to thinking we are all just one small notch above being insignificant in the scheme of things on this planet. It is breaking daylight. My two companions and I are outside the cabin now, glassing the hills. Then back inside for a quick, but hearty, breakfast.

Today we hunt and perhaps run some film through our movie cameras. What to hunt is the question — the sheep that will be on the ridgetops later in the day, migrating caribou, or the moose in willow thickets both up and downstream?

The black mountain sheep that I have been watching for the last couple of days are not in sight, but it's too early — 6 a.m. It's misting a bit, low clouds, not too thick — should clear later. The sheep probably fed all night in the valley bottom and with the lack of warm air currents on the rise, the sheep will be late in heading up the mountain. Regardless, today is the day I will hunt sheep.

Clem is heading upstream to the moose pasture. Dick will try to intercept a nice bull caribou on its way out of the hills. Clem and Dick will be carrying the cameras. To have a successful hunting story, we need to take some animals.

Nobody will be following me with a camera today. That can come later if we have time. I must travel light to get over and around the big boulders I see through the glasses on the big mountain. The mile or so trip downstream was uneventful. The cloud cover is starting to lift. I've crossed the now shallow river without it going over my boot tops. I'm leaving them on this side of the river. I'm now in my tennis shoes. The cloud cover seems to be lifting just ahead of me as I climb. I can now see some of the sheep about a half a mile away. They too are following the cloud cover up, feeding as they go. The valley floor below is beginning to take on that "seeing forever" aspect. Shed moose antlers dot the area, a caribou here and there — several lone sheep way off toward the opposite peaks.

Dick is slowly sidehilling below the opposite ridge, about a mile away, a most colorful carpet of cover under his feet. He stops to glass occasionally. There is little movement in the air. Wisps of clouds slowly rise. The sun will be poking through soon.

I glass in the direction of the sheep. Boy, oh boy, there are some nice rams slowly working upward toward some slab shelves jutting out from the mountain. They are about a quarter of a mile away. I am in no hurry now. I must bide my time for the sheep to settle down before I make my stalk. I need the rest. I have been climbing over house-size boulders — tough going. A misstep would put me into a hole I may never get out of. Clem and Dick know where I am. My arrows are snugly seated in a St. Charles backquiver. A still camera and lunch are in a little sack attached to my belt. My Kodiak bow is lying in some gravel at my side. It transfixes my fantasizing gaze. What will the day bring? I came so far for this. All my preparations, stories read and listened to. A pebble, loosened by my foot bounds down the slope. Sounds like a freight train. How will I ever approach those white critters in this environment? A small flock of ptarmigan, just turning color, lifts off of a slab below. They are the first ones I have seen. Surely that pebble didn't disturb them. The hawk above also notices. He is waiting for his chance. He sails off across the valley — maybe he was just scouting for future reference.

The sun is now out and begins to spread a glow across the hillside. I can feel the warmth as it begins to trickle into my bones. Vapor lifts off of the damp rocks. The sheep also have noticed the warmth. Some have reached the slab rock shelves and are beginning to look like it's snooze time. They are sniffing here and there and gazing out over the valley below. So far, they seem to not have a care in the world. I will wait and watch. It isn't long before it appears they have found where they will have their afternoon siesta. The uppermost band is on a big ledge, about three quarters of the way up towards the top of the ridge.

Although they are quite distant, staying out of sight would be the best approach. I will go directly up and over the top of the ridge and approach from the backside. Hopefully I will find a good ravine to slip down to get into position.

It's about 11 a.m. I am directly above the sheeps' sleeping pad. There are no sheep in sight. But this has to be the place. I am on a grassy slope with shale pockets here and there, lichens in every nook and cranny. Colorful Kinnikinnick berry vines appear to crawl across some of the flat rocks. Should I eat my lunch? The upwind drafts are in my favor. I think better of it.

I start my descent. I am about 200 yards from the ledge. Not bad when you think about what I read about the 500-yard rifle shots. The terrain and ground cover is ideal — humps and hollows. My black wool pants, and black and white plaid shirt should blend in well with the black rock and granite shale. It appears I will be in sight of the sheep for the last 60 yards, while going over some humps. Slowly, I crawled, easing my bow alongside. All goes well — at about 100 yards the sheep come into view. There are nine of them, all full curl, spread out over a 75 by 100-foot area. They are gazing, chewing their cuds, dozing.

I continue my descent. Some of them glance up occasionally, but are not concerned. But, most surely, they must hear something. I carefully take off my shoes — wool socks will do the work from here on down.

Now I am beginning to wonder and worry. Why am I so close and they are not aware — or are they aware and don't care? Such a dilemma! Now I can see there is a mound of gravel and dirt at the bottom of the slope from which the big ledge juts. It is covered with tall grass the full width of the ledge. If I can only get into that ditch, it will put me about 25 yards from the sheep. Slowly down — some shale slides loose. Yes, they hear. Some look. Still no concern. The winds and God are certainly with me so far. Inching my way over the last rise in view of my quarry, I am all but breathless. Now I am out of sight and inch my way into the ditch. With no apparent reason to make a hasty shot, I choose to take stock of my luck. According to the "experts," I am in an impossible situation. No one, but no one, gets this close to nine big rams. Can something be wrong? Am I missing something? Yes, it worries me. I'm actually sitting down, trying to think it out. I've come 3,000 miles to experience this moment. All of my homework — is this the payoff? What situation could be better than this?

Now there is slight crosswind — still in my favor. Through the swaying tall grass I can plainly see the sheep are still not concerned. My watch and heart seem to pound in unison — loud! I must get on with the program. I carefully unload my back quiver and lay ten arrows in the grass. I must be ready to shoot like a machine gun! None of the critters are looking my way. I nock an arrow and slowly rise and shoot. I frantically reach for and shoot arrows until all are gone. *I have just flock shot at nine big rams without touching a single one and they haven't even bothered to get up off the ground! Now I know what was wrong, but too late. Why didn't I think about this? These sheep had never seen a human being! Never had been harassed or shot at. I am standing in full view and they simply look at me almost as dumbfounded as I am. But who is going to believe it? We continue to stare at each other. One is getting up. It stretches its legs and stands, still looking. A few more seconds and I have my wits about me. I slowly walk toward them. At 15 yards, the rest are getting up, not real concerned — curious. Several stretch, stand up. They are standing for a bit. Now they are slowly starting to walk down the slope. I can see my arrows ground into the rocks. The last ram is starting to follow the rest and I am only seven or eight yards from him. Incredible! They are doing everything but help me pick up what is left of my arrows! They are slowly walking away and joining others below them.*

I cannot believe what is happening! I retrieve some arrows that look salvageable. I am limp as a rag, trying to reconstruct the errors I've just committed. Was I relying too much on my reading — did I psyche myself out for too long before the shot? Questions will be with me forever. I finally bring myself to eat lunch and put new heads on five of the arrows worth using. I file the heads and load them into the backquiver. I am too unnerved to try for another stalk on the same band now out of sight. Perhaps another day, if there is time.

I was about 3-1/2 miles from the cabin. I headed back over the boulder-strewn route, peeking over every cliff, every bench. I did spot another nice ram directly below me and at the base of a cliff — a shot of about 30 yards. I could have dropped a rock on it. It was a difficult try with the limb of the bow between my legs, all of the time trying to keep from falling over the cliff. The arrow looked good. I ducked back, looked again. The ram was looking directly at me. My arrow had just grazed his back. With another arrow nocked, I looked again. He was gone. What luck! I continued on my way in disbelief at this day. I was haunted by what had happened.

One thing I learned for sure, never believe the written word of the so-called "hunting experts." Take each hunt at face value. Animal behavior is never quite predictable. Apparently because the sheep behavior was not according to my programming, my behavior was not normal. I know that I am a better shot than that. If only I'd had the movie camera, or if someone had been with me, I could have had that all on film. I second guessed all the way back, stopped only twice — once to rest and once to glass the area for the last time before heading down to the river crossing.

LIFE ON THE TUNDRA GOES ON

Scouting the valley with binoculars from the rim above most always produced interesting episodes somewhere. This particular time, what caught my eye, perhaps a half mile or so away, was a blond grizzly grubbing in and around a 20 by 30-foot granite boulder pile. Brush protruded here and there. The energy that this bear was expending as he dashed from one boulder to another was certainly an indication that something important to him was keeping his attention.

With a little more scrutiny I was able to determine that he was trying to catch a parka squirrel, a tasty morsel, part of a day's work for the bear and very life threatening to the squirrel. The action was so fast and furious, it almost seemed like there were several parka squirrels, the way this one kept popping up in different places. The bear rolled boulders, dug holes, tore at the brush, and all the while the squirrel managed to keep out of reach.

I don't know how long this had been going on before I noticed the chase, but after the 15 minutes that I had been watching, the bear sat down as if to ponder, or maybe it was sheer exhaustion. But no, the bear picked up a boulder and appeared to be waiting for something to happen. Sure enough, across the pile, up popped the squirrel — the bear heaved the boulder at the parka, down went the little head, the bear stayed where he was and up popped the parka right in front of the bear! A big paw quickly gathered up the little squirrel and laid it on a rock. He then began to lick the parka as if to savor it before stuffing it into his big mouth. The tail of the parka which was partly exposed started to flutter. The squirrel had come to life. I thought, oh no, is he going to eat the critter alive? But no — he merely raised the paw as if to smash it. Up popped the parka and dove under a nearby rock! The bear looked at his paw as if he couldn't believe what he was seeing. He scrambled up and the chase was on again for how long I don't know.

The grizzly was a cub, no doubt, as an experienced bear certainly would not have allowed that parka to get away. I headed back to the cabin.

Another day on another part of the valley rim, through my glasses again, I'm watching another big blond grizzly with two cubs, approach a little flat perhaps a mile or so away. This flat had collected itself a little pond into which the three bears jumped — water flying everywhere! They raced back and forth, tumbled and played like there was no tomorrow. After about 10 minutes of this, Ma bear got out, shook herself, sat down, and watched her offspring, who were still wildly mixing it up. She then proceeded to head out looking as if she expected them to follow, but no, they didn't even notice her leaving. Ma bear then lumbered back to the water's edge, apparently trying to get their attention, but to no avail. She then dove into the pond after them, gave each a swat, literally spinning them end over end out of the pond, water flying everywhere! She HAD their attention! Off they went! Child abuse you say? No, just another day on the Little Delta where wildlife never ceases to be interesting.

I Continue To Glass – Day Two

Yes, there still were animals out in force on the hillsides. The wind was now blowing at a pretty good clip and the shadows of low clouds sailed along the valley, intermittently allowing sun to shine through on these colorful slopes. Small bands of caribou heading out of the valleys were fast feeding at a gait hard for a human to match. They would pause and snatch at morsels along the way — two to six in a bunch, ever on the move.

It's about 3 p.m. Dick is on the other side barely in sight, apparently hiding in a well-concealed draw, glassing the hills for the right intercept. Clem is not in sight — perhaps after the big one upstream. A bull moose is feeding on the valley floor directly below me. A cow and a calf are feeding nearby. They are across the river from the mineral lick. All are not too far from Dick's perch, but obviously out of his sight. I head on down to the crossing. A bevy of ptarmigan float out over the slope ahead of me and drop into a blueberry patch below. Two stragglers fall to what was left of my mangled sheep arrows — we'll have them for supper.

I waded the now swollen stream in my tennis shoes, changed on the other side into my boots and headed for the "log barn." The last mile, I did a lot of pondering on what I would tell my partners to make my unbelievable day sound believable. Almost ran into a small black grizzly grubbing for alder roots along the stream bank. He obliged by running off, thus not adding to my already troubled mind.

As I entered the cabin area, a few parka squirrels scrambled for cover over the red carpet of Kinnikinnick berry vines — color that I had never before seen the like anywhere . There was no one around. Clem had apparently come in and left again. Some of his morning gear was hanging from the overhang. I shed some excess baggage and quickly made a peanut butter sandwich and headed for the high slope back of the cabin. There I glassed for the hunters. I was winded as I reached my vantage point, but gradually settled down into my glassing of the humps and ravines on both sides of the valley. While sweeping my side of the slope, something caught my eye about a half mile downstream. Further observation showed someone was moving at a pretty good clip toward the valley floor. Yes, it was Dick running just below the crest of a small ridge, quiver and pack flailing wildly on his back. Right behind him is Clem, bow in one hand, camera in the other.

What in the world, I conjectured. Then — yes! The top of a caribou rack appears barely from the other side of the ridge, then disappears again below the crest. The boys are trying to get ahead of the bull and perhaps others. No matter   the rack I saw was plenty big enough Yes, now there are several bobbing racks — a beautiful hunting scene, if I've ever seen one. Finally all of the bodies seem to arrive near the valley floor at the same time. Dick pulls up, kneels and prepares to shoot. Clem tosses his bow aside and readies the camera from about ten yards back. As Dick crouches low to draw, the big bull moves into sight slightly facing him — it pauses to snatch a clump. It exposes the side Dick wants. The arrow is away! It appears that the bull almost drops in his tracks. No contest! Oh, if only Clem got that on film! At this time, it can be the break we need, with only two more hunting days!

I am now on my way to the scene of this action. My arrival is barely noticed as the hunters are rehashing the shot and exclaiming over the kill. Congratulations were in order, pictures were taken and best of all, Clem felt that he got the much needed movies. Our first real strike! The rack was tremendous!

But now, preparation of the meat for the trek back to the cabin. A slight misting from the cloud cover above was barely noticed and the meat was soon hanging under the cabin's overhang. Yes, we were bushed!

Dick Bolding with first recorded Pope and Young Club Book Barren Ground Caribou.

STORY TIME

It was now 6:30 p.m., time for the happy hour and rehash of the day: Clem had come back early from chasing the moose. This time the moose had a girl friend. Each time Clem would make a stalk, the cow would switch places with the bull between a spruce thicket and a thick willow patch, and finally he found himself trying to get off a shot when he should have been taking pictures and every time he'd go to take pictures it appeared like he should have been shooting arrows. Trying to take good pictures and hunting at the same time does not work out well for anybody. You need two people. Other than getting pictures, he felt like he was wasting his time and returned early. He spotted Dick from the high perch as I had. He headed down the valley and joined Dick about lunch time. The two planned caribou strategy and waited for the right ambush — the one I had witnessed.

They turned in unison to me: "Now you — what happened?" Almost apologetically, I told my story. I offered no excuses except to say that I simply panicked over a situation that seemed too good to be true, and was — by every story ever written in a sporting goods magazine. Oddly enough, the boys were not too surprised. The behavior of the animals in this area was not normal. Early that morning, a hawk attacked Clem's quiver of arrows on his way to the moose pasture. There was no evidence of wolves — caribou unconcerned at our sight — lots of ptarmigan. The few red foxes we saw looked healthy and fat — grizzlies very laid back and curious. Moose did not run clear out of the country. Obviously, the animals here had not been hunted for years or had never seen a human being. Clem felt the moose upstream could be had with two hunters and a little time. Two more days was not much time, and we would have to pick our priorities. The sheep, though plentiful, would have to wait. Already, we were thinking about coming back next year. Tomorrow, September 5th, we would all go to the mineral lick downstream and hunt caribou there and moose in the pasture across the way. Dick would carry the camera. We still needed pictures.

For now, a celebration was in order. As the happy hour progressed, the question came up as to what Dick's huge rack would score in the newly proposed bowhunting version of the Boone and Crockett Records. Earlier, I had detailed to the fellows the progress of the proposal that my committee had given to the NFAA directors on May 1st, that same year. No word had been heard from them, prior to my coming to Alaska. Anyhow, we surmised that Dick's caribou would have to be right up to the top, and the more we drank, the bigger it got!

Next on the program was a supper of ptarmigan. Dick and Clem had each come up with one, and my two, along with spuds, made a scrumptious meal. Lunches were put up, cameras readied, broadheads sharpened. We check the clearing weather. It's about 35 degrees F. Dog tired, we hit the sack. We were again awakened during the night by a tremendous aurora flashing through our tiny windows — awesome to say the least! And we watched it from time to time throughout the night.

DAY THREE

Early morning found us up and consuming another breakfast of blueberry pancakes. Then, gear in tow, we headed out the door, through the usual flurry of scurrying parka squirrels, then downstream, with Clem and me looking for our first kill. Dick, camera ready, would bring up the rear in hope of getting some much needed movies.

As we progressed down the right side of the valley, at an elevation which would best afford a good view of the valley floor, a change in the weather was noted. The misty low-hanging clouds that were there when we started from the cabin were now clearing away and the sun was beginning to peak through. If this trend continued, we would certainly have a comfortable day. We had covered about a mile, when Ma grizzly and her two kids were spotted across the river. It looked like a good setting for pictures. We cautiously made our way down the slope, staying out of sight as much as possible. The bears appeared to be demolishing a blueberry patch. At about 50 yards we set up cameras with the telephotos and started filming. It wasn't long until they apparently winded us and headed up the other slope into a patch of small spruce — the last we saw of them. We did get some footage, however. We then proceeded back up to higher elevation and on down the river. Soon we were opposite the mineral lick. The caribou were going in and out and this appeared to be the place to hunt. Hopefully we wouldn't have to cross the river. There seemed to be plenty of caribou crossing on our side.

Clem headed in one direction, I in another. Dick was to stay on high ground where he could watch both of us and wait for a chance to shoot some hunting scenes. I had the other camera and would try to get some caribou footage near the lick. It wasn't long before a fair bull spotted me and approached, apparently curious. I dug the camera out of

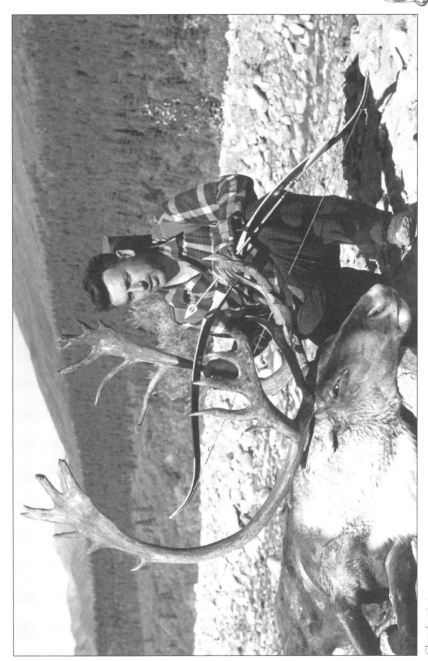

Glenn's prize.

Work begins for Clem and Glenn on Glenn's caribou.

my pack and began filming this curious bull. He started circling me and each time around he would cross the river. When he got fairly close, I laid the camera down and prepared for a shot the next time he came by. He was in and out of some spruce thickets and it looked like a shot was going to present itself. I got all set. The arrow looked good at about 30 yards and smacked the caribou in the right place and down it went within a few yards.

Dick had filmed some of it, having seen what was happening from up above. Clem, who had been shagging bulls for the last hour or so, was hailed down to help with the dressing out and the three mile back pack of meat to the airfield — a long day. The rack on this caribou didn't have much bragging rights. However, it looked awfully good to me! One more day — our last. Clem was getting a little anxious. Nothing that an upended moose or caribou wouldn't cure.

Came that last day, upstream this time, back to the moose willow patch. Dick and I with cameras would follow Clem and see if we couldn't run the "big one" over to him. Yes, the bull was there, alright, and also a cow. Clem could not get in the right place at the right time, although the bull cooperated by moving in and out of the willow and spruce thickets. He was evidently bent on following that cow. We finally had to give up and a disappointed trio headed back to the cabin. We had much to do to get all of our gear ready and packed to the airstrip for a Marc pick up at 10 a.m. tomorrow.

Boy, did we ever hate to leave this place. We hadn't discussed it much, but we were all thinking the same thing — leave the things that we might need for next year! Nothing goes out that doesn't have to. We took last minute pictures — thought about keeping out the bears. No way could this be done. Just leave the door open and hope for the best. Three hours of this preparation. It's only four o'clock.

Moose Pedro

Clem is obviously very disappointed — he had chances — luck was not coming his way. "Hey, we have things about ready to go," I suggest halfheartedly. "There is plenty of daylight left. Why don't you and I take a walk down to the moose pasture across from the lick? It will be twilight till about 8." "Naw," Clem said, "it's too late to get anything out even if we did make a kill." Dick then picked up on the idea. "You guys go and I'll finish up here." Well, the more we kicked the idea around, the better it sounded. We soon found ourselves working more obviously in that direction and going on the last minute hunt! I loaded the camera in my pack — Clem strummed his bow, looked over his arrows, and without any more adieu, we headed out. I was never one to worry about the consequences of any future doing until I was through with the present. My motto was to get them down and then worry about getting them out!

The sky was now overcast. Snowy peaks far back were barely visible. Again our route was fairly high along the right slopes above the swollen river, better to glass the valley floor as we went along. We passed the remains of Dick's caribou. It looked like the wolverines had worked it over — not much left — a bear would have covered it. Sheep could be seen slowly working their way down the black mountain. Caribou fed here and there. Occasionally the clouds would part and let a warm sun ray through. As we neared the lick area, we could see caribou possibilities.

With the glasses, we swept the valley floor and the moose pasture directly to our right and below us. Out of that hollow, loomed what we were really looking for — the white palmated armor of a big one. A moose! He was at least three hundred yards away and chomping in the middle of a willow patch surrounded by scattered scrub spruce trees. It was worth a try.

As we slowly approached this monster, I looked for a place to anchor the camera. At 200 yards I stopped, prepared for filming with the long lens, steadying the camera against a small spruce. Clem continued on down into the hollow, checking the wind as he rolled off the hillside into the bottom. Soon, through the camera I caught glimpses of Clem stalking from tree to tree. Hopefully I was getting pictures. The light was still pretty good. Clem was getting closer and closer and went out of sight at what looked like about 20 yards from the moose which was quartering away from him.

The next thing I knew, the moose was in full flight and seemed to be headed for the nearby river and right past Clem! Surely, he had been hit! I must be getting pictures of the whole scene. Yes, that's it — the critter is headed for the river, apparently to get away from what he thinks are wolves. The next thing I know, I'm off the side of the hill and headed pell mell after the other two scrambling bodies. I catch up to Clem, who is anxiously wondering about the fate of the critter who is wobbling about in water up to his belly. All Clem's arrows are gone. Quite a sight — empty quiver covered with glittering medals. The moose goes down and starts to bump along in the swollen stream. Clem follows along the bank. As the river widens out the water gets shallower and the moose is stranded against a rock.

What to do? We have no rope. Clem wades out and gets close enough to hook his bow over one of the palms, pulls it loose from the rock and slowly drags it closer to shore. I scramble to help, and again get it lodged between two rocks where Clem hopes it can be held until we can figure out what to do. What a predicament! It is now six p.m. Clem cannot stand the ice cold water for very long and all we can hope is the water will not get much higher before it starts to lower. I head for help, three miles away. Clem is in for a long wait.

An hour and a half later Dick and I arrive back with some salvaging gear, a Coleman lantern, rope, and packboards. A rope is now attached around the antlers. The three of us tug and tug but to no avail. The critter won't budge. There is nothing we can do until the river goes down and leaves the carcass higher and dryer.

Clem has already slashed a hole in the carcass above the water line, not wanting it to fill up with silt and sand from the runoff. The Coleman lantern is hung from a willow tripod for use when needed. All we can do now is sit by the fire and wait. The long twilight has set in. Three hours later, there is no change in the river. But darkness has finally set in and I am beginning to wonder if I shouldn't change my

Clem with first recorded Pope and Young Club Book Alaska Moose.

Star-studded sun beams on Glenn and Dick. Mount Hayes in the background.

idea about getting critters down and then worrying about getting them out. He is down all right but there is no way we are going to get him out of this frigid river until morning.

It's a long night. About 1 a.m. it appears the river is receding. At 3 a.m. the water is still knee deep. At 5 a.m. it is daylight, and we are able to get to the carcass and start dismantling it. At 6 a.m. we are taking a few pictures, loading our packs, and heading upriver three miles to the airstrip. It's a tough haul — over rocks, sand bars — you name it. At 7:30 we have dropped the first load and head back for more. There will be at least one more trip for all of us. We are dead tired but have to be concerned about that 10 a.m. deadline! However, Marc will have two loads to ferry down to Portage Creek before he has to think about taking us and the rest of our gear out. It's about 9:45 when we get back with the second load. Clem heads back for the last batch of gear and meat while Dick and I start out to secure the cabin.

HEADED HOME

Sure enough, at very close to ten o'clock, the Supercub appeared on the downriver horizon. It then circled over about where Clem could be and continued on up to our airstrip, looking it over very carefully, and sizing it up for the first landing. Dick and I watched from the cabin, a half mile away. The Supercub finally eased into the strip and out of our sight. We heard it taxiing, apparently over to the obvious pile of gear and meat we had readied to be ferried to the outgoing staging area at Portage Creek. As we busied ourselves buttoning up the cabin, we had our ears cocked for the plane to take off with the first load. Ten or fifteen minutes went by — still no take-off. We began to wonder. After about thirty minutes, we got concerned and decided we'd better head for the strip. The cabin all taken care of, we hurriedly gathered up the remainder of our stuff and, with loaded packs, headed down.

About twenty minutes later, we found the plane parked alright, but with Dick "Mac" McIntyre sitting on our pile of stuff! Nothing had been loaded and we were surprised to find the pilot to be McIntyre instead of Marc Stella! Mac was concerned about the length of our airstrip. It was O.K. for landing. But he did not cotton to taking off with a load and trail the wheels through the tall willow shoots at the end of the strip. He wanted fifty more yards of clearance! Oboy, THAT would take some doing!

Trailing landing gear through the willows, Supercub comes in on our custom landing strip.

The tools? Yes, they were stashed over on the side. About two hours later, we had a swath cut long enough and wide enough to satisfy our pilot. Clem showed up with the last load of moose meat and gear. We helped Mac with the loading. The caribou and moose racks went out, one at a time, strapped to the wing struts. Care had to be taken with the moose palms so that they didn't affect any of the aerodynamics of the Supercub.

Dick and Clem were the next to go to Portage Creek. There, they would wait and eat their lunch or whatever, while Mac took me all the way in to Fairbanks. He would then go back with the Tri-Pacer for them and all of their equipment and meat.

On the way in, over the roar of the motor, I "bent" Mac's ear about what he might know about the history of the cabin we had been in — had he any idea who the trappers were? After a bit of musing about my question, Mac recalled that years ago, when his sporting goods store was situated right next to the Nordale Hotel, there were a couple of fellows who would occasionally hole up in the hotel for three or four days at a time. They had some holdings somewhere in the Delta River country. They shopped at his store and he chatted with them on several occasions. He thought one of them was named Milkoff — yes, that's it, George Milkoff. The other, he didn't remember. They were Russians —

spoke with a heavy accent. Perhaps they are still there. That was all I needed for now!

Upon landing at the small plane strip at Fairbanks, Mac parked the Cub beside the Tri-Pacer, which he promptly cranked up, and headed back to get Dick and Clem at Portage Creek. Meanwhile, I loaded my stuff in Mac's pickup and headed for the Nordale Hotel to check in. I had about 2-1/2 hours to nose around before Mac would be back with the other two. It was now about 2 p.m.

A Russian Trapper Tells His Story

Registering in at the Nordale was overshadowed by my eagerness to check with the clerk about Milkoff. Yes, he was still there! With my stuff safely stowed in my room, I knocked on a nearby door. As the door opened, I was greeted by a weathered looking character, the likes of which you would expect to find in a frontier town. He was the same fellow I had seen paying his rent with gold dust a month ago! Hesitatingly, I stated my mission. His eyes lit up and the next thing I know, I was invited into his quarters. It was cluttered with memorabilia of his days as a miner and a trapper. And soon, through a thick Russian accent, I was hearing the story about the Little Delta trapper's cabin and the mining cabin and buildings below the Portage Creek airstrip. No doubt there was more to this story. He was obviously curious and pleased about our use of the cabin and interest in it. He was more than willing to tell the story. As it unfolded, I was a willing listener for the next hour and a half.

In the early '20s, George and his partner, while prospecting, had found gold in the creeks that fed the Little Delta River at Portage Creek. The find was good enough to warrant putting up a cabin and outbuildings for a more permanent stay. This was done in 1926. The strip nearby was accessed by a trail from the cabin. The strip was put there by the Government for surveying crews that were working in this vast area. George and his partner scheduled flights in from Fairbanks for their provisions and occasionally they would go out for a stay at the Nordale Hotel. When the snow flew and mining was no longer feasible for the year, they took to trapping in the ten miles between the two cabins and throughout the little valleys entering the big valley of the west fork of the Little Delta. The upper cabin we hunted out of was built in 1927.

During the better years of their trapping, they kept sled dogs for their weekly runs to check the traps for wolves, foxes, and wolverines.

They had frequent visits by Frank Glaser, a government hunter whose job was to cull the wolves enough so that they wouldn't have too much impact on the resident sheep, caribou, and moose in the territory. No doubt Glaser's work accounted for the lack of skittishness of the animals thereabouts. We had not seen a wolf while hunting the Little Delta. I asked George about the numbers of grizzlies we'd seen in the area. Had they bothered their cabins or traps? They occasionally ravaged a trap when they found an animal. The sled dogs they kept at the cabin always sounded an alarm when grizzlies were around and seemed to deter them away from the cabin. Whenever they left the cabin for any length of time, the bears would bash down the door and grub out the inside for whatever they could find in the way of food. The trappers hunted sheep, caribou, and moose for food, both for them and the dogs. Games laws were very liberal. This undoubtedly accounted for many of the sheep, caribou, and moose horns found in the vicinity. He was surprised at our being at the cabin and hunting, with a bow and arrow yet!

I questioned him about the huge ridgepole for the trapper cabin and the hewn lumber for the walls. There were no big trees in the area. Where did they come from? The ridgepole had come from the lower valley toward Richardson, as did the sawn lumber and logs for the side walls. All were from a little one-horse mill at Richardson. It was all sledded in on the sled that was still at the cabin. Squatter's rights was the law of the land at the time. Due to the drop in fur prices and diminishing prices in finds of gold, they gave up in 1936. With plenty of money to live on, they were able to make the Nordale their home.

George was happy that we had found use for his cabin. It worried me some that he might be as generous with his cabin with somebody else. As I posed this question, a big grin assured me that our secret was safe — so far as anyone else was concerned, our hunt was some other place.

It was time to get the truck back to the strip. The fellows would be in. It was 4 p.m. I thanked Milkoff for the interesting afternoon and left. I grabbed a sandwich at the in-house coffee shop and headed for the airstrip to meet the guys. They showed up about 4:30. We unloaded — took our meat to a nearby processing plant, our horns to Mac's Sport Shop. We would check them out with the Fish and Wildlife Service in the morning.

It was time for goodbyes. We had settled with McIntyre. Clem gathered Dick and me up with all of our gear, horns, packaged meat, etc., stopped at the Wildlife Headquarters to make the necessary check-out and then it was on to the airport. Dick and I boarded the old Alaska Airlines DC-4 again and were soon headed south for home. Looking out the window of the plane, we saw Clem patting his moose horns as he turned to us with a big smile. Yes, it was all worthwhile and we'll be going back!

First Little Delta Hunt – Upshot

We had been away for nearly a month. It was time now for reflection. What would we find back at the "barn" in Seattle. I had left Margaret with five kids and an archery shop to take care of. It wouldn't be a simple homecoming — it would take getting acquainted all over again.

Dick and I also discussed the possibilities and options for the trip back to the Little Delta next year. There was lots of unfinished business to take care of, like more pictures for the Alaska Airlines film. Hopefully, the transportation and expense contract would stay in place. The big question was: who would be going? who would I ask? and who could go? Dick confirmed his desire to go back — job and vacation time permitting. Clem's military obligations would be a factor. I am sure Fred Bear would love to go, but I would have to consider his tendency to take charge. I had to be assured that nothing got in the way of my obligation to Alaska Airlines. Oh, well. There is lots of time to think about these options. First to get the 16mm movie film developed and see what we have to work with.

Meanwhile, homecoming was all that could be expected from a family that cares. Margaret has to be the most understanding wife there is! Perhaps I should not talk about the next trip until this first one is fully digested.

Of course, there were stacks of mail, but the one piece that I was really looking for was not there: a letter from the NFAA Board of Directors with approval of our North American Big Game Record-keeping Program. Other mail from them indicated their usual concerns over field target sizes, marked yardage stakes, etc., etc. The approval of the record program apparently was not all that important to them. Perhaps I had not done a very good selling job. An incentive for the need was called to my attention about a month later. The newly formed American Bowhunters Association asked about the moose and two caribou we had taken and implied that they were considering recording such kills for their records and awards system! The "fat was in the fire." This quickly got the NFAA Board's attention. Approval was immediate. They had been sitting on it for almost seven months!

The Hunting Activities Committee was ready and, with a little more fine tuning, we introduced the program to bowhunters through-out the country in the February 1958 issue of <u>Archery</u> magazine. The response was very gratifying. Bowhunters at last had a program to which they could relate.

Since the Boone and Crockett scoring system was to be used, we needed their approval and blessing to proceed with their forms. They gave us approval with the provision we not alter their copyright forms. Bowhunter measurers throughout the country had to be trained, and if all went well, the state conservation departments throughout the coun-try would soon have data to prove the effectiveness of the bow and jus-tify, to the general public, their giving bowhunters everywhere more liberal hunting seasons.

By April 1958, the program was well under way. We had records — lots of them. Fred Bear, looking to enhance the program, suggested that we put on a display of bowhunter trophies in Grayling, Michigan in conjunction with the annual July NFAA Field Tournament which was to be held there that year. This took a lot of doing, and with the help of the Grayling Bowhunters, detailed plans for our display and show were put in place and readied.

Meanwhile, the film of our Little Delta hunt was developed. There was a lot of good footage — we needed more. Fred viewed it and promptly asked if he could be part of the 1958 expedition to the Little Delta. Sure enough, his outline of what should happen was a little on the take-charge side and not exactly what I had in mind. A few days later, while I was still pondering how to answer, another letter arrived.

FRED BEAR WANTS TO GO

Now it was apparent that Fred was ready to fit into my plans. Finalizing could be done during the July 1958 NFAA Tournament and Big Game Display in Grayling, Michigan.

Fred asked that I also invite his good friend, Bud Gray, of Traverse City, Michigan, with whom he had hunted many times. Bud, in turn, asked if he could bring his son Mike, whose size and strong back would be of considerable help on such a trip.

PHONE
5061

Bear ARCHERY COMPANY

GRAYLING, MICHIGAN

FRED BEAR
PRESIDENT

December 24, 1957

Mr. Glenn St. Charles
P.O. Box 397
Des Moines, Washington

Dear Glenn:

Thanks very much for the "Glamour Girl" playing cards,
although if I do not keep chasing about the country, I will
seldom have a chance to use them.

In reviewing my recent letter to you, I feel that it sounds
quite dictatorial. I do not mean it to be so. I would like
to go up there with you fellows for a hunt and hope it can be
arranged.

Happy New Year,

Fred B. Bear.

Just got yours about The lion hunt. Sounds like
a perfect setup but I can't make it this year.
Am leaving tomorrow for a try at getting some
duck and goose shooting pictures in La. and
then out to Texas for some stuff on Varmits and
the like. Am too busy. Too much going on. Maybe
we can make the lion hunt next year.
Thanks for writing me.

Fred

FOR THOSE WHO WANT THE FINEST

December 24, 1957 letter from Fred.

Keith Clemmons "Clem," our Alaska outfitter indicated that he would like to go again, provided the Army leave he had requested materialized. He would take care of any additional outfitting for the expedition and help with the chores. He was a good cook and general roustabout. Again, the guide law was not in effect.

Everything began falling into place. Dick McIntyre, who provided the shuttle in and out of the Little Delta last year, was alerted. Meanwhile, he had purchased the cabin homestead from the old Russian trapper, George Milkoff. Thus our hunting area was secured. Dick Bolding, our photographer, got the O.K. from his boss. Nominal expenses and the transportation that I had arranged for in 1957 from Alaska Airlines, through my old scoutmaster Rusty Burke, were still in place.

By July, all was set except Clem's leave which he was sure would happen — but, with the Military, you never know. With more hunters coming, I would have to find additional helpers.

Before leaving Grayling in July, Henrietta Bear and I discussed the food we would have on the trip. She was naturally concerned about Fred. I assured her that we would buy accordingly and all of us would most certainly eat well.

Letters continued to fly back and forth as the time for the hunt approached. It was apparent Fred was willing to take on some of the responsibilities in producing the film for Alaska Airlines. After all, he had more experience in this type of endeavor. We needed more kills. All of us would work in this direction and man the cameras accordingly.

In those days getting the right scenes on film — hunter shooting with animal in the view finder — was no easy task. Snap judgments on the camera light necessary for good pictures were a matter of luck. We really needed lots of luck. I, for one, loved to take movies. I had a history of foregoing a good shot at an animal in favor of getting a good picture.

From the response I was receiving on the Bowhunter Records Program, it was obvious this would be a real time-consuming situation. Little did I know that almost the rest of my entire life would be consumed by it and that my family would feel the strain also. There were problems from the onset — differences of opinion among the NFAA heads on how it was all to happen. I listened, but being closest to the idea as well as being Vice President of the National Field Archery Association at the time, I was in a position to field the pros and cons throughout the process and proceed in a rather dictatorial fashion to be sure nothing would detour us from our goals.

The Grayling display and promotion turned out to be an overwhelming success. One flap did develop as the result of our display. We had billed it as the Boone and Crockett Bowhunter Records. The Boone and Crockett Club informed us that this was not a fact. They had no intention of sanctioning any part of our program. All they were doing was giving us permission to use their forms. They would record any of our record kills taken under their rules of Fair Chase that were large enough to meet their minimums. The type of weapon was of no concern. After a few months, and with the help of capable secretary, Rose (Remick) Malinoski and my family, the record-keeping program smoothed out. I was able to get on with making a living and plan the second hunting trip to the Little Delta.

*   *   *

Art Young, accompanied by photographer Captain Jack Robertson, hunted the headwaters of the Wood River in the early '20s — two trips thought to be 1922 and 1923. He took two Dall sheep. Researching my old topographical map of the Alaska Range, I find a branch in the headwaters of the Wood River that is named Young Creek. Furthermore, the Wood and the West Fork of the Little Delta Rivers both feed off of the Yanert Glacier. Until now, we did not know that the two hunting areas are, as the crow flies, less than ten miles apart. See map on next page.

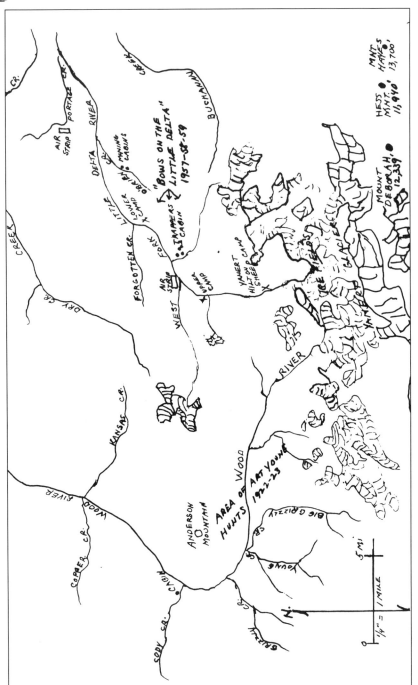

Detail of Art Young hunting area and scene of "Bows on the Little Delta."

11
1958 – LITTLE DELTA HUNT

It's Sunday, August 17, 1958. I am hunched in the rear seat of a Piper Supercub. We are poised, ready for take-off, at the end of the small plane strip just outside of Fairbanks, Alaska. This plane is powered by a big Lycoming engine — the kind of equipment that the guys in this land who literally fly "by the seat of their pants" like to have under them — the kind that doesn't get trapped in box canyons. This was very important last year when Marc Stella, my pilot, took me on a wild ride into the cloud jammed mountains where three of the most impressive peaks of the Alaska Range are located. There we had literally climbed the side of a mountain, through a hole in the cloud — out and over into the beautiful valley where we found that precious little willow-sprouting trappers cabin. It was nestled in the lower reaches of 12,500-foot Mount Deborah on the West Fork of the Little Delta River. It will again be our hunting headquarters.

Dick McIntyre is now at the controls of the same plane a year later. He is the one who brought Bolding, Clem and me off the cabin strip in 1957 — after we lengthened our handmade strip another 50 yards! He didn't like trailing his wheels in the willows at the end of the runway and with a load, yet.

Dick has been ferrying men and supplies into the cabin airstrip since early morning. Yesterday he used the larger Tri-Pacer plane to bring the bulk of the supplies to the larger strip at Portage Creek. From there it will be just a short ten mile hop to the cabin with the smaller

Tanana River as we leave Fairbanks.

plane. Dick Bolding, and Bud and Mike Gray will be coming in later this evening. Fred Bear has been in there since Thursday evening, August 14th. He couldn't wait to get his size 14 boots on the mountain — had to get in touch with the environment. He is one who likes to be alone with nature and knows how to make the most of it. Since I am the instigator of this hunting trip, it is necessary that I hang back and see that everything gets off the ground. But enough of this background! The engine roars, the plane lurches down the runway, and is soon air-borne and out over the Tanana River, heading southeast.

Landmarks, memories of the year before, soon come into view. Moose and caribou dot the flats along the river. McIntyre likes to hug the ground. There is some high overcast, sunshine here and there. About 50 miles out we take a half right and enter the valley of the West Fork of the Little Delta River. The sky becomes patchy with small fluffy clouds and more sunlight sweeps the valley walls. Cloud shadows head on down the valley by us like they are really going somewhere. There isn't much color showing yet, indicating lack of frost. But wow, what a sight! The snow-capped peaks of Mt. Hayes, Hess, and Deborah begin to show. Twinkling glaciers seem to form a chain between them. The Yanert Glacier dominates the head of our valley and furnishes the ice melt, run off from the sun's heat, which keeps the West Fork of the

Little Delta rising and falling each day — down in the morning, up in the evening.

We are cruising below the valley rim. Lush patches of willows, lichen-covered lower slopes rush by. White shed moose antlers dot the hillsides. These will have to be hid lest we stalk a set of bones.

It appears that Mac is now about to take a swipe at the Portage Creek strip, to refresh his memory as to how much stuff is left that needs to be ferried on up — looks about two loads. I drink in the next ten miles of landscape — this is to be our hunting ground for the next two or three weeks! Gee, that has a good ring to it — like saying no hurry, not to worry — no guides to help or hamper us — a great crew — Fred's with his cronies. I'll find out all too soon his first reaction to all of this! He is down there somewhere.

As we make the cabin strip approach, there is movement here and there — a moose in Moose Hollow a half a mile downstream from camp, a few caribou nearby feeding down one of the many slopes. One of the guys is on his way up to the cabin and another is loading his pack among the piles of stuff on the side of the strip. I yell to Mac to make a pass by the cabin to take stock of happenings there. No sign of life. Fred's green pop tent is up. I can only assume that he had noticed all the bear hairs on the trees nearby and had fixed the cabin door so as to be sleeping secure inside.

Now we are heading into the landing. Mac's approach indicates that there is a crosswind. It will be rough, so as a precaution, I put my hands on my head to cushion the bounce. Mac puts the Cub down. We bounce a couple times, wind drives the tail to one side and we head for the brush. He is barely able to get it back on the strip as we come to a stop. No harm done other than the stuff piled around me was shaken enough to make it settle a little more. Jack Albright (Jocko) is the one at the strip, getting ready to head out to the cabin. Bob Arvine is the one we saw on the way to the cabin. Clem is somewhere in between. They haven't seen Fred for three or four hours. He is apparently busy scouting the area.

With the plane unloaded, Mac is headed back to Fairbanks for Dick Bolding, and Bud Gray and his son. He would get them all in before dark, one way or another, and look for Bud to be at the strip about 8 p.m. It's 4:30 now with daylight out there till 9 or 9:30.

Jocko and I load up and head for the cabin, a half hour or so away. The river is quite high. A gravel bar lets us cross without going over our boots. Soon after, we meet Clem and Bob on their way down for

View upriver from airstrip area.

Fred at work.

Bud Gray and Bob Arvine look on as Fred and I put a more permanent fix on door.

another load and it isn't long after crossing the last creek that we level off on our trek to the cabin. Amid all of the grunts and groans as the packs peel off our backs, a face appears from within the dark interior of the cabin. Fred's grinning like a Cheshire cat and exclaims: "You really found it this time, George!" That's all I needed to hear! It made my day! Hey, there's something different about Fred — he's wearing camo! He had brought some for all of us. It was a new thing!

Yes, he had noticed the bear hairs and put a fix on the door. The cabin had been all cleaned up, utensils in place ready for use. For now it was chatter time for Fred and me. An hour or so later, Clem and Arvine were back from the airstrip with their pack loads and began sorting things out in preparation for supper. It wasn't long before five of us sat down to a sumptuous meal, with moose from Clem's Fairbanks freezer as the main fare. At 7:30 p.m., Fred and I head for the strip to film Bud when he arrives.

It wasn't long before we heard the Supercub on its way in. A few bounces on the airstrip boulders and coming to a stop, out popped Bud exclaiming, "Wow! What a ride! I hope you got some good pictures of that landing to show the "brass" back home." Mac hurriedly turned the Cub around and took off for Portage Creek to ferry the other two, who had been cooling their heels for the last two hours at the Portage Creek airstrip, ten miles downstream. There was no need to wait for them. Bolding knew the way to the cabin.

Most of you reading this will have read Fred Bear's Field Notes Book about the 1958 Grubsteak Bowhunt in Alaska. So I will try not to be repetitious beyond what is necessary for a semblance of clarity.

1958, this year's hunting crew consists of hunters and packers. Bob Arvine and Jack "Jocko" Albright, hunting partners of mine from years past and Mike Gray were brought in to pack, set up camp, or do whatever is needed. Outfitter Keith Clemmons "Clem," and Dick Bolding were my hunting partners here last year. The packers would hunt, time permitting. All of us, including the hunters, would share chores, like trips to the creek to fill the water bucket, cut firewood, wash dishes, and cook.

It's August 17th. Hunting season opens the 20th. All of us are now here. There is much to do. Tomorrow, two tents, food, and related supplies must be packed downstream to set up Camp 2. This camp will be directly across the river from a caribou pasture alongside of a mineral lick at the base of the black mountain.

The day began early. A mountain of stuff was moved by the packing crew. By evening, Clem, Bob Arvine, and I had it all set up and secured. Other than a little polishing, Camp 2 was ready. Fred, Dick Bolding, and I would hunt out of it. Bob Arvine would cook, oversee the camp, and hunt when possible.

The cabin, considered base camp, is now being secured by the other half of the crew, Bud, Mike Gray, and Jocko. Clem would be in charge.

Meanwhile, Fred and photographer Dick Bolding are scouting the area with movie cameras, hopefully getting necessary background footage of terrain and animals. Tomorrow we hunt. Fresh meat was needed so all would be on the lookout to tag an eatin' size caribou.

We were up at 4 a.m. Arvine had prepared a hearty breakfast of bacon, eggs, pancakes, and lots of coffee. With lunches packed, we headed out. Fred and Bolding would cross the river and attack the Black Mountain for sheep. I would climb the valley's east slope in back of camp. Armed with a 57-pound Kodiak and razor-tipped arrows, I made my way up the slope, glassing occasionally. About half way up, I spotted a small band of caribou feeding on a plateau below me to my right. The plateau rose about 200 feet above the river floor — a perfect place to make a kill and get the meat to camp.

Twenty minutes later, I'm approaching the herd. They spot me but do not seem too concerned, like they are wondering what I am. It was time to bring the movie camera into play. This really got their attention! They were transfixed. A small bull proceeded to come toward me — apparently curious. He kept coming and I kept filming. He began to circle me at about 40 yards, and gradually closed the circle to about 25 yards at a fast walk. Occasionally he would glance at the rest of the herd, still watching intently with ears extended — strange. I took another caribou near the river last year the same way. What I am doing is working. I slowly set the camera down, nock an arrow and take him completely by surprise. Down he goes about a hundred yards from the edge of the plateau. Yes, it is an eatin' size alright!

After applying the tag and dressing him out, I was able to drag it on over the edge and down to the valley floor, barely 300 yards from camp. From there I would need help. At camp, I found Arvine. The two of us made short work in cutting up the caribou and getting it to a meat pole we put up behind the tents. Arvine wasted no time preparing the backstraps which we would have for the evening supper. As for the ribs, they were set aside for Fred to roast. He loved to roast ribs over an open fire.

Fueling the tanks for the day's hunt.

The next two days I spent hunting the black mountain with Fred and Dick. We saw lots of sheep — mostly ewes and lambs. Lone rams were spotted here and there. It was only a question of time before a good stalk would be made and someone would certainly make a kill.

It's Friday, August 22nd. The three of us again cross the ice cold river — generally in tennis shoes or high top rubber boots — carrying our dry hiking boots and socks. You simply cannot climb mountains with wet feet. After an hour or so of looking in many nooks and crannies, I decided to head out on my own to a higher slab bench. The approach was a grassy slope where I had seen a band of feeding sheep. There were some nice rams. Suddenly, they would disappear. Occasionally, one would wander out onto a prominence and look out over the valley below. This would happen generally around two or three o'clock in the afternoon. I must find out where they were disappearing to. Another hour of climbing got me to one of the prominences. I followed the ledge around to the right and there they were at the top of a long narrow canyon, treacherous looking but negotiable. I found a place at the approach to this canyon where there was a pile of big boulders one could hide behind. It appeared by the trails, that this band of sheep would feed on the valley floor early in the morning, and wind up to this higher plane as the sun warmed the hillside. I would be back another day.

On the way back to camp I spotted Fred and Dick far off climbing down the mountain. About 30 minutes later, I'm in camp, out of my boots and heading for a cup of coffee at the cook tent, when I hear Fred and Dick crossing the river. They are both with grins a mile wide. Fred had a nice full curl set of sheep horns sitting on top of his back pack! They had found a lone ram bedded a couple hundred yards away. They stalked it with a camera, getting much footage, and Fred finally got close enough. As Fred prepared to make the shot, it stood up and gave him the picture he wanted — the arrow did the rest — all on film.

It was time for rejoicing. Jocko wandered into camp just in time to be commissioned to help Bob and Bolding bring out the meat from high on the mountain. Some of the meat would stay in Camp 2. The rest of it would go with all of us to base camp (the cabin) for a rib roast cookout and a declared happy hour. Sheep rib has to be the tastiest wild meat of all.

It was about dark when the cookout broke up. It was time for Bud and me to have a day together on the sheep mountain. Fred and Bolding would hunt out of the cabin. Arvine and Mike Gray would tackle the caribou at the mineral lick near Camp 2.

It was a tired bunch that trekked by lantern light back down to camp. And so to bed to be up at an early hour for the hunt tomorrow.

At 6 a.m. Arvine gave us the call for breakfast, and a hearty one it was. He had sandwiches ready and we had our pick of whatever candy bars we wanted. It was now time to glass the surrounding hillsides for sheep before striking out toward the mountain. Meanwhile, Arvine and Mike crossed the river and headed for the caribou pasture by the mineral lick.

Bud and I, glassing the mountain, found sheep all right but they were still pretty low in the shadows. The sun would have to warm the mountain before they would begin their climb to the higher regions. It was time for us to do a little stump shooting. There was time to do a little plinking with blunts to get ourselves in tune with the environment. A few rotten logs we found down there took a beating.

Bud, one of Fred's hunting cronies, had been on several hunting trips with him. His home is Benton Harbor, Michigan, not too far from Grayling; but more than a flight arrow shot, however. Bud shot with an Apache draw — three fingers under the arrow. His bow is a 60-pound Kodiak, his hunting arrows aluminum tipped with Bear Razorheads.

We occasionally glass the hillside and when the sheep, ewes, and lambs, and three or four rams off to the side slowly work toward the

Glenn admires Fred's ram.

upper regions, we dispose of our blunts and proceed to make the river crossing. I decide to leave my bow in camp — you can't do both, take movies and hunt. A half hour later as we approached the grassy benches, the sheep went out of sight. There are numerous sheep trails. Water trickles down every little crevasse, blueberry patches here and there.

We are just entering a little flat about to start our climb to the higher elevation. There, about a hundred yards before us, was a grizzly bear squatting — a beautiful blonde grizzly — beautiful as in he appears not to be sizing us up for a meal. We are not quite sure what his thoughts are. He is intently watching our approach. We stop and

Fred roasting ribs.

begin to eyeball each other; me, armed only with a movie camera, and Bud with his bow, and the ever-present lethal broadheads. The bear is armed with you know what. We have no intention or inclination to confront this critter and hope he is in the same mood we are. The fact that he is sitting gives us a little assurance.

Considering the fact that continued staring might create a misunderstanding and change of mood, we gingerly pick our way around the bear, *waaay* around, trying to be as nonchalant as a mother duck with ducklings travelling over an open body of water, with a pair of hunting eagles overhead. The bear evidently takes the cue and disappears into the tall grass away from us. We continue up the hill. From a higher elevation we spot him below in a big blueberry patch shoving "handfuls" of the succulents, leaves and all, into his hairy face. O.K., so he has lots of other food. What a relief! He is truly a sight to behold. The long hair on his back waving as the grass nearby, the hair seemingly changing colors as the breeze flows through it.

About now, my judgment is to be questioned. What a setting for pictures. Such a chance seems to smother any idea that this critter might not like to be photographed. Bud apparently is not a gambler. I have to reason with him that the sheep above can wait. We can go down the hill, get under the bench the bear is on, slip up to the edge of the flat, and be about 20 yards from our subject. The slightly downhill hop, skip, and jump from the bear to us, does not look good to Bud, and even makes me have some concern about my sanity. Of course, Bud has reason to be concerned, wondering if he would be required to become an instant "Art Young." The grizzly season will not be on for another week. Any hitch in our thinking, like a miscalculation, will have to come under the heading of self-defense or perhaps better be described as suicidal.

Our sneak on the bear works! Instead of 20 we are about 15 yards away and slightly below the bear. You can see his back as he slowly moves among the blueberry bushes. Now, it is a question of checking the camera for light settings, lenses, etc. It is not going to be easy to hold a camera steady. Can my face look as pasty white as Bud's? I caution him that I really have no idea what this bruin will do when he hears the "whirr" of the camera. Be as ready as you can with that "stick" (which I am thinking is not looking quite as potent as I would like).

The moment of truth is at hand. I am pointing the camera, pressing the trigger. The bear is literally exploding — digging out with all feet! The turf is flying! All away from us, thank God! He's going — about ten yards. He's stopping — he's looking back — he's taking off! I'm pushing Bud toward the bear for a picture. To Bud, it looks like I am literally throwing him to the lions!

It is all over — just seconds — the bear's gone. Our heartbeats are slowing down. Bud's bow and arrow are in disarray. Bud is fumbling with something on the ground. "How do you get the hammer back down on this thing?" He's got a 44 Magnum he's never shot and doesn't know how to operate it. My, oh my! You never know! There is a gun in camp!

That was enough excitement for the day; we headed back to camp. The bear pictures turned out great. They can been seen in Fred's movie: "The Grubsteak Bowhunt."

A day or so later, Bud was accompanied by Bob Arvine in the same area and they spotted a nice Dall ram. It was parked on a prominence on the same mountain overlooking the bear pasture. Arvine kept him in sight while Bud made a stalk around behind the ram. Arvine, using a white handkerchief and hand signals, walked Bud right in to the critter. The shot was almost too close to record. It was a beautiful head. The Pope and Young Records needed this.

The 1958 hunt was drawing to a close all too soon. Fred and Bud had to head out to Wyoming and left with a simple goodbye. The rest of us would gradually schedule trips out. Dick Bolding had to get back

Bud with ram.

to work, Jocko had business to take care of, Arvine didn't seem to care if he ever left there. On the day I was to go out, it was simply a case of heading down to the little strip. My gear was already there.

MIKE ELOTT'S DILEMMA

I was surprised to find Major Milan "Mike" Elott and his wife Sandy camped beside the airstrip. These folks I had known from years past. He had once been stationed in the Seattle area and now at Ladd Air Force Base, Fairbanks. On this particular day, Sandy was cooking breakfast. "Where is Mike?" I asked. "Oh, he's in the tent over there getting his gear together to attack a grizzly bear if it should pass by here. He saw one coming over yonder mountain from the direction of Mt. Deborah, headed this way." "Well, where is the bear now?" "Oh it went by about 15 minutes ago." Sandy replied. "Mike is still in the tent!"

Sure enough, I found Mike sitting on a box, apparently in deep thought. He confided to me that he didn't have any confidence in his shooting. He had a malady he referred to as "target panic." Couldn't get to a full draw and he was in a dilemma as to how to take care of it. I suggested to him that he switch from right hand to left hand as a cure. That I had done so ten or fifteen years ago. Like everyone else, he protested that he could never shoot left-handed, it would be too awkward. I cited others that had changed, master eye notwithstanding. The only thing Fred Bear did left-handed was shoot a bow. Many others went through the same process, including myself. I simply left him with the idea to just do it. The Supercub came in soon; I left. AND guess who wrote a book about switching from right to left and the cure for what he now calls "It"? Later as a Colonel, Mike wrote the book called "Why We Miss" and referred to our discussion on the West Fork of the Little Delta River!

UPSHOT

Upon my departure, Mike and Sandy moved into the trapper's cabin with Bob Arvine. Bob, as the last one out, secured the cabin. Yes, he hated to leave.

The 1958 trip had produced two sheep, Fred's and Bud's, several caribou, and a moose. God willing, the film would turn out to be all we had hoped for. I had not taken a sheep — perhaps another time one would stumble over me and somehow break all its legs.

Yes, our film was good. We had enough for our movie. However, upon reviewing the whole thing, Fred reasoned that it could be better if Alaska Airlines would give us one more year, so here we go again! We had an excuse! The last thing Fred said when he climbed aboard the Supercub was, "Let's do it again in '59!"

Clem, Jocko, and Fred heading out to airstrip.

Bud, Jocko, Arvine, and Fred loading the Supercub.

The entire 1958 gang. Left to right: Clem, Fred, Mike, Bolding, Bud, Arvine, Glenn, Jocko.

12

1959 – LITTLE
DELTA HUNT

During the ensuing year, plans were formulated for a '59 hunt at the trapper's cabin. This time, we would have more hunters and help. There would be 14. Keith Clemmons would not be with us — he had opted to set up his own camp elsewhere. This was to be the year — I would set up my own sheep hunt, one that I'd been considering for the last two years. Jesse Rust, a friend from Seattle, would be my companion and helper. We would head up the left branch of the West Fork of the Little Delta and reach for the Yanert Glacier and its lower moraines where I had been observing many, many bands of sheep.

If I were to feel good about leaving this operation with all the diverse hunters, I would need to find team members with the right attitude to fit each hunter, plus I would need to have a real take-charge person, an organizer to be the camp manager. Without much thought, it was easy to determine that person would have to be Bob Kelly, my hunting partner of many years. He was a counterpart to Bob Arvine. Those two were a team and always worked well together in any endeavor. Both served in the Navy together as Seabees. Kelly was also an excellent cook. Yes, he would have to be the man. When I approached him on the idea, it was go all the way. Obviously, Bob Arvine had helped in Kelly's decision by painting a pretty good picture of his experience on the 1958 hunt.

Bob Arvine was more than willing to go again and, like last year, would have charge of Camp 2 downstream. He would be the hunting

K.K. Knickerbocker checking out the dog sled at cabin.

companion to K.K. Knickerbocker, Fred's longtime crony. Another plus was the fact that both Arvine and Kelly played cribbage, a must in any camp with K.K. Knickerbocker. Bob Arvine was briefed on K.K. and relished the opportunity to hunt with him. You have to know K.K. to understand him — a prince of a fellow, a proverbial joker who liked to bait people around him and give them a bad time, such as: On the way to a hunt on the Salmon River, Idaho, with Fred and cohorts, we stopped for breakfast at a roadside eatery. K.K. loved to deliberately complain about most everything around him — the food too cold, etc., just to get the waitress' goat. Recognizing what was happening I went

A card game in full swing. Left to right: Bolding, Fred, Kelly, Russ Wright.

to the kitchen and told the waitress that no matter what he says, stand up to him. Don't take his guff! She played her part so well, Knick left her a $50 tip!

At Camp 2 with Bob Arvine, Knick announced that he didn't care what time dinner was, as long as he and Arvine could have a happy hour before. He loved to play cribbage — in fact, it appeared at times he was more interested in that than hunting. Sometimes they would have a game before dinner, during the happy hour.

This year the river seemed to be extremely high from the glacial runoff, making it almost impossible to cross. Subsequently a bridge of fallen trees was set up across the river, complete with handrail yet. This was quite a classic accomplishment and all of us were able to keep our feet dry.

A blind was put up across the river at a caribou lick. Dick Bolding built a makeshift tree stand to take pictures of Knick shooting a caribou, but alas, all Dick got were pictures of Knick asleep with caribou streaming by. One day, Knick came in from his day's hunt and noted to Arvine that the drinking water in the bucket was a little muddy. Bob suggested that he dump it out and get himself some more. Knick com-

Hunter checking out bridge.

Lower level view without railing.

plied. Knick wondered to Arvine where he was to take care of his morning constitution — Arvine simply handed him a shovel. Again Knick took care of that situation. When Knick needed firewood for his tent stove, he cut it. Never have I ever seen a bowhunter have so much fun doing everything but hunt. I can still see him slapping his thigh and laughing over a cribbage match when he and his partner got the advantage. Fred, of course, was always a part of this scene. Bob Kelly and Fred or Bill Wright would generally team up against Knick and Arvine.

One afternoon we were surprised to see a small plane flying toward us up the valley. As it neared our area, it came in real low and dropped a shiny object which fell like a chunk of lead to the ground. It was several hundred yards away near the river bank. We heard a clunk and the plane flew back toward Fairbanks. Those at camp struck out toward the place where the object fell. There we found a gun hunter standing over what had been a five gallon can of food. Now it was nothing but a three inch layer of mash in the bottom of the can. Feeling compassion for this fellow, we fed him for the next two days, until he took off downstream where he was to be picked up by his pilot friend at the Portage Creek strip. So much for dropping perishables out of an airplane without a parachute!

REACHING FOR THE YANERT GLACIER

Before Jesse got into camp, I had established a sheep hunting headquarters about two miles upstream from the trapper's cabin where another small creek joined the West Fork of the Little Delta River. From there we would start our sheep hunt. On the appointed day, Jesse and I loaded up with the necessities, tent, etc., for a five day hunt in the glacier area — glaciers that looked close enough to touch. We knew better, but didn't know enough to realize what we were getting into. They were very, very far away.

A couple hours upstream, we sighted a band of sheep feeding on patches of lichens on a boulder-covered flat. We pondered how to approach and perhaps get a shot. Apparently one of them spotted or smelled us and spread the alarm. No they didn't run. Noisily jumping up and down on the ground, making a drumming sound, they gathered together. You aren't going to believe this, but they made a charge toward us, in a pack. I thought maybe this would be the time one would run over me and break all his legs so I could tag him. This was serious. They meant business! We took refuge on top of one of the

Changing into boots for river crossing to Camp #3 upstream, jumping off place for sheep hunt.

nearby boulders only to watch them sail by us, less than ten feet away. We were too disconcerted to even consider shooting. I've often wondered if any other sheep hunters ever experienced this behavior. Perhaps they thought we were something that needed a show of force. A bear perhaps. Who knows. It was all over in seconds — the sheep headed for the hills.

As we pondered this episode, we continued up the valley which was beginning to narrow considerably. The terrain intermittently opened into small flats between huge, bare, rocky mountainsides that only a sheep could climb. Sheep trails seemed to crisscross every inch of the bare ground. In one gully, we spotted a lone sheep bedded down in a maze of boulders. I attempted a back door stalk while Jesse was to divert the sheep's attention and walk me into it with the old handkerchief trick. Apparently Jesse got bored waiting for me to appear and was looking elsewhere when I needed him. I had no way of knowing from the backside where the sheep was bedded and subsequently stumbled in to it. No shot was taken.

We continued our trek on up the valley. The blue ice glaciers were right out there and we couldn't tell that we were getting any closer. A lunch was in order. As we ate, we concerned ourselves with next moves. We would go as far as we could before dark. It would appear

Sheep trails everywhere.

that anywhere from now on would be good sheep hunting. This was verified by binocular sightings along the valley and canyon rims.

About 8:30 p.m. we put up our small tent beside the river. The sky had been clear most of the day, but now a few clouds were drifting over Mt. Deborah and the glaciers before us. To be sure, tomorrow would be interesting, as we would begin our attempt for the sheep that appeared

Snow made sheep hunting impossible. Camp was in valley below.

so accessible. It was time now for a meager meal. Soon we found ourselves in the sack and conked out from our strenuous hike.

The morning found us in about six inches of snow! The hills were
covered, the temperature dropped enough to hold it. The mountainsides looked especially treacherous. The white sheep would disappear
from view in the snow. Yes, they would leave the high country in due
time. The question was, could we stay long enough to wait for that?
Jesse and I slogged around in that environment for the next three days
and found footing impossible. The pictures on these pages tell the story.

We finally packed up and headed back to the main cabin camp;
arrived there Friday, September 11, just in time for one of Kelly's fine
dinners. The upstream Camp 3 was evacuated to the landing strip. We
spent the next few days hunting, filming, and trying to keep track of
animals downed. Gradually our gear was funnelled to the main cabin
and then to the airstrip. The Supercub would be in about noon on the
17th to start ferrying Fred, Russ Wright, Dick Bolding, and me out to
Fairbanks with our gear, one at a time. We would then head for Cor-

Cabin with new roof. Tree in foreground where grizzlies left their claw marks — show of territory.

dova, Alaska, where we would board the Valiant Maid for a brown bear hunt with Ed Bilderback on Prince William Sound.

HOW NOT TO CALL A MOOSE

Came the morning of our departure, we had finished breakfast and the guys were beginning to pack personal gear to the airstrip for the pickups. Fred was to go out first. Someone spotted a huge moose wandering down the mountainside across the river about a mile upstream. Since it would be another three hours before Fred had to get to the strip, he got out his birch bark moose call and began to beller the likes of which I've never heard before! On and on it went. The moose didn't budge. After all, he was over a mile away. The moose finally disappeared into the willow thicket, not too far from the end of the airstrip. This was the same thicket that had attracted moose year after year. We never could get to them. Pedro was the name we applied to those that were swallowed up in that thicket. Fred continued on the call until he got so hoarse he was no longer making enough noise to count. Bill Wright took over the job of bellering at Pedro.

Finally, it was time for Fred to leave for the airstrip. Always the innovator, he decided to take a roll of toilet paper with him. The Super-

Yes — the ribs were good. Bolding and "Moose" Bill Wright, otherwise known as "Wire Whisker Willy."

cub's takeoff would head right over the thicket where he would toss the roll out trying to pinpoint where the moose actually was. Meanwhile, Bill Wright continued to bellow at Pedro — nothing. The Supercub came in and took off with Fred and his gear aboard. We watched with binoculars. As the plane headed over the willow thicket, the side window on the Cub opened and out popped the white toilet paper. As it played out, it got caught on the tail structure. The last we saw of the Supercub was a long streak of white paper being towed behind it. Some of it made it clear into Fairbanks, 90 miles away!

In a couple hours, I would be the next one to go. We kept watching for the moose. An hour or so later, it appeared and started feeding downstream, traversing along the mountainside. At this point, Bill Wright, who would be staying on with Kelly and Jocko for a few more days, opted to go after the moose and try making an intercept on one of the well defined trails he was coursing down. I got the rest of my gear together and went with him, at least to the airstrip.

Judd Grindell drops two caribou — side by side.

Bill Wright

Mr. Fred Bear   June 14, 1959
Grayling, Michigan

Dear Mr. Bear:

     Please forgive me for not writing sooner we had planned to go back to Alaska in May. Have considerable equipment stored in Fairbanks and had entended to bring it back here to Oregon City. Now we find out we can have it hauled from Fairbanks to here much cheaper than I could do the job. We have bought a home here and intend to live here. I do not intend to cut myself off from Alaska, after living up there steady for 44 years that would be hard to do that. I will be taking out hunting and fishing parties during the summer months and spend the winters here.

     I was quite surprised to find you and your party had that part of the Little Delta to yourselves. It may be that you were there in the early fall before the Air Force men from Big Delta Base started hunting there. I know that the past 8 years they have done lots of hunting there.

     The last ten years that I worked for the Fish and Wildlife Service we made many landings on the river bars in the summer with a Super Cub with dual wheels. We could land in very rough terrain with this type of landing gear. Besides killing wolves from the air my job was counting big game in this locality. This was just a short run from Fairbanks and we covered that part of the country as much as several trips per week, especially during the winter with ski equipped Super Cub. I made every effort to reduce the wolf population in this part of the Alaska Range.

     Wood River, Dry Creek, Little Delta and Day Delta Rivers had a large population of big game during the 1920's and early 1930's. Then when I was devoting full time in the Arctic the wolves increased to such an extent that by 1948 the sheep and caribou were at a very low ebb. Now I am glad to say that the sheep and caribou are coming back strong.

     The little Delta has 3 forks on the right, going up stream is the west fork the middle fork is Buchanan Creek the main fork on the left is called east fork and it heads in a large glacier on the north west slope of Mt. Hays. This is the best fork for sheep. Up to about Sept. 15th the main bunches of old rams are in the gulches long side of the glacier moraine. You would not expect to find them here.

Frank Glaser's letter of June 14, 1959 to Fred Bear, continued on next page.

After about a half hour of waiting, McIntyre showed up with the Supercub. From above, we could see the moose, headed Bill Wright's way. It looked like Bill had found a good ambush spot. While all this was happening, Fred was taking care of business in Fairbanks. He then came out to the airport to pick me up. McIntyre headed back to the cabin airstrip to pick up Russ Wright. He would pick up Bolding the next morning.

The snow had all but left the area. Moose sightings were now more frequent. Caribou were still very much in evidence. The fellows remaining would loose some arrows. While we were still at the small-plane Fairbanks Airport, McIntyre informed us by radio that Bill had shot Pedro. We could imagine the celebration that was now going on at the cabin. They would be busy getting the critter off the mountain — hangovers would not help. There would be another rib feast.

In 1954 and 55 I counted over 225 big rams in these gulches on both sides of the moraine. Some of these gulches are up ten miles along the moraine. These rams leave this summer range any time after the 10th of Sept. but they do not join up with the bands of ewes and lambs and young rams until some time in October. In 1954 we landed in one of these gulches on the west side in August 20th had dual wheels on the Super Cub. The last count I made of caribou in this locality was in the spring of 1955 snow on the ground we found over 1,500 caribou. This is quite a difference from 1920 and 21 when I trapped in this district then the caribou bands numbered over 200,000 one finds some find bulls in this district. At one time it was a wonderful grizzly country still quite a few there and moose are increasing too.

I envy your bowhunting. One has to be a real hunter to stalk game close enough for a good shot. I was in a sniper outfit in first World War and after I got out and back to Alaska April 1919 used scopes on every gun that I owned. Still I always liked to get as close to an animal before I shot. I tried to get up as close as possible to a grizzly and hit him in the neck or chest one shot generally done the trick. They are no harder to kill than a caribou. Am enclosing a sketch map from memory of the Little Delta district hope it helps.

Sincerely yours,

Frank Glaser
Vista Motel
430 Pacific Highway
Oregon City, Oregon

P.S. East fork of Little Delta is the best for big rams. They will be found around the glaciers during August. At the very heads of the streams and range, separate the females and lambs. On the east fork glacier gulches come into the moraine several miles above the face of the glacier. Up these gulches you will find full grown rams during the later part of August and until Sept. 15. By that time the new snow will drive them lower down. The west side of the moraine on east fork is the best and several years ago we were able to land on the bar in one of these gulches with a Super Cub. These bar landings can change from year to year I have trapped wolves in this district on every one of the rivers since 1915. We made sheep and caribou counts from the air several times since 1948. In 1954 about 1,500 caribou were in the vicinity of Little Delta River.

Frank Glaser's letter to Fred Bear, continued.

Bolding came in to Fairbanks the next morning with all the details. Bill had climbed the mountain above where the moose was traversing and was able to ambush it at close range with one arrow. It was a monster, overshadowing the one Keith Clemmons had shot there two years ago. And so it was — the saga of another Little Delta hunt.

Regarding the map and the letter to Fred Bear from Frank Glaser dated June 14, 1959: This copy I received from Fred after the 1959 Little Delta River hunt. Why this did not surface before, I do not know. It seems that the letter was in a pile on Fred's desk and he did not get to it until his return from Alaska. It happens — I have mail on my desk now that has to be at least six months old. It could have made a difference in where we hunted. Note the airstrips and cabins dispersed here and there, some closer to the glacier areas.

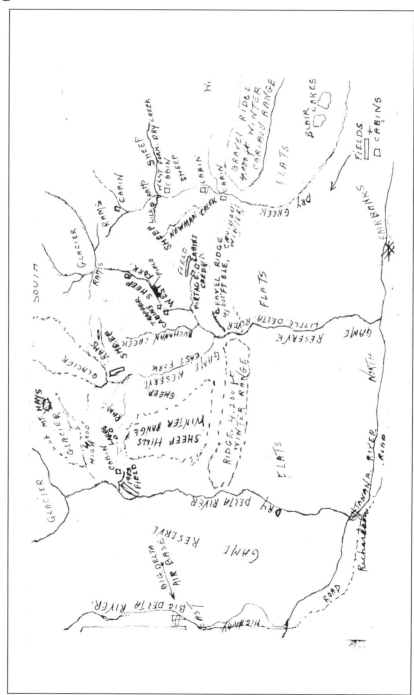

Frank Glaser's rough sketch map.

13

PRINCE WILLIAM SOUND/ BROWN BEAR HUNT/ VALIANT MAID – 1959

Our flight from Fairbanks took us through Anchorage. Ed Bilderback was at the Cordova Airport. Obviously, he was happy to see us. The fruits of the talks we had last July were about to gel.

The Valiant Maid was ready and, with everybody else willing, it was simply a matter of getting our gear on board and turning the Valiant Maid loose. With Ed at the helm, we headed for the open water.

Little did we know at the time that we were in for the trip of a lifetime. There would be no dull moments hunting and plying the beautiful Prince William Sound, which was home to Hinchinbrook Island and the Columbia Glacier. The countless inlets and islands would be thoroughly scanned for signs of the great brown bear, seals, sea lions, all akin to this environment. Fred's "Field Notes" tell the basic story, but there is more — mainly about the antics of Ed, our guide.

GETTING TO KNOW ED

When I first met Ed, about July 1st of this same year in Cordova, I was impressed with this bundle of energy. On the way to his home, we had spotted several Sitka deer in a flat not too far from the road. He stopped his truck, gathered up a handful of grass, selected a blade from the bunch, held it to his mouth, and blew a squally noise which immediately got the attention of the deer and drew them within 20 yards.

Cordova Airlines DC-3.

I had movie film with me of some of Fred Bear's previous hunts. Ed literally commandeered the local theater, getting the manager to cancel the night's show and put Fred's hunting movies on the screen.

Hunting from a boat is a very unique experience. The arenas are always changing. The unknown is around every inlet of water — on every beach. During a lull in the action, Ed would entertain us with his M-1 carbine. He had boxes and boxes of 32 cartridges aboard. The M-1 ate them up like there was no end to its appetite. A catsup bottle thrown into the air would come down in pieces. Even the cap was never overlooked — and Ed is shooting from the hip!

We liked crabs. The Sound itself was literally a crab hatchery. We had a crab pot with us for awhile. It either got lost, stolen, or forgotten at some anchorage along the way. We didn't cotton to "borrowing" the succulent creatures from the numerous commercial pots along the way, so Ed decided to build one. He spent the whole of one night on the project. The next morning, he rushed out of the cabin, grabbed his creation of wire and fish netting, tossed in some bait, and threw it

The Valiant Maid at dock.

overboard. One small problem — he forgot to attach a rope! We all watched as it disappeared into the depths below.

Ed was a hair seal bounty hunter. He got three dollars for every nose he could bring into the Wildlife Headquarters in Cordova. If he took the time to skin them, the hides brought him more income, as they were were used for the very popular coats and hats. Therefore, while scanning the shorelines, flats, and thickets for bear, we were always on the lookout for seal havens — the rocks and little islands off shore.

We had just returned to the Valiant Maid from a bear sortie on a nearby flat. While waiting for the cook's call to dinner, Ed spotted seals on a small, low-lying gravel bar about three quarters of a mile away. So it is another one of those Chinese fire drills! All but Russ Wright and the cook head for the skiff that is tied to the side. Ed fires up the 35

Glenn holding down the fantail.

horse Evinrude! The M-1 carbine is cradled in the bow, Bolding's on the next seat, and Fred is standing tall with his arm wrapped around the net's snubbing 4x4 post in the middle of the boat. Ed and I are sitting together on the back seat. As usual, Ed has the throttle wide open. It's charge, all the way! As we near this 30-yard long island, Ed heads for the bow and yells something. I'm not hearing above the roar of the motor, so I'm sitting there dumb and happy, assuming all is well on Prince William Sound. Of course, the motor will most certainly shut off and we'd glide gently to the shoreline. But NO! We hit the beach going FULL BORE! Ed sails off the bow and hits the beach, with the M-1 going FULL BLAST! Dick and the board seat he's clutching leave next! Fred is lying, just barely on the beach, his feet in the water with his arms still wrapped around the post, and I wind up on TOP of him!

Yes, you guessed it; the yelling that I didn't hear was "TURN OFF THE MOTOR!" The blasting M-1 got four seals. The rest of the critters disappeared off the far end of the bar.

Now we have a problem — a small hole in the bottom of the boat where the post ripped out. The bar we are on is disappearing in a fast-running tide. "Not to worry." Ed, with his knife, simply removes a metal patch from another part of the boat and with a rock, nails it over the hole in the bottom. With the four seals loaded, we head for the Valiant Maid and dinner — it's just another ordinary day!

Dick and Glenn preparing to hoist the skiff overboard. Note post in center Fred ripped out when we hit the seal island.

We are returning from our excursion to the Columbia Glacier where we watched the huge ice wall calve icebergs, large and small. If they didn't fall off naturally, all Ed had to do was toot the boat's horn. The vibration did the job nicely. We found the glacier and the icebergs very interesting. We were much impressed when a very small berg, with very little energy, put a neat hole in the small skiff while Dick was filming the Valiant Maid against the glacier wall and the bergs. Not wanting to be caught in these chunks of ice all night, we headed out for the run to Hinchinbrook Island. We would be crossing a lot of open water. However, Ed always kept safe havens in mind.

That evening, while sitting around the stove in the galley slurping coffee, Ed told this story: Several years ago, he and his wife, Doreen, were coming back from their mail route on the way to Cordova, 50 miles away. It was a night run. Seas were running pretty high, visibility fair. Then it happened! They struck an iceberg, one that had apparently survived the warmer open waters and where no one would suspect it

Columbia Glacier

A small berg can punch a big hole in a small boat.

Ed in wheelhouse.

could be. It put a hole in the bow below the water line. The Valiant Maid began to take on water. Ed, surveying this critical situation, quickly went into action. With little outside light from the boat, and what little there was coming from a cloud-dodging moon, he winched up his 15-foot skiff, slung it over into the water, filling it, and then lifted it into position off the aft end of the boat opposite the hole, thus tilting the boat enough to keep the hole out of the water! They slowly made their way to Cordova, arriving mid-morning — a story both alarming and assuring.

ROUGH WATER FOLKS WE AREN'T

Fred, in his "Field Notes," touched upon our following experience, but, I feel, only too lightly. Yes, we were about to cross approximately the same open water. The seas did get rough, gusts to about 55

Back of cabin. Note stanchion in middle of deck where I rode out storm.

knots. All of us but Ed got seasick, or at least, squeamish. Ed was at his post in the wheelhouse in his not-to-worry stance, one eye on the water ahead and the other on a paperback book. His foot is operating the wheel. The rest of us? Dick Bolding is holding his own in his bunk, occasionally looking in on the rest of us as we agonize over the situation. Russ Wright is making many trips outside from the cabin galley to the deck to retch over the rail. At times, it appears that he is about to go overboard and really doesn't care.

We can't get to the "head" which is outside on the windward side of the boat. Waves constantly engulf the door, assuring that it can't be used. A driving rain is crossing the deck in sheets. I'm in full rain gear, boots and all, hanging on to a 6-inch iron stanchion anchored to the deck. The wind, water, and rain are the only things that are keeping me from losing it. At one time, I had to make a diving grab for Russ' leg to keep him from going overboard.

Fred was inside the cabin. He had no idea what was going on outside because he was too busy taking care of his own needs. Picture, if you will, Fred sitting on a bucket which was careening back and forth across the floor, with him hanging on for dear life. It wasn't long before the door to the cabin burst open and Fred, glassy-eyed, hands me the bucket and says, "Here's a bucket of stuff for you!" That's all I needed! In my condition, I felt it was prudent to toss bucket and all overboard! The morning found a shaken bunch moving into a sheltered bay on Hinchinbrook Island.

The next day the wind subsided enough for us to continue hunting. We drop anchor in another sizable bay. There are several small creeks coming out of the heavily forested hillsides. Apparently, the creeks are full of spawning salmon, because the beaches are practically solid with bald eagles waddling here and there. There are many flocks of crows and gulls diving over the whole scene, all looking for their share of the spoils. Most interesting of all, Ed has sighted a couple of bears working the mouth of a nearby creek — looks like they are literally walking on salmon.

We lower the skiff as quietly as possible, the four of us climb aboard, and Ed slowly rows it to the beach. We make our way through the eagles. They are so full of fish they are unable to fly, and there isn't room for them to make a run and set their wings for takeoff. They simply squawk and shuffle aside. This sortie fails and we head back to the boat. It's lunch time.

We no more than get aboard when Ed sights two more brown bears on another creek. They look very approachable and Ed paddles the skiff ashore again. It's low tide and the bears do not see or hear us from the higher ground where the creek enters the bay. Bolding and I are on the movie cameras, while Ed and Fred stalk the bears. At about 40 yards Fred nocks an arrow and shoots at the nearest brownie — then another arrow, and another, all he has in his bowquiver. All three missed. The bowstring has fouled up on his open jacket!

The bears do not notice the errant arrows and continue fishing. They do not notice as Fred digs one of his arrows out of the gravel, sits on the bank, and sharpens the insert and the blades. We abandon our cameras because the foliage is so thick it appears the creek is running through a dark cavern. Once again Fred is ready to sneak a little closer to one of the bears. Some brush hanging over the creek obstructs a shot. When the bear is in the clear, the arrow is away and as it finds its mark the bear literally explodes out of the water. Both bears are now

Bob Kelly, the cook at Little Delta cabin, 1959 hunt.

frantically headed for the thick tag alders. We all wait, flatfooted, and listen. At one point, Fred hears something in the brush and yells, "Is that you in there 'George'?" "No, I'm right behind you." A startled Fred suggests, "Must be the bear, then." It's time for Ed and the 375 Winchester to take over and he slowly makes his way toward the noise. He finds the bear duly dispatched. It's beautiful — long dark brown hair, perhaps about two years old, between 400 and 450 pounds. Another day on Prince William Sound.

Alaska Upshot

From this trip, Fred and Ed had struck up quite a hunter-guide relationship and made several other hunts throughout the area, resulting in the taking of more monstrous brown bears. Believe it or not, one of those hunting trips to get a bear was made necessary to replace the hide of a mounted bear that Fred transported around the country to trade shows. The public, by touching and stroking it, had picked it almost bald.

Ed eventually took the Valiant Maid to Hawaii, where he introduced some of his fishing know-how to those waters. The latest word I have on Ed is, he is back in Cordova and is working a gold mine on a nearby beach, one his dad discovered many years ago.

Grayling, Michigan. Fred and Bob Kelly the day Bob became president of Bear Archery Company.

Bob Arvine must have done his work well. K.K. Knickerbocker left him most of his hunting gear.

Bill Wright's moose now hangs in the Fred Bear Museum in Gainesville, Florida.

There were many other hunters from the Lower 48 who hunted out of the trapper's cabin and in nearby camps. In 1960-61, these hunters included Bob Lee, Dale Marcy, Dick Mauch, and Wayne Trimm.

Upon our return to Seattle from Cordova, Fred stayed an extra day here to unwind and evaluate what had happened on our Alaskan adventures.

Fred indicated to me that he wanted Bob Kelly to someday be part of the Bear Archery Company. Fred would determine the time. Meanwhile, Kelly continued his work with the West Coast Engineering Company, makers of the new concept retrievable targets for indoor archery lanes. Kelly oversaw the opening of these new lanes throughout the country. Howard Hill and Dale Marcy were part of these openings, putting on their coin-shooting programs.

May, 1963, Fred Bear's call came. "Where is Kelly?" he asked. "I need him now." My reply: "At the moment I don't know but I will find him." Kelly was in Denver opening a new archery lanes. I asked that he call Fred at the Bear Factory. The next day, Kelly was in Grayling, Michigan and was hired as the Bear Archery Company Sales Manager! Kelly subsequently became President of the Bear Archery Company.

The Alaska Airlines film? Yes, it was produced and delivered to their office here in Seattle and was promptly lost. Alaska Airlines was having problems and, in the throes of reorganization, the film disappeared. I never saw it. I can only assume it was the same as the Grubsteak Bowhunt film but with the Alaska Airlines format.

Fred and I shared the rest of the movie film and still-pictures. Time permitting in the future, I may do something with the 5,000 feet of movie film — history from 40 years ago.

As for me, I'm frantically trying to get the story all down on paper before I forget. I have many files and notes to draw from. Fred's classic "Field Notes" portrayed the day to day happenings. My role has been to circumvent the wall-hanging events and bring us into the realm of why we hunt — to recall the things oldtimers really remember when their bodies no longer can shift into the "YA GOTTA GO GETTUM" gear!

14

GO NORTH, BOWHUNTER, GO NORTH!

*Because of many inquiries after the 1957 Little Delta Hunt
from bowhunters wanting to go to Alaska,
the following article was printed in the March **1959** <u>Archery</u> magazine.*

Yes — you, too, can hunt in Alaska! Many inquiries have been received in the last few weeks, and these, added to the inquiries I have received in the past two years, make it almost mandatory that I skip the hunting yarn this month and explain just how you, too, can hunt in Alaska.

Basically, there is no difference in hunting in the Far North than there is in any other state. The main difference is the transportation involved. First you have to get to Alaska, and then instead of traveling on wheels, almost all travel to the hunting areas is by air. For years, Alaska had a guide law which made an outfitter or guide a must. This cost the hunter from $75 to $100 per day. In 1957 and 1958, the mandatory guide law was not in effect, which meant all you had to do was get your own gear together, get to Alaska, fly into a hunting area and set up your own camp. However, for those of you who prefer the added convenience of a guide and outfitter, there are many available.

Alaska Airlines has a very excellent schedule out of Seattle. Their Deluxe Golden Nugget DC-6C will take you to Fairbanks in five hours — a tremendous trip over some of the most rugged mountains in the world. The round trip fare is $202.24, including tax. Northwest Orient Airlines will take you directly to Anchorage with a round trip fare of

$166.86. From these two cities, the bowhunter can get to some of the best hunting areas in Alaska. Some of these areas may be as little as only 45 minutes away. Bush pilot service in Alaska runs from $40 to $75 an hour, depending upon the size of the plane. A Cessna four-place float plane can take a good-size load into almost any of the lakes where you can camp practically in the middle of a big caribou herd. Much of the flying, however, is done by the smaller Supercub which will take you into less accessible airstrips. These small planes cost less per hour, but also haul less, making more trips necessary.

A bush pilot taking you on a caribou hunt will know ahead of time where the main herds are, and can set you down on a lake nearby, where you can set up camp and be ready to hunt in a very short time. Don't plan on going into any hunting area for less than a week. A two week trip is much better. Be sure, though, if you plan on staying more than a week, that there is more than just caribou to hunt. In the better caribou areas, your permit could be filled within a day or two. In most of the caribou areas, you are allowed three caribou. Keep in mind the places that have the most caribou are generally the ones which have less of any other animals.

The C.A.A. has a list of about 90 bush pilots who are qualified to take you into a good Alaska hunting area. And, if you have any ideas about hunting up north this year, I would suggest you immediately write for this list. The address is: Civil Aeronautics Administration, Fifth Region, P.O. Box 440, Anchorage, Alaska. This list includes the names of the pilots, locations, and what animals they can make available for your hunting. Make contact with one of these fellows as soon as possible and let him know what you are after. Whether it be caribou, moose, sheep or bear, you can be sure you will be hunting in the most fabulous hunting area you can ever imagine.

Assuming a party has all of its own gear, a ten-day trip originating at Seattle, Washington, costs as little as $600 per hunter. This includes transportation for the hunter and gear to and from Anchorage or Fairbanks, bush pilot service, $50 hunting license, food, and the bringing out of at least one big game animal. I know of two fellows who made a caribou hunt out of Anchorage for $475 each. You can spend as much as you like. Costs rise depending upon your own individual choice of food and equipment. Transportation of animal carcasses out of the area is another big cost factor. This cost does not allow any living expenses for much of a layover in any of these towns, where milkshakes are $.75 each and eggs cost $1.00 a dozen!

Now the question arises, what should one take up there in the way of camping equipment and clothing? I would advise the usual necessities, but to save weight and expense, these necessities should be in the form of lighter and concentrated equipment. Weather during the hunting season can be very good or very bad. You shouldn't think of Alaska as a polar region during August and September. However, the nights can be very cold. I would say that on the average, most places between Anchorage and Fairbanks, you will be in temperatures, during the day, between 40 and 60 degrees. Nights will be 25 to 35 degrees. One season, while hunting 200 miles north of the Arctic Circle, it was so warm we hunted at least half the time in our shirt-sleeves. This was an exception.

Footwear probably will be your most important equipment. Much of the country where moose and caribou are found is tundra — mushy, oozy tundra, and for this type of hunting, I have found a snug-fitting rubber boot with a ten-inch top the most practical. Where you are hunting sheep and goats, this same boot is not very practical. It will not hold your foot firm enough, where a turned ankle is a possibility. On these steep hillsides, waterproof footwear is not always necessary either as the area probably will be fairly dry. A good arch-supported climbing shoe is the best for these hillsides. It should have a rubber cleat sole. It must fit your foot perfectly so that downhill travelling will not allow your foot to slide forward. In the mountainous glacial areas there will be streams which will rise during the heat of the day and go down when the cold again strikes the glacial ice. These streams are full of glacial sand. When this gets into your shoes and socks, it is impossible to get out and will cut your feet. Hiking in wet shoes and socks will definitely limit you and keep your feet constantly soft and swollen. In these areas, waders or hip boots are a must to cross the streams — or allow for a change into tennis shoes.

A hunt for moose and caribou could place your camp in a fairly flat valley where the ground is extremely wet — waterproof ground cloths for your shelter will be essential. The atmosphere will be damp — plastic or waterproof sacks of some kind for storing clothes and some of your food will be very handy.

The shelter you take should be large enough for sleeping, cooking, storage and the drying of clothes. A small heating device, other than your Coleman cooking stove, should be a part of your gear. Above all, be sure you have plenty of gasoline for cooking and heating. You may be going into an area which has no wood of any kind. There should be some extra gasoline to spare in case of emergency.

Your pilot may be delayed for the fly-out because of a storm. In many of the hunting areas, a twig to tie down a tent is hard to find. Your tent or shelter should be complete with all poles and stakes necessary. Keep in mind the flat, open countries of the Far North can be very windy, making tie-downs very necessary for your shelter. Lots of light, strong rope will be needed for many things.

You should have sacks to take care of any meat you acquire, and a good covering of black pepper will go a long way in keeping flies from taking over the fresh meat. A goodly quantity of salt will be necessary to take care of any hides or skins which you will want to bring out.

We have found it most practical to buy the food in Alaska rather than ship it up there. It may be more practical, however, to buy concentrated foods down here and ship them up. Freight rate on hunting equipment to Anchorage is 23¢ per pound or $17 per hundred pounds. To Fairbanks, the rate is 40¢ per pound and $19 per hundred.

Some of you may have some questions as to hunting equipment for these animals in Alaska. As you know, some of the animals are sizable, and for all practical purposes for moose and bear I would recommend a bow somewhere in the neighborhood of 60 pounds. For caribou, sheep and any of the other inland animals, you would require a bow no different than you would use down here for hunting big game animals. I personally use a short, fast, 57-pound Kodiak bow for most of my hunting, and Razorhead-tipped glass arrows.

I hope this article, in some measure, will help you with any Alaska hunting plans you may be making, and that I have covered most of your questions regarding such a hunt. Undoubtedly, I have forgotten something which your bush pilot will certainly help you with. Keep in mind, however that your bush pilot will not be responsible for any big game animals you may collect, but he will be responsible for flying you in and bringing you out. As a last reminder, be sure someone else besides the pilot knows about where you are camped during your hunt. If at all possible, do SOME hunting with a movie camera. You'll never regret it!

Good luck and good hunting!

15
COUGAR
IN THE YAAK

It was December 6, 1957. Light was just beginning to spread over the area as we passed the sign indicating we were in Libby, Montana. We had been driving all night from Seattle.

The call I had been expecting came yesterday afternoon. The simple message: "This is Tom in Libby . . . The big cats are up . . . Be here, crack of dawn." My gear was ready. Now it was just a case of notifying my hunting partner, Bob Arvine, that we would be leaving my place about midnight for the seven hour drive to Libby — with coffee breaks. Meanwhile, I would take a long nap.

We took off at the appointed time with a fine lunch my wife Margaret had prepared. The highway and weather were clear all the way to Spokane. There we found ourselves entering an area with light snow flurries. This continued until we reached the Montana/Idaho border. No new snow from there on. Tom DeShazer was not particularly a guide for hire, but spent much of his spare time during the winters hunting cats for bounty. I hunted cougar with him the year before. We had only been able to garner a bobcat apiece. Tom figured the lack of snow kept the deer from herding up, thus the cougar found the food supply easier to come by elsewhere. When Bob and I pulled into the driveway, Tom was feeding two Bluetick hounds, Joe and Blue. The third one, Mollie, a Redbone, was now too old to take to the trail. The hunting last year was certainly exciting. Hound dogging really gets in your blood — looking for tracks — the baying of the dogs!

A bobcat, 1956.

The ideal combination for such a hunt is at least three dogs plus perhaps a couple in training. We were to go with two only — good experienced hounds.

Now, the dogs were sensing some action and yelping in between gulps of food. Inside the house, May, Tom's wife, ushered us to a table heaped with breakfast food. Alan Appling, Tom's helper for this trip, was already at it. The four of us made short work of this fine breakfast while we discussed plans for the day. We were to head back west of Libby about 30 miles to the small town of Troy. Then north into what is known as Yaak country, the extreme northwest part of Montana.

Timber companies were keeping the main roads free of snow while they cut and hauled logs. Tom was known to give $10 for a call on a fresh cougar track. He was particularly interested in one trucker's call and that's where we would be headed. Snow was deep in the high country, about ten inches of fluffy stuff on top of five to six feet of packed snow. Cat tracks today would be undisturbed. We would need snowshoes. The big cats were feasting on deer that hadn't made it to these roads. At this time of the year, nature dictates that, in the wilderness where you find deer, you most likely will find cougar.

With breakfast over, it was now a matter of Bob and me checking in at the nearby motel while Tom and his helper loaded the dogs and gear for the hunt. This would include lunches and survival food for four and the dogs. My friend Bob would be manning my 16mm Bolex movie camera.

With the dogs and Alan holding down the rear of the old International Scout, and Tom, Bob, and me in the cab, we headed out toward the Yaak country, a few miles north of Troy. Tom began checking all the side roads. He had one particular wilderness area in mind where the track had been sighted. From my seat, I saw a good-looking track. Tom had noticed it also but drove right by saying that it was a lynx. This I couldn't believe and questioned. Tom backed up, had me step into the snow beside the track. I sunk clear through the eight to ten inches of snow as would a cougar. The large foot pads of the lighter lynx held to the top of the snow. 'Nuf said. You learn.

Deer tracks were everywhere. The dogs constantly sniffed the air and every time we made a stop the dogs would sound off sensing that they were about to go to work. It wasn't long before Tom, with a glance at his map, took off on one of the side roads. A quarter of a mile in, the dogs let out a whoop and Tom announced, "This must be it and there is the track!" "Fire ONE!" Tom yells to Alan and the older hound Blue takes off like he really knows what he is doing — he is hot on the trail. We hear Blue far over the hill beside us. Tom listens intently. "It's a live one alright! Fire TWO!" Tom yells and away goes Joe across country directly to the yelping.

Now it's our turn. Snowshoes come out of the truck, two pair of bear paws and a couple of trail breakers. With our day packs loaded — lunches, flashlights, candy bars — we are ready to go. Tom is also carrying dog food and leather dog booties in case they are needed — could be a long day. Tom heads out with us right at his heels. He is anxious to keep in touch with the dogs. The trail is up and down through gullies, but generally climbing. The area harbors hillsides of ponderosa pine, lodgepole pine thickets, and rimrock bordering huge outcroppings of boulders. Today there is a buttermilk sky. About a quarter of a mile out, we sight the first cougar deer kill. It is old. It is one of several we find along the way.

On the trail.

The yelping is getting more faint now and we need to get to the top of the slope we are on. We cross several bobcat tracks but so far the dogs do not seem distracted. At the top the hill, we are hearing the dogs clearly. It appears they are circling to our right below a rimrock cliff. Tom stops again to listen. "Could be chasing deer," he says. "They are circling, getting closer." He starts shaming them about deer chasing. The dogs are a bit confused. Now we see what probably caused some of the confusion. There is a small band of big horn sheep up in the rimrocks, a natural place for them to be at this time of the year, where the wind has kept most of the rock free of snow, exposing the lichens that the sheep feed on for survival.

Tom ties up the dogs while he and Alan sort it all out. Bob and I set up the movie camera with a long lens for sheep pictures. About a hundred yards farther out, Tom finds two different tracks — they cross. He decides both tracks are of the same cat, one fresh but the other made the night before. The dogs are loosed again on the fresh track. They are headed out over flat country away from the sheep which are now disbursing off the back of the rimrock. Now, the dogs are sounding off more positively, like on a pretty hot trail. We hurriedly fold up our camera gear and head out once again.

It's approaching noon, we are tired and hungry, the dogs are baying. There is no time to rest. Bob and I are not used to this snowshoeing. Tom suddenly stops and listens again. "Treed!" Tom announces. "Now we must pick up speed before something happens like Joe getting bored and not all that attentive at the tree. Blue will be circling to be sure that the cat doesn't give them the slip. A cat jumping from tree to tree can get away."

Yes, we are anxious and Tom feels like we have about three quarters of a mile to go. A few gullies and lodgepole pine thickets later we approach the racket — sure enough, the cat is lodged in a small pine at the base of a ten-foot ledge. The cat is about eyeball to us as we approach on the ledge. The cat climbs to about 30 feet off the ground but only a slight angle from where I would stand on the ledge for a shot. Tom and Alan scramble down the ledge and tie up the screaming dogs while we contemplate our next move.

First thing, we need to rest. A sandwich sounds good to all of us. The growling, not too passive cat isn't going anywhere. There is time to look at all the angles and what I am seeing is not good. The only picture I would have of the whole episode would be filming the cougar into a bright background of sky. The cat would be simply a silhouette. Not a good situation.

I gotta have pictures! Excitement, you bet! The shot would only be about six or seven yards. It couldn't be any better than this! God, what a beautiful, poised creature, every muscle ready for action like a coiled spring. *Suddenly it sunk in to me — "Like shooting fish in a barrel!" That thought started me to figuring out what I could suggest as an option without having Tom blow his stack.* Maybe we can get the cat down — let the dogs tree it in a better area, hopefully nearby. There is still lots of daylight. Tom is not too happy with the idea. I can tell he is pondering the fact that there is many a slip between the cup and the lip. A $75 bounty — the next tree could be worse, the cat could be further away.

I am not about to do in this critter with the odds the way they are. It even passes my mind that this could be an ideal catch and release situation. The guys sense my reluctance. Tom finally agrees to try to tree the cat at a another location. With a glance at the sky, Tom suggests we could have snow by nightfall. Alan moves the dogs a ways off to quiet them down. We throw sticks and snowballs at the cat. It reluctantly begins to oblige — comes down head first. What a sight! It heads out through the timber.

The dogs were loosed, and again the chase was on. Joe was right on the cat's tail as it bounded up over the ledge, and on up the slight slope ahead, covered with a series of lodgepole pine gullies. The cat was making a real run for it. Soon all the critters were out of sight, engulfed in a brushy sidehill below the flat we were on. With all the racket, the chase was not hard to follow. There they came up off the hillside, onto the rimrock again where the snow had blown free, leaving bare rocks. The chase really picked up speed now. The cat, realizing that perhaps he had a better chance dodging through pine thickets, went down into one, perhaps looking for a tree to climb. None were very sizable.

Tom was really concerned that we might lose the critter. This cat was not prone to tree. Hopefully, it would eventually head for a stand of larger trees. The three animals went out of sight down into a gully. Suddenly, there was a different sound in the air! Not as much noise. Tom climbed a nearby boulder and started looking for them with his binoculars. Surely three animals went into the gully, but only two came out! "NOW what?" Tom exclaimed.

The snowshoes were really being pushed to the limit. It took us about ten minutes to reach the gully and, in the bottom, what we DID find! Joe, flat on his back in the snow, all four feet in the air, like dead as a mackerel! Tom yells: "That darn cat killed my dog!" (Boy, I thought, I'm going to feel the heat now!) Tom rolled Joe over. Couldn't find a mark on him — nothing! About then, Joe's legs began to move, and with a yelp he jumped up, shook his head, and took off after the others. What a RELIEF! Joe had apparently been knocked out by the cat's tail!

Soon we were to experience more concern. Blue wasn't sounding quite so noisy, perhaps getting tired. We were in a low spot where we couldn't see. Again the sounds changed — startling to Tom. "Could be a fight!" he exclaimed. "The cat, perhaps getting tired, and knowing he only has one adversary, is standing his ground. Now we could be in REAL trouble!" Joe, screaming after them, needed to get there right NOW! Tom, again getting to a high observation point, verified the unmistakable sounds of a fight. "Oh boy!" Tom exclaimed. "This is where we should have had another hound!"

Again we push on. Uphill, through gullies. The sounds again change. Tom briefly listens and announces that Joe has joined them.

The chase is on again. As we top the gully ridge we see them all headed for a tall ponderosa pine stand. We are about a half mile away. There would be no need to hurry now except for the fact that we need to know if Blue suffered any damage. You never know — dogs are hellbent to go the limit.

Fifteen minutes later, we reach the fight area. Yes, there are drops of blood! One of them got ripped — probably Ole Blue. With glasses, we could now see the dogs terrifying the cat in a tall, bushy Ponderosa. Another 20 minutes found us at the scene. Joe is frantically trying to climb the tree and Blue, tossing his head, is circling. There are drops of blood all over the place. Tom quickly grabs and examines Blue. He finds that there is a one inch slit in the flap of his left ear. It's bleeding pretty good. This bleeding is soon stopped by taping the slit together. Blue is not too much the worse for wear.

Meanwhile, the cat is hiding in some low branches on the pine about 35 feet off the ground, possibly resting. He soon moves with an awesome show of muscle to a higher perch, about 25 yards on two large parallel limbs. The cat's left side and belly are exposed to us. Good for a shot, but will be at a very steep angle from the ground unless I choose to shoot farther out from the tree. Bob checks the light meter and finds there is barely enough light. Tom wants to get out of there before dark. A light snow is beginning to fall. Tom notices that I haven't made any moves toward getting into action. He is again concerned with what I am thinking.

Mustering once again the necessary nerve, I suggest that the morning light from the east would be better and the dogs surely won't mind keeping the cat up the tree all night! Even I am surprised at what I am saying and the rest of the crew think, of course, that I must be out of my mind.

I really am aware of what a long night is out in the woods in the snow, having done just that last year, laying out all night with three dogs and no fire. Our only heat was from the dogs. We had been too far out to get back to the truck. Anyway, I was willing to do it again, and announced that if Alan would stay with me, he would be the proud owner of a new Bear Kodiak bow!

Obviously, I was taxing Tom's patience to the limit. On the other hand, I've got to have pictures! *Without really realizing it, I was prolonging the agony of shooting that cat — that defenseless cat — out of a tree.* "O.K.," Tom said reluctantly. "Could be a lot of snow tonight — no guarantee the cat will be in this tree in the morning." "That's the chance I'll have to take," I replied.

Bob would be going out with Tom. Preparations had to be made. Dry wood for a fire was gathered, dogs were fed, what little food that was left for Alan and me was put on a tarp with all the waterproof clothing they could spare. Drinking water was to come from melted snow. The dogs were chained and bedded down on a tarp at the base of the tree. They were still belching an occasional yelp.

The cat, broadside to us, appeared settled down and resigned to his fate. Yes, it would be a long night. Folks, you don't how long until you have experienced such an outing!

The fire was fed by pushing dead dry poles into it. Gradually heat formed a hole in the snow about three feet deep and eight feet around. The side walls kept in the warmth. The sky darkened. Night was setting in. It was snowing pretty good. The dogs under the tree were now entirely covered with snow and asleep. The rising and falling of the snow with each breath indicated their whereabouts. The cat, too, was covered and the trees all had a new mantle of snow. Our fire kept us fairly comfortable.

It was time for small talk, time to reflect on the day. It was wild. The chase. The confusion over the tracks. The sheep sighting. The constant baying of the dogs. Damn, it was FUN! My thoughts eventually turned to tomorrow and doing in the cat — mixed feelings. Hindsight tells me that I should have got it over with on the first contact, but no, that was not to be. Finally the exertion of the day overcame us. We got to know what is meant by cat-napping. Many times we awoke during the long night. I considered how stupid a man can get — the better word is obstinate. I had to be the ultimate. Determined to play out what was to be just a simple cougar hunt, I had to be miserable, but by choice.

Although our watches told us otherwise, we looked for indication that the sky in the east was changing. We looked for some sign that the guys were on their way back in. We even imagined that we saw a faint light flash in the tree tops far down the slope. But no. The night went on and on. Finally the black sky in the east turned to gray. The snow had stopped and we again turned to the slope below looking for any sign of the guys. Gad, I hope they don't forget the coffee!

Suddenly, there it was, a glint far below. We are about to be "rescued." Perhaps another hour or so. When finally they came puffing into camp, salutations were brief. They unloaded their day packs, and hot coffee, fried egg sandwiches, and apples — just like downtown. Tom fed the dogs, examined Blue's ear, and declared him O.K. A flashlight beam to the snow-covered cat showed he was still in place. Possibly he had shifted some but was still very much a part of our day.

By the time our breakfast was down, daylight was pretty much full upon us. Not the best camera light but plenty to get the job done. The cat tree faced easterly toward a sun-shrouded, cloudy sky — a flake or two. The snow had played itself out. The moment of truth was surely upon us and Tom was definitely in a no-nonsense mood. The dogs, sensing some action, began to get a little excited — a yelp or two.

While I readied my gear, Tom and Alan collared the dogs and anchored them away from the tree. Tom wasn't about to let them loose until he knew the status of the cat. He wanted no part of the dogs tackling a wounded one. The trees, all covered with snow, branches pressed downward — yes he was a pretty critter — a powerhouse of muscle.

With the camera rolling, I loosed an arrow. A thud. Bob yelled, "You hit a limb!" Yes, one the cat was laying on. It stood up. Another arrow. All hell broke loose! A cloud of snow enveloped the tree and surrounding area. No one remembers seeing the cat. Nothing but cascading snow. We ran to the base of the tree looking beyond. Tom screamed, "Look out, we may have a wounded cat on our hands!" Such bedlam! There was nothing *beyond* in sight.

It was all over with within seconds. Tom had two eager dogs straining to take up the chase — any chase — and he was not about to let them loose! I glanced down at my feet, looking for blood — any sign. There, practically under my foot was the end of the cat's tail! The cat was attached to it alright, but six feet down into the snow, stone dead! The dogs spotted it as we hauled it out and the bawling began. It was then the dogs were allowed to chew lightly on the spoils. We were all smiles.

Yes, Bob thinks he got the pictures which proved out back in Seattle. A great day in the Yaak country! Boy, look at those powerful front legs, heavy paws and claws, which came within an ear flap of removing Blue's brains in the fight! Tom produced a big heavy canvas bag to be used as a sled to get the critter out of there. This cougar, a male, weighed out at 180 pounds. It was eight feet long from nose to the tip of the tail. My two-year quest was over!

Tom got his bounty, Alan his bow. The dressed-out cougar was hauled to Seattle, hide removed, and put in a cooler for use at a sportsman banquet two weeks away. There it was barbecued on a spit, relished by all — wonderful meat. It sure caused some misgivings when after the meal it was announced they had just eaten a cat!

Glenn with Tom DeShazer and hound dogs Blue and Joe.

Cougar Upshot

Two months later 1958, Bob Arvine and I went back to Libby for another cougar hunt. Bob took a nice tom cat on February 22nd. It was a no-nonsense hunt. I was the cameraman.

Our guide, Tom DeShazer, was hard pressed to justify keeping his dog as a money maker. The bounty and the hunting fee per hunter, balanced against the dog's upkeep, was a losing situation. It came down to keeping them just for the thrill of the hunt. Believe me, hunting behind hounds is a thrill! Bob Arvine was completely hooked. He offered to keep one of Tom's dogs, Joe, through a winter at his home on Vashon Island, southwest of Seattle.

To Bob, *having Joe* was quite an experience! He soon learned to keep the windows closed while driving with Joe in his truck at night. Joe would even react to the truck headlight reflection on the end of a pop can! He'd jump out the window thinking it to be a cat. Pets on the island also took a beating. There were many complaints to the sheriff's office about lost pets. Finally, after several threatened lawsuits, and possible jail time, Bob found it prudent to take Joe back to Libby, Montana!

I personally do not wish to kill another treed cougar with the aid of dogs. I would, however, like to go on more hunts, tree the cougar, and let it go. The thrill of the chase is very exhilarating, good exercise, and as my cougar hunt portrayed, anything can happen. My cougar hunt occurred before the Pope and Young Club records came into existence. I did not keep the skull. Fair chase was a consideration at the time. I had a gut feeling that it was not right. As a result of this feeling, it seemed proper within the Pope and Young Club to put the brakes on recognizing numbers of such kills by individuals. Thus, in the beginning, only one cougar or one bear taken with the aid of dogs could be entered by a hunter.

At the Denver Pope and Young Convention in 1972, club members involved in hound hunting successfully lobbied to eliminate any and all restrictions on numbers. The reasoning: if it was legal to tree and kill with the use of dogs in the state involved, it should be acceptable in our records.

For what it's worth, for several years after my hunt, I acquired frozen cougars from Tom. They were shipped out of Libby by freight. These cougars were used for sportsman club banquets and considered the finest of delicacies. The hides should have had real value. They didn't. I could hardly give them away. There were few takers at any price, some citing the fact that it would cost them at least $5 to have them tanned! Today those same hides, if you could find one, would go for about $300.

16
NASON CREEK
MOSSBACK

Saturday, November 7, 1959 started out to be no different than any other weekend hunt to the "Mountain."

On this day, I was accompanied by my nine-year-old son Jay. He was always eager to be a part of any hunting sortie. We were headed for the "Fort," our log cabin, tucked away in the timber on the north slope of Thompson Ridge about 200 yards below the crest.

Jay and I had a late start, so we elected to take a so-called trail-less shortcut up the steep south side of Thompson Ridge from Chiwaukum Creek. Bench by bench, we climbed upward making much noise. Our packs were cumbersome and slowed us up considerably. With Jay lagging behind, I neared the top of the slope. A salting of fresh snow began to show on the ground.

As usual, when I'm about to crest anything, I stop to rest and nock an arrow before cautiously proceeding, especially so in this area where many big bucks have been taken. I could hear Jay puffing and blowing below. Then out of the corner of my eye I noticed movement on my left. A nice buck was sneaking out of a thicket. The pace quickened and he made a break directly away from me. Instinctively I readied my shot and let fly. I watched my arrow looking good all the way. It appeared to disappear in the maze of horns which framed his rear end as he went over the top, I would guess 40 yards away!

Immediately I had second thoughts on what I had done. Should I have taken such a shot with less than an hour of daylight left? There

The Fort — Babe, our pack horse, standing by.

really hadn't been much time for thought. There were three redeeming features however: a fresh light snow on the ground, a clear sky, and only 15 minutes from the Fort where tracking lanterns were kept. We decided to head for the cabin, diagonally away from the heading of the deer, where we could unload and timing would be right to start look-ing. If it was a good hit, the deer should not be far away, perhaps 300 yards from the cabin. If not, we would be in for a long night! Needless to say, we made tracks for the cabin, found everything in order, and headed for the scene of the shot so as to pick up the trail.

Yes, we had him. Jay found the critter piled up about 60 yards from the crest, on a bench on the other side of the hill. A magnificent animal! A real Mossback, not too heavy, but HORNS, did he ever have HORNS! Seven on one side, five on the other, rather fragile but long, long, long! Punctures in his chest indicated many recent battles. We managed to dress him out before dark and laid the carcass across a cou-

Left to right beneath their respective P&Y trophies are: G.H. Malinoski, 1959, 151-2/8; Glenn St. Charles, P&Y World Record Mule deer, 1959-1962 at 182-6/8; Bob Kelly, 1960, 155-5/8; George Wells, 1960, 168-3/8. The center trophy, 162-6/8, was taken by Les Eide (not shown) in 1952. These deer were all shot within a half mile radius of each other, Nason Creek Bowhunting Area, Washington State.

ple logs to keep him off the ground. We draped some of our smelly clothes over him in hopes it would keep predators away.

The next morning after a hasty breakfast, Jay and I headed out to take care of our prize only to find a windstorm — 100 mile an hour winds yet! — that was snapping huge trees off about 30 or 40 feet from the ground! It was not the time to pack out the meat, but time to get into a thicket of smaller trees where we wouldn't be demolished by the hail of limbs, trees, etc., falling around us. I did take time however, to take the horns and skull plate off the carcass to a safe haven in a near-by aspen thicket.

The storm blew itself out a couple hours later and we were able to make it back to the cabin, which was unscathed.

The next day, we made the trip out to civilization and brought in a pack horse to retrieve the kill. It was a nice deer with a rack scoring enough to hold the Pope and Young Club world record between 1959 and 1962. Even though you may not be hunting for trophies, sooner or later, the law of averages will bring one to you.

17
TREE STANDS
OF YESTERYEAR

Between 1950 and 1960, one of our most productive parts of the Nason Creek hunting reserve was Thompson Ridge, a steep south slope of ponderosa pines. Our log cabin, the "Fort," was nearby on the other side of the ridge.

We had four shooting stands on the crest of the ridge. They were about 6 by 8-foot log platforms built between trees. They overlooked the steep hillside where an occasional migrating buck would appear climbing up out of the bottom far below.

The four of us, Bob Kelly, Bill Jardine, Bob Arvine, and I each had our own platform. They were about 15 feet off the ground, accessed by a pole ladder. I was not prone to stay on one very long. The cold and boredom would get me. I needed to know what was going on where I couldn't see from the platform. I never killed anything from my platform.

One episode from Bill Jardine's stand proved quite interesting. He shot a big buck that was traversing uphill through a foot of snow. The rest of us witnessed the shot. The buck instantly rolled over and slid down the bank and came to rest against a log. It appeared to be stone dead. We all got down from our stands to congratulate Bill. Our bows were parked against the trees nearby. Bill proceeded to light up a cigarette and relish what he had done. While we contemplated the next move to take care of the carcass, the legs started to move. A few seconds later, the buck scrambled to his feet and took off, right before our eyes!

Kelly in a real tree stand.

Nobody had bothered to check out where the arrow had hit and there was no sign of blood, nothing. We tracked him for half a mile or so to be sure that we weren't just dreaming. We never saw the buck again. All we could assume was that the arrow had hit a nerve somewhere that simply knocked him out.

My only other tree stand attempt was on a hunt with Jack Williams in the Oregon elk country near LaGrande. Jack spent several hours putting a small platform between a couple of pines. It was about 20 feet off the ground, astride a well-travelled elk trail. It was complete with safety straps and he checked it out. He could swing and lean off of it in every direction. A perfect set up except for one thing. I climbed up some obliging tree limbs to get into it. When I looked down to the ground there was no way I would be able to shoot from it. I had never learned to shoot a bow with my arms wrapped around a tree! Tree stands are not for me.

WINDMILLS, PIT BLINDS AND TIPIS

It's 1981. Jack Williams and I met George Moerlein and Jim Scott at Glenrock, Wyoming, and proceeded to the King Ranch, where Scott Showalter had set up his tipi which he had brought all the way from Garden City, Kansas. Talk about a hunting camp, this was it!

The first morning I found myself in the crib at the base of an active windmill, which overlooked and supplied a nearby waterhole. Although it was there primarily for sheep and cattle, the place was alive with deer, antelope, and a multitude of critters, birds, badgers, and other small animals. There was a wood platform built into the metal framework about 20 feet off the ground, which would have served as a higher observation post. However, I preferred the comfortable crib on the ground which allowed for much more movement.

Besides my bow and quiver full of arrows, I was armed with a new Super Eight colored-movie camera and was anxious to try it out. I didn't have long to wait. Eagles, buzzards, you name it, fluttered in and out. About an hour into the wait, a nice buck antelope headed for the water hole. He was accompanied by a bunch of does and lesser bucks. I judged his horns to be about 14 inches long. Now I had to decide between shooting the buck with the camera or the bow. I figured that the day was early and there would certainly be more antelope in at a later time and proceeded to take pictures. I got a lot of footage and noted the number of animals in the bunch. Soon after they left, a badger decided that my crib needed some attention. He crawled up on the rail and passed in front of me about three feet from my nose — a bit "hairy" to say the least.

Being in this crib was like a lesson in animal behavior. I learned how the ewes and cows sheltered their young from the sun. The pump keeps a steady kerchunk, kerchunk. You feel yourself counting how many kerchunks per minute. Life at the water hole kept my camera busy. I shot no arrows, but prepared to when, about four that afternoon, I spotted and identified the same bunch of antelope coming that had been there earlier in the morning. The heavy-horned buck was not with them! No arrows were shot that day.

Scott was due in any time now for the pickup. I was ready to call it quits. I told him about the antelope and how they came back without

Picture for the record. Left to right: Jim Scott, Jack Williams, Scott Showalter, Glenn, and George Moerlein.

the big one. "Oh," he remarked, "he's in the back of my truck. I shot him about an hour ago at the last windmill down the road!" There he was, a beautiful antelope. Yes, it was the one I had seen that morning.

My next experience was by another water hole at the bottom of a sizable slope. I dug a pit in the side of the hill, piled sage brush all around, leaving an opening for a shot. Again, I found it more interesting to get some good footage with the camera. Several times I found myself laying the camera aside and firing a feathered shaft. The critters beat the arrow every time. I found the pit blind to be rather restrictive and decided that the windmill crib was much more comfortable. I wound up getting a nice antelope from a mill platform the last afternoon of our hunt. We all filled our permits.

My last-day Wyoming antelope.

A visit from Billy Ellis and Chuck Kroll helped liven up one of our evenings. They were hunting in another location nearby.

When you hunt with Scott Showalter, otherwise known as "Atterbush," you hunt out of a tipi. It was quite an emotional experience with that gang of characters. Jim Scott, from Alaska, a poet of sorts, kept us entertained all during the evenings with his spontaneous poems of the north country. And, as the Schnapps dwindled in the bottle, the better the poems got. Just when you thought you had seen it all, you found Moerlein cranking up his ever-present bagpipes and marching back and forth through the sage brush; quite a sight and sound — especially with a full moon shining down upon the scene — almost eerie. When it was time to hit the sack, ear plugs were a must! Atterbush and Jim appeared to be trying to out-snore each other!

1978 hunters host Ed Coy, front center

Showalter and Moerlein riding herd on the ol' man during 1978 hunt in Wyoming.

Salkaho Pass, Montana, 1980. Left to right: Jack Williams, Jerry Salter, Glenn, and Joe St. Charles.

This was not my first experience hunting out of a tipi. I once owned a 22-footer, complete with liner and inside fire pit equipment. Jack Williams, his son-in-law, Jerry Salter, and my son, Joe, set it up at the summit of Salkaho Pass, Montana, in 1980, for a go at deer and elk. You really haven't hunted the old-fashioned way until you've done it from one of these Indian houses. The tipi changes the whole atmosphere around you. The circle of friends with bows and quivers hanging from a rope circling inside, the smoke rising and reaching for smoke flaps adjusted to draw with the wind, the stories — this all adds up to memories that will be remembered long after the kill has been forgotten.

18
RIVER-OF-NO-RETURN

The year is 1961. We are hunting sheep where the River-of-No-Return (Salmon River) in Idaho cuts its way through some of the most rugged "hills" known to man. (It has been said that if Idaho was ironed out, it would be the largest state, and you'd better believe it!)

Historically, this is also known as "Sheepeater Country," where wayward Indians of the 1870's lived on the sheep they took with bow and arrow from their rock pit blinds. One hundred years later, these durable pits still stand and overlook the many sheep trails.

We have just worked our way out of the river canyon below on one of these torturous sheep trails. We are taking a breather. Fred Bear chose to plunk his size 14 boots on a waiting rock, thus to get a bird's eye view of where we had been. I chose to lie on a clump of dry grass and take in some of the much needed mountain air. The sight before me was pretty awesome! The hills and canyons that seemed to go on forever — the river — the tall lean figure. A picture was the only way I could lend any credibility to an otherwise indescribable scene.

Adding to the aura of the past that seemed to surround this particular area was our near encounter with primitive man on the trail below. We had just passed a rock pit blind. My partner reached for an odd-looking stone on the edge of the rocky sheep trail. It was a grinding stone. Nearby was an awl and two obsidian arrow points — tools apparently dropped by a Sheepeater. "Perhaps a Shoshone," he remarked as we looked over the find. "We'd best leave them. He may be

Discussing strategy at upper sheep camp. Left to right: Our guide Lucky, Glenn, Bill Vanderhoef, K.K. Knickerbocker, Roy Brian, Fred Bear.

back — looking." "But, Fred," I exclaimed. "These probably have been here a hundred years or more!" "I know," he replied with that mischievous grin.

Upshot – River-Of-No-Return

The trip was a disaster as far as producing any big game. However, I will say that it was one of the most interesting trips I have ever been on. The trip was put together by Bill Vanderhoef of Boise, Idaho. He was on that trip. The Salmon River courses through the most spectacular canyon. Part of our hunt took place on the upper ridges of it. The rest was by jet boat on the river, thus allowing us to go everywhere, through rapids, shallows, etc. We saw it all.

At one point in our day along the river, our guide spotted a black bear on one of the slopes reaching from the river toward the mountains. The jet boat was beached at the far end of a backwash. The guide and Fred took off after the bear, which appeared to be absorbed in a grub-infested log, or perhaps it was berry picking.

Meanwhile, Dick Bolding and I found ourselves a nice shady spot at the side of this backwash. There were little patches of standing water here and there among rocks of various sizes. The wash was surrounded by thickets of lodgepole pine, some dead or dying, some had fallen matchstick-like over the wash. Some were laying out there 30 or 40 feet or so, the ends three or four feet off the ground. With nothing else to do, Dick and I thought it was a good time to eat our lunch. It was a very serene and peaceful setting until, about five minutes into our sandwiches, a far-off whistling sound came to our ears. Quickly, it became louder and louder. We glanced into the sky to see two black blobs side by side headed our way — straight down. In seconds, as the sound got more ear-piercing, the two blobs turned into two dark brown torpedo-shaped birds. Now we could see one was a little ahead of the other. Most surely they would crash head on into the rocks. But no — a split second before ground zero, out popped the wings, the legs, the claws. The lead bird appeared to tap the end of a 5-inch pole about 30 feet out over the wash and flew on. A grouse tumbled about four feet to the rocks below. The second bird, without missing a beat of its wings, scooped it up with a claw! Folks, this is a simple strike in the day of a hunting pair of Golden Eagles! It was the most incredible show of nature in the raw that I have ever witnessed!

We were dumbfounded. We hadn't even noticed the grouse, and Dick, with a movie camera at his side, had no time to even suggest taking pictures. By the time Fred and the guide got back, Dick and I had regained our composure.

How many of you have ever seen a hatch of moths the size of hummingbirds? We did, on a flat beside the river. They literally covered a patch of yellow flowers that looked like wild sunflowers. The moths looked like hummingbirds and flew like hummingbirds. We found it interesting enough to take movie footage.

The headquarters for our river hunting was an old log cabin beside the river, where our guide spent time with fishermen during the fishing season. This was not that time of the year. K.K. Knickerbocker, one of our party, was also a very dedicated fly-fisherman — treated it like it was a ritual. Knick was constantly trying his luck on the river.

Cabin on the river.

One day while he was casting flies on the river in front of the cabin and having no luck, the guide, a tall, raw-boned, bewhiskered character, one of the old school, watched Knick. He ducked back into the cabin and soon came out with a length of quarter inch rope to which he had attached a big lead weight and a huge single hook. On this hook was a sizable piece of bacon. He hauled this gear down the river bank beside Knick and remarked: "So you want to catch a fish!" He whirled the business end of this so-called tackle around his head and plunked it out into the middle of the water. Then he handed the end of the rope to Knick! 'Nuf said.

K.K. Knickerbocker working the river.

19

ANTELOPE HUNT
IN NEBRASKA – 1979

Out of the dark, I heard a voice exclaim: "You say that old man got that critter? It had to be luck! There just aren't that many of these animals around." "I heard that, Turpin. It would have been luck to have gotten one the way we have been hunting the last three or four days. The idea of you go there and I'll go here and we'll drive them by you, simply doesn't work with these critters. They've been pushed too far, and you, above all, should realize that." (The Turpin I refer to is Dick Turpin, a Wildlife Agent for the state of Nebraska.)

To get that animal I simply pulled something out of the hat from bygone days. It was one of my better stalks — a one-on-one situation. I found a ridge between two flats that had enough brush for cover. Before long, a small band of antelope seemed to come from nowhere, feeding in a direction that would bring them about 200 yards from my hiding place. I made a sneak, literally crawling, for about a quarter of a mile in a direction to intercept their path. The moment of truth came when I could just barely see the buck's horns above the tall grass in front of me. With my bow at ready, I slowly raised up. His head went down to grab another bite. I'd caught him flat-footed. The arrow looked good, but I ducked so as not to spook the rest of them, and saw no more.

Not wishing to spoil a stalk by somebody else that might have been after the same bunch, I waited to let the evening shadows come around me. The buck apparently had gone down practically on the

A Nebraska antelope.

spot. By the time I had him dressed out and ready for transportation, darkness had set in. Now, how to get him out. I did not want to leave the animal, as I might not be able to readily find the spot again. The answer to my situation came soon. Headlights of autos began to show here and there — they were looking for me. After a few yells in their direction, I could see a flashlight headed my way. Denny Arrowsmith, a huge man, arrived on the scene, gathered up the antelope, threw it over his shoulders and we headed out. Luck, you say? Think again. You fellows just haven't lived long enough.

This was a 1979 hunt in the vicinity of Chadron, Nebraska, in the northwest corner of the state, not far from the Wyoming border. My hunting partners were Dick Mauch, Dr. Schneider, Gail and Dan Martin, Turpin, Arrowsmith, Ben Rogers Lee, the famed turkey caller, and my son Joe. We were staying in the old Fort Robinson Army barracks,

Barracks where hunters were housed.

the officers' quarters, no less. It had much to do with past history of the country, Indian wars, etc. It was here that Chief Crazy Horse was held after his capture, and where he was shot by a disgruntled guard.

There were no more antelope taken. Dick Mauch made a beautiful shot to take a full-blown mule deer.

"SAM"

I did experience another interesting episode, however. While travelling down the main highway between Fort Robinson and Chadron, we were passing a huge landscape slightly sloped toward the highway, allowing us to notice that there were a lot of blowouts in colored rock formations. There were many polished rocks of all descriptions strewn about. My interest in agates and arrowheads came to life. The area also

Joe, where the great Sioux Chief Crazy Horse was held.

looked like good antelope hunting territory. Since Dick would be coming back by there after his shopping trip to Chadron, I suggested they let me out at this area, and he could pick me up on his way back. I would most certainly hear the honk of his horn.

After entering the area, for about a quarter mile I picked through the rocks, sand, etc., feeling as if being watched. Sure enough, swivelling my head, I discovered a big jack rabbit nearby who in turn was watching me, very closely. Of course, I was immediately tempted to shoot, but for some reason, there was something different about this passive confrontation. The rabbit, instead of running away, started hopping slowly toward me. At about 30 feet, he stopped, looked at me, sat down, and we simply stared at each other.

It was then that I got a little bit concerned, remembering that these critters do get rabid, and that President Carter had written that he had been confronted by a rabbit in some of his travels; and if I remember right, that rabbit was dispatched accordingly. But there was something about this particular rabbit that made me feel at ease. So, watching him out of the corner of my eye, I went on with my rock searching. Sure enough, he followed me. Wherever I went, there he was, almost like he was lonesome and simply wanted some company. Crazy as it may sound, he followed me all the rest of that afternoon, for at least two hours, sometimes practically at my side. I found myself calling him Sam.

When the horn on Dick's car sounded later that day, I was concerned with what was going to happen to Sam. If he followed me out — he might get run over, as many do. I tried to chase him off. He went off a little ways and simply watched as I left. Yes, I was touched.

20

HUNTING THE
SANDHILLS OF NEBRASKA

Some of my most memorable times and hunts took place at Carol and Dick Mauch's Keim Place ranch near Bassett, in northcentral Nebraska, between 1962-1989. This is sandhill country, through which the treasured Niobrara River flows — a haven for migrating sandhill cranes. Ground cover on these rolling hills is native hay, myriads of wildflowers, and grass — cattle country. Game birds of all kinds abound. It is a shot-gunner's paradise. Many abandoned ranches, bought out by cattle barons in the '50s and '60s, dot the countryside. There are deep limestone canyons through which many creeks flow. The surrounding hillsides and flats are covered by gnarled pines, cottonwood, oak thickets, patches of sumac and walnut, and nearby lush fields of corn and sunflowers — all home to Merriam turkeys, whitetail, and mule deer.

Being a prospector of sorts and an armchair archaeologist, I am intrigued by the fossil finds of bison, mastodons, elephants, rhinos, deer, and horses in the limestone and volcanic ash formations on the Keim Place. There in the late '20s, a famous paleontologist, Morris Skinner, had unearthed complete skeletons. One, a fossil three-horned deer he found, was named for him. If looking for fossils was not enough, Indian digs here and there kept me busy.

It was in 1962, my first trip to the Niobrara Valley, that I killed a Nebraska deer. When spotted, his barely visible rack was moving pretty good through a sizable patch of fall-colored sumac. I was thinking whitetail all the way. The shot would have to be threaded through an

Glenn, Dick, and Fred checking out some fossils with Morris Skinner.

The gang at Mt. Rushmore. Left to right: Joe St. Charles, Gail and Dan Martin, Glenn, and Mauch, 1979.

opening — any opening. No time to pick and choose when or where. Just as I loosed an arrow, Dick Mauch, watching the action from the hillside above, yelled, "Mule deer!" Too late. The shaft had found its mark. A three-point by western count. It lacked the branched third points — looked like a whitetail to me!

Bowhunters invited there before 1982 found housing either in an 18-foot trailer parked on a flat beside Plum Creek, or in the only hotel in downtown Bassett. They might even find space in Dick's home on the outskirts of Bassett — at least four blocks from Main Street.

It's 1979. Remnants of the Chadron, Nebraska, antelope and deer hunting crew had just reassembled at Dick Mauch's place. We were unwinding from a side trip to the Dakotas, to visit Mount Rushmore and the site of the Crazy Horse Monument. Ben Rogers Lee, a champion turkey caller, was anxious to show his stuff. But first, he had to take the grand tour of the hunting area and ranch with guide Dick Mauch.

The rest of us scattered to the four winds in search of turkeys or deer. Gale and Dan Martin went to an area they had looked over early on. Joe and I headed for another deer pasture where Joe downed a nice mule deer doe. It was hot — very hot. We needed a cool place to keep the deer.

Meanwhile, Dick dropped Ben Lee off to hunt with us, and took off shopping in nearby Ainsworth. After much stewing around, the three of us decided that nearby Plum Creek would be the place to cool off the deer. We lowered it into some shallow water. It immediately became engulfed in sand!

We hadn't thought much of it until Dick showed up and announced that we really BLEW it! A butcher's nightmare! So it was for us rookie hunters. After much hosing down, most of the sand was removed. The butcher was able to save the meat. However, I will have to admit the remaining sand probably ground a little off some of our teeth.

Gale and Dan Martin had an interesting afternoon. Dan made a good stalk on a nice whitetail buck, but it didn't cooperate. Their stay was limited to one more day which we all spent with Ben Lee. Boy, was he ever good with the turkeys! He brought some in to where we all had some shooting. Dan and Joe connected. Gale picked off an unsuspecting sharptail grouse on the way in from the hunt. Yes, knowing how to talk to the birds does help.

The next day Dick cranked up his Comanche and flew Gale, Dan, and Joe to the airport at North Platte, Nebraska, for their trip home to Washington. Ben Lee, Carol, and I were left to hunt the ramparts.

Everyone has to have a place to unwind, relax, and just do the things that set it apart from the work place. The Keim Place was just that, a place where Fred Bear could get together with his cronies, names that some of you may or may not not recognize — K.K. Knickerbocker, Dr. Judd Grindell, Gordon Ford, Doc Strider, Bob Munger, Bob Kelly, Dick Mauch, host, and yours truly. Most of these fellows were not only bowhunters, but shotgunners as well. Fred loved to go after the feathered critters. He handled the scatter gun like a pro. When this crew got together after a day's hunt, there was a happy hour, stories, laughter, and lots of lies.

For many years, come fall deer and turkey season, you would find us prowling the many ridges, gullies and flats of the Keim Place, ever on the lookout for critters to fire an arrow at. Fred was a many-faceted person. He was known by many as a great bowhunter and communicator,

Joe with doe deer at Mauch Ranch.

Happy turkey hunters Joe St. Charles and Dan Martin.

Dick Mauch making the "fixins."

Chowing down.

but you have to recognize he was also a good salesman. One supported the other. A fact of life. He was an innovator, always looking for something that appeared to be needed to improve the quality of bowhunting. Time in the field proved up his products and selling them put him out there. Grousehaven was his PR workshop. There he entertained his customers, the likes of distributors, dealers, vips, suppliers, and the media. They would come to visit with Fred, mingle, and get a taste of the good life — bowhunting the local whitetails. However, that was work and not the relaxation that Fred needed — the Keim Place was the place to be.

Through the years, it became apparent that the Keim Place should have a hunting lodge or cabin. We badgered Dick about this until the day came in 1982 when Fred Bear, Dick Latimer, Carol and Dick Mauch, and I descended into the Plum Creek canyon — there it was. A 28 by 28-foot log cabin of 8-inch pine logs. On a table inside was a book Fred had sent to Dick titled, "A Cabin in the Woods." The inside was fully furnished. Bunks to sleep six people and an 8 by 16-foot kitchen, with all the appliances you can find in today's homes! Well, needless to say, it was time for celebration. A happy hour and a scrumptious dinner!

There were two double bunks with Carol's blue denim draw curtains. Dick, in the tradition of what he had witnessed at the main lodge Safarilandia in Mozambique, where hunters and guests wrote and drew on the walls, invited Fred and me to initiate each set of curtains by inking our logos and names on them. Through the years, other names followed — a guest book yet!

A shed hung on the side of the cabin was filled with machines to maintain the spread. Fred spent some time here, tinkering and making needed repairs. Other times he could be found picking the apple crop from the lone tree beside the cabin, or fine-tuning the dinner bell, a huge iron wagon rim hanging beside the kitchen door.

Water piped from a nearby artesian spring supplied the cabin. This spring surfaced into a beautiful little pond of watercress, and other water plants. Little green frogs scurried here and there and occasionally launched themselves from the lily pads. The spring also supported three fish ponds. Each held a different fish — bass, trout, and bluegills. Fly-fishing gear was on hand for the visitors to use at any time.

The trout pond was home to a lot of one-pounders. I'll swear Dick had them trained to his way of fly-fishing. I probably had cast a fly on waters before Dick was born, but I could not play a fish the way Dick

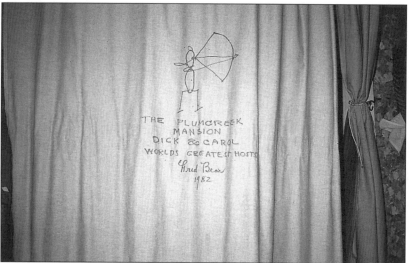

Fred's mark on curtain.

thought it should be. Fred could be seen most any morning and evening trying his luck on the trout — one of his favorite pastimes. Yes, we did catch some, enough to keep the cooks and guests happy.

These ponds were also home to several colonies of beavers who were constantly building dams and ravaging the nearby poplars and cottonwoods for food and building material. Between the pond and the cabin, a camouflaged outhouse, a remnant of the past, stood in all its glory.

There were shooting butts of hay nearby. A varied assortment of archery equipment could be found there at any one time. Many arrows were shot and many empty cans felt the sting of these expendable missiles.

For those of you who conjecture or wonder about Fred's shooting style, perhaps the following will help. During one of our practice sessions, Fred was shooting his Kodiak and some metal arrows painted black. In the middle of the action, he suddenly left the bales and parked himself on a stool at a nearby picnic table. He proceeded to scrape all the paint off, with this explanation: during the process of drawing he needs to look down the shaft as if it were a gun barrel, to better concentrate the eye to shaft to target. The shiny shaft made it easier.

For those who have heard or read that Fred would not or could not shoot a compound, let me explain. I can only assume that he prob-

The book Fred sent to Dick Mauch.

The beavers have to eat too.

ably had the same trouble with the compound that I did. My instinctive inner computer could not relate to the "clunk" when it valleyed out. The bow had to be altered to put the valley beyond my draw. On one occasion, I brought an altered bow for Fred to try out. It worked for him as it did for me. However, he still would have no part of it — that it was too late in life for him to cope with the new gadget!

The surrounding country supported a lot of nice whitetails and mule deer. Stories of them had time during the happy hour. Turkey hunting in the fall got most of our attention. Dick had access to all the local ranches. There were turkeys, hundreds of them. We had many encounters. Hunting turkeys consisted of checking out all the known feeding areas and roosts. There we would hope to pick them off with our arrows as they left a tree.

A typical day found us going through many gates — I mean gates that obviously some 300 pound muscle-bound Nebraskans put togeth-

Fred with his old reliable Kodiak Take-down.

Trying out the altered compound.

er. We had a "thing" going about gate opening. There were "Generals" and "Privates." Your particular status depended upon years of hunting on the place, age, etc. The "Generals" rode in the front. "Privates" rode in "the back of the bus," whether it be a truck or station wagon, and opened all the gates. This particular day "General" Mauch was driving his pickup truck. "Generals" Bear and K.K. Knickerbocker were in front with him. "Private" Dick Latimer, lowest on the totem pole, the designated gate opener, rode with me in the bed of the pickup. I was the helper, if needed. After a few obstinate gates, Latimer groaned and exclaimed, "Now I know why Fred brought me out here." "Smart boy!" K.K. remarked. "Smart General!" Fred quipped.

Dick and Carol Mauch are perfect hosts on their extensive holdings and grazing lands of the middle sandhill country near Bassett, Nebraska. Among other things, they own and operate a cattle ranch of prize Salers, the kind of cattle that prompted the phrase: "BEEF, it's what's for dinner." However, they have been careful to let others carry on the work of the ranch so that they can pursue their hobbies of hunting, fishing, and throwing an occasional shotgun blast toward the feathered critters. Both are gourmet cooks and the meals we all had there were proof of it. Two bird dogs helped to keep the freezer full of pheasants, grouse, ducks, and geese.

The evenings during and after dinner found us carrying on discussions on many subjects. Plans for hunting trips to other lands were gelled there. Even the Pope and Young Club got some attention because there was a time when Dick Mauch, Fred, and I were all officers or directors of the club.

We all were very grateful to Carol and Dick for the many years that we were allowed to unwind at their wonderful ranch. I truly believe Fred's quality of life was certainly enhanced, especially in the waning years. On a trip there with him in his early 80's, I can still see him as he was, one icy morning, standing as ready as any 20-year-old would, on the edge of a wild cherry patch looking very alert over a well-used trail, to catch some unsuspecting whitetail on his early morning constitution. I had walked with Fred there. My ground blind was a little beyond. It was cold, very cold, and as I occasionally glanced at the motionless figure, it concerned me as to how he was doing. I asked him if perhaps it was time to head back to the barn. "No, George. Let's hang tough a little longer. It gets awfully cold in Michigan, you know."

It's fall, 1984. Fred phoned, "George, let's do it one more time! A get-together at Dick's," he said. "I need to talk." He sounded troubled. Dick picked us both up at Omaha for the 150 mile trip to the Keim Place. Fred was troubled about events at the factory. Dick and I listened. Carol kept us fed. We managed to catch enough fish for dinners. Little thought would be given to the deer and turkeys this year. Fred needed some shoulders to lean on. When we parted company about ten days later, we didn't know that this would be Fred's last trip to the Keim Place. He passed away in April of 1988.

And so it was in these lush Nebraska hills, until the fall of 1989 when I wanted Margaret to share in my next trip to the Keim Place. She had a great time taking pictures of turkeys, frogs, livestock, windmills, a cooperating photogenic porcupine, sumac, bittersweet, prairie dogs, you name it.

Something new had been added. An overturned canoe lay on the bank of Plum Creek. The canoe was to be our way of exploring the many islands in the creek where you would find fossils deposited from the spring runoff. Margaret and I spent a whole afternoon doing just that, gathering interesting pieces from the distant past. Carol took us to some Indian digs nearby. Finding a chip of flint or arrowhead vividly reminds one of the exciting past, and helps to make you a little bit heady as to what you might find next.

Meanwhile, seven fellows including Dick Latimer, all sporting new

"Generals" Kelly, K.K. Knickerbocker, and Mauch (standing right), with "Privates" St. Charles (standing left), and Latimer and Doc Strider, (kneeling).

Stetson cowboy hats compliments of Bob Kelly, retired President of the Bear Archery Company, arrived at the Keim Place. Kelly had planned the trip to coincide with our time there, but at the last moment he was not able to come because of health problems. This gang set up camp in tents and the trailer. They were hell-bent to scour the entire ranch for turkeys and deer.

Dick Mauch thought this would be a good time for the rest of us, Carol, Margaret, Latimer and me, to take a side trip to Valentine, Nebraska, for a buffalo and Texas longhorn cattle auction. This proved to be quite an exciting experience, watching how the handlers took care of getting the animals in and out of the auction area. One huge buffalo bull just about demolished the fence where we were sitting in the audience. Looked like he would come right through it! Quite a vicious looking beast up that close, like about three feet from us. To me the most interesting part was the pies that the farm ladies had made and brought to the auction to sell at lunch time. Were they ever good! We were back at the Keim Place late that afternoon. The Stetson hat crew straggled in and none had hide, hair, or feather to show for their day.

The very next morning, while I was manning a whitetail crossing near a harvested corn patch, a flock of turkey jakes came out of a deep canyon and proceeded to feed on a freshly mowed hay pasture. They wandered a little close. I fired an arrow at them. I would like to say the arrow was directed at one bird. Truthfully that was not the case. But after they dispersed, low and behold, they had left one with its head lopped off. "Hey, that's some shooting," I heard someone yell quite a way off. It was Carol. Little did she know that I was flock shooting.

The white hat fellows, after a week of turning the Keim Place inside out, headed for home. Most of the arrows they left had no trace of blood or feathers on them. However, one of the guys had connected on a button buck, which was later cooked up for Kelly's annual big game feed in Gainesville, Florida. And, as Kelly would say, "They were happy as clams on an incoming tide!" Latimer stayed over a few more days to spend some time reminiscing about Fred Bear and the earlier good times. That was really what this trip was all about for the rest of us. Perhaps one would call it a wake. Latimer, Dick Mauch, and I spent two or three evenings sitting around the table . . . four chairs, one vacant — Latimer emotionally "felt" that Fred was there. Reminders were all around. The signed curtain. The wagon-wheel dinner bell — it had to have just the right tone. His trout pole leaned in the corner by

Latimer and his turkey get some attention.

Margaret and me on Plum Creek.

the door, tattered jacket nearby. All reminders of the good days when the after-supper stories flowed freely. Fred had a huge sense of humor. One anecdote we recalled was from a discussion about new gadgets that were coming on the scene — sights, etc. Fred's remark, "Oh, but you fellows don't use these latest accessories. I have first hand experience. I had been experimenting with the new-fangled clicker which could be used with a hunting arrow. I though I had it pretty well perfected and put one on my Kodiak for a hunt for moose into British Columbia. I sneaked to within 15 yards of a nice bull feeding on some willow shoots beside a creek. I was so close, I felt that I must wait till he turned his head for he would spot me in any kind of a movement. The moose finally turned his head away as if to bite something near his rump. Just as I drew, the moose passed some gas. Thinking it was my clicker, I released prematurely. The last I saw of the moose, he was headed "south" with my arrow imbedded in one of his palms and the clicker dangling in the feathers!"

Each day of the wake, Latimer, though emotional, became more and more relaxed. He told us he was convinced "Papa Bear" was there, listening and laughing. When it was time for Latimer to leave and goodbyes were said, I thought to myself as he got on the bus, *there goes*

Kelly's "White Hat Gang." Standing: Neil Rouse, Carlos Garero, Mark Toth, Harold Hatfield, Dick Latimer. Kneeling: Glenn, Roger Hatfield, Roger Cusick, Dick Mauch.

one of the two, outside of the immediate family, truly entitled to use the endearing term "Papa Bear." The other is Frank Scott.

As for the hunting, Dick and I continued to beat the countryside for whitetails. For two days, we stood vigil in a cottonwood patch just off a freshly mowed alfalfa field. We had spotted whitetails feeding there each morning. They would leave the field and enter the cottonwoods. Two abandoned rolled bales of alfalfa, about ten yards from the main exit trail, afforded me a good blind. Dick went to the far end of the grove and made a slow one-man drive upwind through the deer bed areas, probably figuring that I would miss. I did. Two different mornings I had shots and for the life of me I could not hit those critters. Never touched a hair! A hay stacker beyond took the brunt of my two arrows. Dick never saw them after they went by me. However, when I got back to Seattle, I found that I had brought home a beaut of a poison ivy reaction! When Dick was told of this, he suggested that that's why those two rolled bales were left there! How in the heck was a "Western Southerner" to know that those two hay rounds left there were abandoned because they were possessed with that demon weed!

21
THE DEVASTATOR

It's March, 1987, the 15th Pope and Young Biennial Awards Program and Banquet in Tulsa, Oklahoma. Fred Bear and I are in his hotel room having a cool drink, reminiscing over the past, and generally trying to solve the world's bowhunting problems. (That's what off-season bowhunters do, isn't it?) His feet were parked on top of his wheeled oxygen bottle, the bottle he carted around with him, all the while claiming that it was really a disguised bottle of Schnapps.

In the course of conversation the subject of crossbows came up. We discussed the inroads the crossgun was making into the bow seasons and it was being touted as directly archery related. "Hah," he said, "I can see you need some experience with one first hand! When I get back to the plant, I'll send our latest — the Devastator!" He was BAIT-ING me!

The following letters and notes pretty well tell the story.

Margaret and I made the trip to Florida in February of 1988. In Fred's office, I presented him with a stuffed duck and the story of my experience with the Bear Archery Company's Devastator Crossbow. The duck was one I had picked up at a local swap meet. He read aloud the story of my experience. Dick Latimer videotaped the presentation affair, a video that we now have in the archives! That's what friends do to each other, isn't it!

56730

BEAR ARCHERY
Subsidiary of Walter Kidde & Company, Inc.
KIDDE

Rural Route 4
4600 S. W. 41st Boulevard
Gainesville, Florida 32601
904-376-2327

Toll Free (800) 874-4603
In Florida (800) 342-3403
TWX-810-825-2325

25683

DATE 4-1-87

SOLD TO:
GLENN ST. CHARLES
NORTHWEST ARCHERY
19807 1ST. AVE, SOUTH
SEATTLE, WA, 98148

SHIP TO:

DEALER NUMBER	CUSTOMER ORDER NO.	TERMS NET 30 DAYS	TRADE DISCOUNT	SPEC. SHIPPING INSTRUCTION
5715-B735				

QUAN. EA.	CAT. NUMBER	LENGTH	SIZE OR WGT.	COLOR	L.H.	DESCRIPTION	PRICE	AMOUNT
1	8900					DEVASTATOR		
2	1005					ARROW 3 PACK		
1	1987	CATALOG						
						NO CHG,		
	843-6004	413-B						

Hi GLENN — IT WAS GOOD TO HAVE A CHANCE TO TALK
WITH YOU IN TULSA — ENJOYED SEEING JOE ALSO.

AM SENDING THIS RIG TO YOU — SUGGEST THAT YOU
ASK MARGRET FOR A WEEK OFF SO THAT YOU
COULD FIGURE EVERYTHING OUT AND GET IT
SHOOTING AND THEN YOU WILL NEED ANOTHER
WEEK TO TRY TO FIND OUT HOW TO GET IT TO
WITHIN SHOOTING DISTANCE OF A DEER.
WE ARE ABOUT TO COME OUT WITH A CARRIAGE
FOR IT — THIS WILL HAVE SORT OF A TRIPOD ON
IT LIKE A MACHINE GUN.------
QUIT YOUR WORRYING — HAVE FUN — ENJOY LIFE.

Salesman _____

Purchaser _____ Fred

MOORE BUSINESS FORMS, INC., JACKSONVILLE, FL. M

19807 1st Avenue South
Seattle, WA 98148
July 30, 1987

Dear Fred,

A long overdue letter--Yes, the 14 lb. thing-a-ma-bow arrived
soon after I got back from Tulsa! Before I could get it all
together, Bob Marquart and Colleen Klineburger discovered
that I had it. They and Doug Walker were getting ready to go
to Africa. Colleen had a Devastator to take with her and
needed some more bolts. We gave them ours from this set you
sent us. That ended the crossbow saga for a time. More cop-
outs cropping up--we were remodelling our kitchen and dining
room--we put on a 3 day Boone & Crockett workshop to train
14 more Boone & Crockett measurers--Margaret's mother became
critically ill early in June and passed away July 3rd.

Now the good news--I found a couple of BIG 3 ft. Wagon Wheels
at the swap meet with which I am building a carriaage for that
"machine". Jay and I will then trundle it out into the Washington Wilderness to see what it will do. I'll keep you
posted and may even send you pictures of the results--I may
even send the results! Hang on--we're in a "devastating"
mood.

It was great seeing you again in Tulsa, Fred. Let's have
more of these get-togethers. Margaret and I will probably
come to Gainesville after Christmas to see her brother Robert
and his wife. Will look you up then--I still have't seen
that museum.

Relax, you say--how can I? I'm booked up with things to do
till I'm 150.

                              Yours truly,

                              Glenn St. Charles

                              Glenn St. Charles

BEAR ARCHERY
Subsidiary of Kidde, Inc.
KIDDE

Fred B. Bear
Chairman

Rural Route 4
4600 S.W. 41st Boulevard
Gainesville, Florida 32601
904-376-2327

September 10, 1987

Mr. Glenn St. Charles
19807 1st Avenue South
Seattle, Washington   98148

Dear Glenn:

On July 30th you wrote me a letter extolling the
virtues of the Devastator.

I sure am glad you liked it and I know your hunting
success will improve continuously as you sally forth
with this fine weapon.

Mostly, this letter is to tell you how great it will
be to see you and Margaret when you come to
Gainesville after Christmas. I will write you again
in early December, just to jog your memory.

Best regards,

BEAR ARCHERY COMPANY

Fred B. Bear
Founder and Chairman

19807 1st Ave. South
Seattle, WA 98148
February 11, 1988

Fred Bear
Gainesville, Florida

Dear Fred,

With this letter, find one very dead duck, obviously done in by a bolt. As
I promised, we gave the DEVASTATOR a real shakedown in our rugged country
with intent to capture one of our elusive wildlife. However, we did have a
little trouble.

Because of its massive weight, 14 pounds, it appeared that we would need a
carriage to properly transport it into the woods. I shopped the local swap
meet for a pair of 40" buggy wheels. A piece of 1-1/2" water pipe served
as our axle. To this, we attached a 3' wide by 6' long wood platform,
complete with tongue and all the trappings so two people could pull. The
back end was extended so a third person could push. The DEVASTATOR was
mounted on a 4-way swivel for easy aiming in any direction. Because we
would be travelling in rough country, we aimed it diagonally so in case the
thing went off it would not hit the front pullers. Because our hunting laws
are so obsolete (crossbows not legal), we decided to hunt in a remote region
where we would not be noticed. We parked our truck on what looked to be an
isolated road and unloaded the carrier near what looked to be a fresh deer
trail. Then away we went, bolt in place, safety off for quick delivery. My
sons, Jay and Joe were the pullers, and I brought up the rear, pushing
against the tail piece. We had gone about 200 yards, cutting through brush,
over logs, rocks, etc.--tough going. Out of the blue, one of the boys
yelled "Duck!", so duck I did--the back end of the carriage went down with
me. A twig set off the trigger with a WHOOSH! We heard a THONK! And low
and behold, this mallard fell down practically in my lap! Some odd feathers
continued to drift down and we were trying to gather our wits when a whole
bunch of officer types descended upon us. They had heard the commotion. It
appeared that we most certainly had run AFOWL of the law. What we didn't
know: on another road close ahead of us was a State Game Department hunter
checking station. They were on the boundary of a National Park and helping
to man the station were National Park and U. S. Forest Service personnel.

We were cited for the following crimes: Parking our truck illegally in a
National Park, trespassing with a carriage across National Park land without
a permit, defacing forest lands, hunting with an illegal weapon and killing
a duck out of season--and no duck stamp yet--all punishable by fines of up
to $1100 and possibly 6 months in jail.

In spite of all this, I did want to show you how successful our hunt was. I
killed a duck with a rock in the neighbor's Pond in order to trade for the
duck with the bolt in it. The Feds fined me for the other duck also, but
gave me my prize. We of course plan to appeal the fines and jail term on
the basis that we were out of our minds. Take good care of this duck. We
may need it for evidence.

> Your friend--with reservations,
>
> *Glenn St. Charles*
> Glenn St. Charles

P.S. We have engaged an attorney who is looking for somebody to sue--sooo
you and Tom Jennings hold onto your hats!

StC.

Fred Bear

Margaret and I had also brought six Magnum Bows which Fred signed for us, with the question: "What do you do with these?" "Fred," I replied, "we donate them to bowhunter auctions where money is being raised to perpetuate the cause of bowhunting." "Sounds great," he remarked. "But when are you going to cut me in on this?"

We left him on the morning of the 17th, whereupon he wrote the following letter.

2-17-88
11:30 AM

GLEN —

You just left. I was to give
these bulbs to Margret.
The candle piece I carry in
my pocket when hunting. Its a
lifesaver when a fire is
needed and everything wet.
Its also handy for dressing the
shooting glove – to grease a nail
or screw going into hard wood
or to slick a door or drawer.

Have fun

Fred

The candle he referred to is what Fred does. Like most folks with desk drawers, they fill them with stuff. The flat piece of wax with the wick still in place I slipped into my jacket pocket. Within a week, it was used. One cold morning, a car key would not enter the door lock. My hand seemed to be drawn to my jacket pocket where I felt the candle. I rubbed some on the key and it slipped right in. You never know! Some folks just know how to be remembered!

22

BOONE AND CROCKETT CONNECTION

As a hunter, interest in the Boone and Crockett Club had been with me for many years. However, a more direct interest took place in 1957 when the National Field Archery Association Hunting Activities Committee decided to go with the Boone and Crockett system of recording big game animals taken with the bow. Subsequently, John Yount, NFAA Secretary at the time, obtained permission from the Boone and Crockett Club to use their copyright forms under the NFAA heading. I contacted their headquarters to see if B&C measurers would be available to measure our bowhunting racks and heads. Their reply was that they would not ask their measurers to accommodate us, but they could if they so desired — fair enough, however, we would need more — our own measurers.

Meanwhile, from Mrs. Grancel Fitz, Secretary of the Boone and Crockett Club, we obtained a copy of a measuring manual on how to score big game heads. With this manual in hand, the NFAA Hunting Activities Committee took to measuring every barn-hanging rack we could find. Finally, after some knowledge of what we were supposed to do, I measured a small blacktail rack, boxed it up, and sent it with a score sheet to Sam Webb, B&C Records Chairman, for his assessment of my work. His answer came back in the form of a certificate of appointment as a B&C measurer. That was all I needed to get us off and running to process our own measurers.

RECORDS OF NORTH AMERICAN
BIG GAME COMMITTEE
———
SAMUEL B. WEBB, CHAIRMAN
99 JOHN ST., N. Y.
MILFORD BAKER
285 MADISON AVE., N. Y.
FREDERICK K. BARBOUR
120 EAST 79TH ST., N. Y.
ALFRED C. GILBERT
NEW HAVEN, CONN.

ADDRESS CORRESPONDENCE TO:

MRS. GRANCEL FITZ, SECRETARY
5 TUDOR CITY PLACE
NEW YORK 17, NEW YORK

BOONE AND CROCKETT CLUB

July 2, 1958

TO WHOM IT MAY CONCERN

Mr. Glenn St. Charles, National Field Archery Association,
Seattle, Washington, is hereby appointed an Official
Measurer of North American big game trophies for this
organization, which is internationally recognized as
the official repository for records pertaining to North
American big game.

Mr. St. Charles has demonstrated his fitness to act in this
capacity and willingness to abide by the required standards.

Samuel B. Webb, Chairman

SBW:bf   RECORDS COMMITTEE

Next, if we were to some day emulate the club to some degree, we needed to know more about the structure of the club itself — how to go about forming our own club. Again, I contacted their headquarters. Frederick C. Pullman answered with a Boone and Crockett manual, complete, except for all the membership names. The Boone and Crockett Club was very helpful in getting the Pope and Young Club off the ground.

My favorite animal to hunt was one that we in Washington have always called the Olympic elk, otherwise known as Roosevelt's Wapiti. Large numbers inhabit the western forests of Washington, the greatest concentration being on the Olympic Peninsula of western Washington. However, its range continues on down through western Oregon and into northwestern California.

What does the B&C club have to do with my interest in the Olympic elk? Just this. Today these unique elk are recognized in the B&C and P&Y records as a subspecies, aside from the more common American elk. I like to think I had something to do with this happening.

1958 — NFAA pioneer bowhunting measurers in Seattle. Standing: Audrey Bryan. Seated, left to right: Bill Jardine, Warren Berg, Wayne Hathaway, Jesse Rust, Bill Neve, Glenn St. Charles.

(In 1963 I wrote the following letter to Mrs. Grancel Fitz.)

19807 1st Avenue South
Seattle, Washington 98148
November 8, 1963

Mrs. Grancel Fitz
5 Tudor City Place
New York 17, New York

Dear Mrs. Fitz:

Re your letter of October 18 regarding elk, I have Olaus Murie's book called "The Elk of North America," copyrighted 1951 by the Wildlife Management Institute of Washington, D.C. He is recognized as one of the world's foremost authorities on American elk and by many as the greatest authority. From his book, I find the following:

Cervus canadensis canadensis: These are the Eastern elk or Canadian elk and at one time they considered the American elk or Rocky Mountain herd as part of this form of elk until Bailey in 1935 described the Rocky Mountain animals as a distinct branch. The Cervus canadensis canadensis is extinct and the present Rocky Mountain or American elk is now called the Cervus Canadensis Nelsoni Bailey.

Manitoba Wapiti, Cervus canadensis manitobensis Millais: This form ranges through Manitoba and Eastern Saskatchewan, and the only difference between this form and the canadensis is that they are a little darker and have smaller antlers. The ranges of the Manitoba and American elk overlap and have no definite line between them; therefore, there would be much interbreeding.

Olympic Wapiti: Roosevelt Wapiti; Western Wapiti, Cervus canadensis occidentalis: This herd is a very distinct type living in the rain forest regions of British Columbia, Vancouver Island, Washington, Oregon and the very northern part of California, Kodiak and Afognak Islands in Alaska.

Arizona Wapiti, Cervus merriami Nelson: This type as such is extinct. They do now have elk in Arizona and they are harvested; however, this Arizona herd is now the American Wapiti as the result of a transplanting years ago from the American or Rocky Mountain herd.

California Wapiti; Dwarf Wapiti; Tule Wapiti; Cervus nannodes Merriam: This elk is now restricted to the Owens Valley of California and a fenced preserve at Tupman near Bakersfield. In other words, as far as hunters are concerned, this form might as well be extinct.

To sum this up, one would gather from Murie's book that the only two herds or forms of elk left which are now harvested by hunters are the American or Rocky Mountain elk and the Roosevelt elk. They are two distinct forms and have very distinct ranges. The Rocky Mountain herd has been used extensively for transplanting to all parts of the country including Argentina and Canada. The only exception apparently is they have not been taken into the Roosevelt ranges. Likewise, the Roosevelt herd has also been used for transplanting to various areas including Kodiak and Afognak Islands in Alaska. The Kodiak and Afognak herd is now quite large. Fishing boats and guides report that it is not uncommon to see elk and brown bear feeding on the beach flats of these islands a hundred yards or so apart.

The Roosevelt range is pretty much the same as our Blacktail deer; however, it would seem that the best defined line between the Rocky Mountain and the Roosevelt elk would be Highway 99 which runs straight through from Canada to Mexico. You could be sure that an elk taken west of this highway would be a Roosevelt elk. These smaller antlered Roosevelt elk are magnificent animals, generally larger bodied than their Rocky Mountain cousins. There are thousands and thousands of them harvested every year and it seems to me and many others that it is a shame that these animals are not listed as a separate category with Boone and Crockett and an added shame that the very animal that bears the same name as the founder of the Boone and Crockett Club is not even recognized by the Boone and Crockett Club.

Sincerely yours,

Glenn St. Charles

GS:rm
cc: Robert S. Waters

Judges and consultants at 15th Boone and Crockett Awards, Atlanta, Georgia, 1973. Left to right: Elmer M. Rusten, Dr. Philip L. Wright, Clarence Cottam, Ms. Dorothy G. Petrovsky, Bernard A. Fashingbauer, Glenn St. Charles, Arnold Haugen.

My letter was referred to the B&C Records Committee. I find no reference that I ever received an answer and forgot about it until ten years later — 1973, when I was appointed a judge for the 15th Boone and Crockett Awards Program in Atlanta, GA. This was to be a very busy travel year for me. I have always been one to want, as the saying goes, to "kill two birds with one stone." Since I was going to be in Atlanta for the measuring session, what else could I be doing on that side of the country? For one, I would be staying with my daughter, Linda, a school teacher there. Timing was right to attend an antique gun show in St. Petersburg, Florida, the following weekend. Fred Bear got wind of this and invited me to spend a couple days with him in Orlando, Florida, on my way to St. Petersburg.

Came the day. Linda picked me up at the Atlanta airport and took me directly to the warehouse where the B&C measuring would take place. I was greeted by a crew opening crates of the usual skulls and bones. On hand were the other judges: Dr. Philip L. Wright, Charles Erwin Wilson, Jr., Bernard Fashingbauer, Clarence Cottam, Arnold O. Haugen; and consultants: Frank Cook, Dr. Elmer Rusten, and George L. Norris. Arnold Haugen was a bowhunter — we had some reminiscing to do. He was NFAA President and I was NFAA Vice President in the years between 1948 and 1950.

This 15th Awards Banquet was the year of the North American Big Game Awards (NABG), sponsored jointly by the National Rifle Association and the Boone and Crockett Cub. Harold Nesbitt was the coordinator between the two. About 60 heads were to be measured over the next two or three days. Evenings were spent enjoying the southern hospitality and bull sessions among the measurers over the day's work. It was during one of these sessions that I mentioned my concern over the Roosevelt's elk. Dr. Wright immediately picked up on it and we struck up a lasting friendship.

Dr. Wright, head of the Zoology Department at the University at Missoula, agreed that the Roosevelt's elk possibly could be recorded as a separate species. Further research might show that its antler configuration had unique differences from the American elk, the main difference being the crowns, or what I call the "Bones of Contention," in and around the fourth or royal point of the Roosevelt's elk racks. His interest spurred me on and we would take up the whole matter at a later date.

With the measuring over, it was time to go to Fred's in Orlando. I was to come back to Atlanta after the gun show as the "clean-up guy" to measure the heads that came in late. Fred met me at the airport and we wound up at his condominium, located in a beautiful park-like setting on the outskirts of town. His wife, Henrietta, had lunch prepared. We made short work of it. Fred assumed that I would want to go see Disney World — it was a case of when. Well there was no way I would want to waste my time there. Let's just talk. Fred liked that. As a gesture to get my feet back on the ground, he took me to a men's club nearby where he proceeded to beat me in a game of pool.

Later that day, Fred took me to an abandoned orange grove. It was only after he assured me that I wouldn't be attacked by resident coral snakes and chiggers, did I leave the truck to pick the oranges. He had all the equipment — ladder and orange picker attached to a pole. Boy, did we ever get oranges — tree-ripened yet — a truck full! We hauled them back to Henrietta's kitchen and proceeded to squeeze the juice

The Bear home in Orlando, Florida.

The orange picker.

Fred and Henrietta.

out of all of them, much to the apprehension of Henrietta. Yes, we made a mess! Henrietta let us know in no uncertain terms we were to clean it up! Folks, you haven't tasted orange juice until you've had the likes of this. We must have produced several gallons and drank most of it. The upshot of the orange episode was that Fred packed some oranges for me to take home.

We talked about many things. The "chemical pod" for one. Fred always had been concerned about bowhunting wounding losses and looked for solutions. I went away from there with the complete understanding that we agreed the pod was not a solution. It would never be accepted by the bowhunting fraternity.

My next stop was St. Petersburg, a beautiful waterland city full of retired folk. A taxi took me out to the antique gun show. There I found myself standing at the entrance to a building that looked to be a quarter mile long and a hundred yards wide. Inside were rows and rows of tables jam-packed full of old guns of every description. These shows are otherwise known as "Rust Conventions."

All of the vendors were wearing Confederate uniforms. The backdrops were all Confederate flags, etc. A kid's band in uniform was marching up and down the aisles making the most awful racket you can imagine. Ear plugs would have been a blessing. As I looked over three or four piles of stuff, and as the band approached, I yelled above the noise to one of the vendors: "Hey, I thought the war was over a hundred years ago!" Just at that point, the band stopped playing! Everyone within a hundred feet heard me! An authoritative-type person approached me and asked: "Where you from, Boy?" "Washington," I replied. Noting his bushy eyebrows start to bristle, I quickly added, "The STATE of Washington!" He consulted with others nearby, came back and said: "Y'all can stay. We consider you a Western Southerner!" How about that! A colonel, no less!

On my return to Atlanta, I found two Boone and Crockett racks to measure and add to the list. I bade my daughter goodbye and headed back to Seattle with a feeling of accomplishment. The trip had netted me "four birds with one stone."

For the next several years, I became more and more involved with the Boone and Crockett Club as a measurer, instructor, and judge for their Records Programs. The Roosevelt's elk status was discussed throughout the years and always pointed to the fact that there would have to be more research done, to prove that the crown points were indeed unique to the Roosevelt's elk and could be paired.

December, 1979, I brought one shed antler of a crown point Roosevelt's elk to the B&C Records Committee meeting in New York. I was a guest of Dr. Wright. They, perhaps for the first time, saw the odd configuration and concurred it certainly had potential and warranted more consideration. Meanwhile, the Records Committee had seen enough information to prompt them to begin accepting the racks for measuring and recording in the 18th Awards Program in 1983. This acceptance was to begin January 1, 1980. Hunters and measurers in the areas of these elk were very enthusiastic about the prospect.

However, until some real difference was proved to warrant a different score sheet than the American elk, the same scoring would prevail. I was to continue my mission with the encouragement of Dr. Wright, who proved to be a doer, an innovator, and always looking for new horizons in the measuring and recording field.

In December of 1980, I was elected to membership in the Boone and Crockett Club. In the fall of 1981, my wife and I made a trip into the heart of the Roosevelt's elk country to see if we could establish a distinct difference between the antlers of the Roosevelt's elk and the American elk. The November 21, 1981 letter to Dr. Wright was the result of that trip.

This research established the fact the Roosevelt's elk antler configuration was distinctly different than that of the American elk. The Roosevelt's elk would have a separate recording form.

Dr. Wright came up with this interesting "aside" regarding the naming of the Roosevelt's elk: C. Hart Merriam, the father of American mammalogy, was a great splitter. He named 86 species and subspecies of brown and grizzly bears. President Roosevelt and many others thought he was odd, but when he decided to name the elk for Teddy, the latter tamed down and felt highly complimented. Later, the consensus became that Roosevelt's elk was at best a subspecies and Teddy complained in a letter, "Where has my glory gone!"

Through the ensuing years, my involvement with the club was strictly as a member of the Records Committee. I was a judge in 1973 and 1977. I was Chairman of the 1979 judging session and a consultant for the sessions of 1983 and 1986. Additional work was done in the form of participating in Measurers' Training Workshops for new measurers. One in Spokane, 1981, then one with Dr. Wright at the University of Montana, and 1987 in Seattle at the St. Charles Museum of Archery. We were prepared here with all the necessary racks, horns, and skulls, complete with blackboard, etc. Fourteen new students showed up for this class, and believe me, it was something special. Walter White, Chairman of the Boone and Crocket Records Committee, Dr. Philip Wright, Rusty Lindberg, and I were the instructors.

November 21, 1981

Dr. Philip L. Wright, Chairman
Records of North American Big Game Committee
Boone & Crockett Club

Re: Sub Committee Report on Roosevelt's Elk, by Glenn St. Charles

The following report is the result of research carried on to determine the point
configuration of a typical Roosevelt's elk. This project was recently culminated
by a four day trip around the Olympic Penninsula of Western Washington. The eastern boundary is Highway Interstate 5 running from Canada, through Seattle, to
Oregon. The other boundaries are Oregon, the Pacific Ocean and Canada. This prime
Roosevelt's habitat is basically rain forest--about one half of it averages 200
inches of rainfall per year.

My wife, Margaret, assisted me and took many slides and pictures which will be
shown at the December 2nd Boone & Crockett Records Committee meeting in New York.
We looked at approximately fifty heads and racks. They were found in homes, cafes,
motels, shacks, garages and a game farm. They literally came out of the woodwork
and there are many more.

Eighteen of these sets of racks appeared to be trophy size and could possibly meet
the Boone & Crockett minimum of 290. This would depend on how we finally decide to
measure what I call the "BONES OF CONTENTION". These are the points above the
fourth on most racks six points or better, counting the main beam as a point.
Hereafter, I will refer to them as crown points. The majority of racks, however,
have only one crown point on each side and they are in the fifth position. They
protrude at varying angles. On most racks they are adjacent to and between the
royal fourth and the main beam.

Sometimes, the crown point has a common base with the fourth point. Again, it may
be attached to the main beam or it can be based equally between the two, forming a
web. This point plus the fourth and the main beam appear almost as a crown not
unlike the stags of Europe. There are large and small six and seven point racks.
Regardless of size, the crown point appears on two thirds of all the racks we ob-
served--most generally on each side, but sometimes only on one. Only one rack, an
eight point, had two crown points on each side. Taking all this into consideration,
it appears that THE TYPICAL TROPHY ROOSEVELT'S ELK HAS CROWN POINTS.

Thus far, I have not been able to locate a crown point elk from Oregon. The
Canadian herd on Vancouver Island does grow the crown points--about 50% according
to Boone & Crockett measurer Wilf Klingsat, who has observed and hunted these
animals. The Raspberry Island herd of Alaska also grows crown points, but what
percentage I do not know.

Acknowledgments for Help in this Research:

     Lloyd Beebe, Olympic Game Farm, Sequim, Washington
     Dr. Randall Byers, B & C and P & Y Measurer, Moscow, Idaho
     Wilf Klingsat, B & C and P & Y Measurer, Kamloops, B. C., Canada
     Reg Lutzvick, P & Y Measurer, Aberdeen, Washington
     Bob Mayton, P & Y Measurer, Aberdeen, Washington
     Jack Smith, Chief Biologist, Olympic Penninsula, Washington State Game Dept.
     Aubrey Taylor, B & C Measurer, Port Townsend, Washington

CROWN POINT "BONES OF CONTENTION" ON DIFFERENT
CONFIGURATIONS OF ROOSEVELT'S ELK RACKS

F = Main Beam; G = Points; CR = Crown Points;
H-4 = Fourth Circumference; L = Left; R = Right.

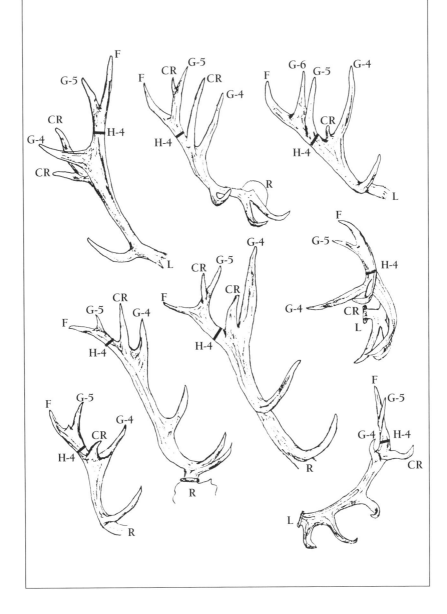

Dr. Wright started by introducing the program, and carried on for a couple hours. The look on the faces of the students was really something. Phil had literally mesmerized them as if he was conducting an orchestra. We called a break to give Phil a needed rest. It was time for Walter, Rusty, and me to take over. We talked about it and agreed that neither one of us wanted to follow Phil's superb performance. We concluded that Dr. Wright should continue, if he felt up to it. He agreed, that with a break now and then, he could carry on. He was enjoying himself, certainly he was doing what he does best. His performance was one that the students and Walter, Rusty, and I will always remember. This whole measuring session was topped off with an afternoon picnic and pictures.

BOONE AND CROCKETT UPSHOT

The 1986 measuring session in Las Vegas was to be my last. Being a consultant doesn't really define that it's any different than being a judge. You are one of the measurers crawling around, in and under tables, moose, caribou, and elk racks. This 75-year-old no longer felt up to the task. If the truth were known, I would say that the feeling was mutual with the Records Committee that my judging days should be over. A character at my age can get a little cantankerous.

In the following years of my membership, other bowhunters became members of the Boone and Crockett Club. They were, in succession: Fred Bear, 1982, Dr. William C. MacCarty, 1984, Billy Ellis, 1986, Dr. C. Randall Byers, 1988, and John O. (Buzzi) Cook, III, 1990.

In 1991, I asked for Emeritus membership consideration citing the fact that I was 80 and had a lot of unfinished business to take care of like writing this book. Emeritus membership was granted.

Let it be known that Boone and Crockett is a first-class and honorable club. When a hunt culminates in putting an animal in their records book, that entry has real meaning. I am very proud of the club's accomplishments in the field of conservation, and am honored to be a member.

Judges and consultants measuring horns in the snow for the 17th Boone and Crockett Awards Program, at Jefferson City, Missouri, 1979. Left to right: Glenn St. Charles, Washington; Scott Showalter, Kansas; Glen Sanderson, Indiana; Dr. Philip Wright, Montana; Frank Cook, Alaska; Jim Murphy, Missouri; Bill Crump, Wyoming.

Boone and Crockett Measuring Workshop, instructors and trainees, 1987. Standing, left to right: Charles "Rusty" Lindberg, Oregon; Dr. Philip Wright, Montana; Dean Cook, David Sanford, John Stone, Larry C. Lack, John Durst, Washington; Roger Atwood, Idaho; Russ Spaulding, Buzzi Cook, Washington; Walter White, Minnesota; James F. Willoughby, California. Kneeling, left to right: Glenn St. Charles, Bob Byrne, Bob Mayton, Reg Lutzvick, Jay St. Charles, Washington; Ron Sherer, Idaho.

23
HUNKERING DOWN

Every bowhunter should some day experience a hunt out of a tent camp where he has to hunker down. By that, I mean when you are hovering over a small pile of smoldering wet willows, trying to fan a flame to keep from freezing. The Nason Creek characters I hunt with, Bob Kelly, Bill Jardine, Bob Arvine, and I certainly have had our share. However, I wouldn't wish the following experience we had on anyone.

We are in our cabin high in the Cascades in the Nason Creek Bowhunting Reserve. The 1965 hunting season is over. We've shared a deer or two with each other and most of the venison is now home in the freezer. We are buttoning up the cabin for the winter, a winter that will probably dump from six to eight feet of snow on the cedar shake roof of this Chalet. Out of nowhere, I hear a remark: "What we otta do is come up here in the middle of winter just to see what it's like." "Yeah," someone answered, "it could be interesting." "Well," I said, "if we have any idea it will be this coming winter, we'll need more wood for the "Toad" and we'll have to hang a shovel outside on the building about seven or eight feet from the ground so we can dig out the door."

Now, we're all scurrying around acting like the "wild" hair idea of making a two mile trek into this haven is a done deal. Word got around to others on the outside world. The occupants of the Bucktail Lodge, another cabin about 200 yards from ours wanted in on it. We even went so far as to ask, as a guest, a game department agent who was a bowhunter. Surely, we could make some brownie points with him!

The Chalet in January.

There would be about 10 or 12 of us. Some would be going in on cross-country skis, others on snowshoes. We planned the trip for after the end of the year. As the time approached, we contacted the local sporting goods store to rent clothes — when you're into winter sports, you've got to look like a winter sport!

Came the day. Three cars headed out of Seattle and over the 4,000-foot Stevens Pass. We met about 15 miles beyond at the Oxbow, a combination tavern and coffee shop, about a mile from our take-off point. It was a hale and hardy crew that left the Oxbow about 9 a.m. on a Saturday morning. We figured we should be at the cabin by noon. We parked near our starting point by heading our cars into a snow bank far enough to get off the highway. We all carried packs stocked with a change of clothes, a smattering of food, candy bars, and one contained a big chunk of venison to roast on the "Toad." Two of the fellows brought sleeping bags.

The sky was cloudy, a flake or two was drifting down on top of about six feet of snow. The snow was wet and slick. Our skis worked real well on the flat that we were on. Soon all this was to change. Most of it would be uphill, winding through jack pines, firs, and spruce. About thirty minutes into the trek we were beginning to realize that this would be no cake walk. Any sign of trails was non-existent in this

On the way in.

winter setting. Someone yelled out and suggested, "If we had any brains, we'd go back to the tavern." The remark drew a lot of flack. About then I realized that my choice of skis over snowshoes was a big mistake. The last time I'd been on skis was when a single strap held your shoe to the ski.

We were soon on a compass heading, up, up, up. Skiing we weren't. It was a case of walking on skis, one step at a time, trying to lift about five pounds of snow with each step. This sapped the energy real fast and, if that wasn't enough, one of my ski poles broke. So now I am like on crutches and to top that, scrambling around the tops of some vine maples, the crotch of my black wool pants split! I was exposed to the elements! Others were having problems. It wasn't the way we'd planned.

Our unsure path took us to a deep ravine. During hunting season this ravine probably had a creek running through it. Now it was frozen and partly filled in with snow and ice. We couldn't recognize it. Somehow we had to get across it so we had to take our skis off and try to throw them to the other side. One of mine went down a hole in the snow and disappeared! Now, what do I do? Well, I did the only thing I could — crawl and slide down into that ravine, crawl into the hole, and try to reach the ski.

Ordinarily, the guys would get a big kick out of my predicament, but we were all in such sad straits, it just wasn't funny any more. I had to get so far down into the hole to reach the end of the ski, I couldn't get out. A couple guys had to pull me out by my feet. All three of us were then mired in the mess. The snowshoers were not in as much pain. One of them threw us a rope which they had tied to a tree, so we could pull ourselves out and up the steep hillside. We had only covered about a half mile of the two we had to go.

Needless to say, this outing was turning into a disaster. At the top of the ravine, we found a pretty sizable bench. There we decided to regroup and figure out what to do next. *Someone produced a compass and we all decided that compass had gone bad! Another was pronounced bad, and when the third one agreed with the other two, we KNEW we were hopelessly lost!* The only thing we could figure out at that point was that maybe the compasses were reacting to some iron deposits under the snow we were standing on. By now, we were at about the 4,000-foot level. Clouds were not ABOVE us any more. We were IN them.

Nearby was a cedar snag about three feet in diameter. The snag suggested that we go no further. It was about two o'clock in the afternoon and we had thought we'd be at the cabin by noon. No way! Most of us were in no condition to try to get back out of there before darkness set in. Someone produced a belt axe. We hacked enough splinters off the side of that snag, set fire to it with a cigarette lighter and began settling down for a long, long rest of the day and a long, long night.

We soon had ourselves a 100-foot torch reaching into the cloudy sky. Anyone at the bottom of this mountain who could see it would probably assume that there had been a lightning strike. They would never assume that anyone would be dumb enough to do what we were attempting to do. The heat from the burning snag began to melt the snow around us. We made ourselves as comfortable as possible. A couple cans of sardines were produced; we emptied and used the cans to melt snow for water. Not the tastiest water to be sure! We promptly ate what lunch food and candy bars we had, and saved the venison roast for later.

A couple hours of this and the heat lowered the level of this whole operation. We finally found ourselves on the ground in a little amphitheater about 20 feet in diameter and 6 feet deep. As we gradually recuperated, a joke or two could be heard. There was a little levity in the crowd. I even dickered with one of the guys for his sleeping bag. I would trade him a brand new Kodiak just to use it for the night. He

The guys hovering by the torch!

wouldn't bite. *Our Game Department guest was not favorably impressed but took it all in stride.*

For supper that night, we laid everything out on a dry part of the ground. It was a couple loaves of bread, some potatoes, and the big hunk of venison. Roasting sticks were produced from some nearby vine maple branches, and Bob Kelly tied a white handkerchief around his head and announced that he would be the chef! In due time, the meager meal was laid out. It was relished by all. We then settled down for the long, long night by curling up on the ground around the bottom of the tree, which at this time was pretty dry. All this time, the burning snag was shedding embers which were burning holes in our rented jackets and pants. Yes, we had a miserable night! Another inch or two of snow fell.

As daylight slowly came upon the scene, we heard a faint train whistle. We scrambled to our feet and looked far down the slope from our bench into the valley below, which was now clear of clouds. There was a train threading its way parallel to the highway. The compasses that had gone bad instantly repaired themselves and snapped to attention! Now we knew where we were! We had no further desire to find the cabin. We just wanted to get out of there! We left our still-burning torch, our savior, and headed down.

Bob Arvine making the best of it.

Headed out.

During the night, I had made myself an improvised ski pole out of a branch with a wadded-up bunch of rags and belts strapped near the bottom, so that it would operate somewhat like a ski pole. I managed to get down the hill, but found myself bringing up the rear along with the snowshoers. My problems were not over going downhill. The skiers ahead would run over the vine maples that were bent to the ground by the snow, and when I got to them they were popping up. My skis went under them and I would find myself time after time bent over these branches, flat on my face in the snow.

Yes, we all got out of there safe and sound, but that was not the end of our troubles. I had left my car lights on. It had to be jumped. We all got to the Oxbow. This time, its priority was that it was a coffee shop and we were hungry. It was there we decided, because of the snow that had fallen during the night, we perhaps should take another route home. Stevens Pass, our route in from Seattle, could be socked in. We would try going over Bleuett Pass. As it turned out, we stayed at the Oxbow too long, or long enough, to get trapped along a river road by two avalanches that plugged the road behind us and in front of us. We waited there for two hours for snow plows to clear the highway.

Our rented ski outfits were worthless. Needless to say, we had to pay for them!

Yes, we Nason Creek bowhunters know about hunkering down!

24

QUEBEC LABRADOR CARIBOU

1982 Hunt

The scene of my 1982 Quebec Labrador caribou hunt was Bobby Snowball's Tunulik River Camp, at the head of Tunulik Lake in northern Quebec. Twenty-two made the trip — 4 rifle hunters and 18 bowhunters. Fourteen of us flew from Vancouver, B.C. to Montreal, where we met the rest of the group who had come in from various parts of the country. From Montreal, Nordair Airlines flew us into Fort Chimo, one of their regular stops on their daily run to the far North. Fort Chimo is on the southern end of Ungava Bay, 900 miles north of Montreal.

From Fort Chimo, air transportation was a ten-passenger Twin Otter, an incredible airplane. It literally dropped into the short gravel runway on the edge of Tunulik Lake. The previous group of hunters left on the same plane, which lifted off in less than 100 yards. We were the last hunters for the season. There were five hunts before ours. The success for all was 100%. The later the hunt, the more foul the weather — but, in turn, this weather brought us the largest antlered caribou.

We were met at the airstrip by our guides in 20-foot freighter canoes powered by outboard motors. It was a half mile trip to the camp, which consisted of 11 plywood huts with oil heat — four hunters to a cabin. Nearby, there was a big cook shack staffed with native women, wives of the guides, as cooks. In their spare time, some

20-foot freighter canoe.

of the wives made moccasins and gloves from native-tanned skins and others made wool caps, all of which they sold to the hunters. Bobby's 80-year-old mother occupied a tent nearby. She worked the leather goods and helped with the cooking chores.

The head guide and owner of the camp was Bobby Snowball, a college-educated native Inuit (Eskimo). All the guides were Inuits. They are the native people ranging clear across the northern reaches of Canada. They don't like to be called Eskimos. Bobby Snowball's main helper was a Canadian from Toronto, who acted more or less as a liaison between the hunters and guides.

It was apparent from the start that the guides knew nothing of Pope and Young or Boone and Crockett. "Fair chase" was something we hunters had to actually work at. Most of the guides spoke very little English, and to convey to them that you could not shoot the animals in the water was very difficult. For some of the guides, "Yep," "Nope," "I think so," and "Maybe" seemed to be the extent of their English vocabulary.

Hunting was done out of the freighter canoes with two hunters and two guides in each. Options for the hunters were: the guides would either stay with you, or drop you off on the beach and come back for you later. They would cruise the lake, watching the low-lying hills for

The vast region of Tunulik Lake, Quebec.

migrating caribou. They could spot the caribou at incredible distances. Sometimes, in search of caribou, they would cover the full length of the lake for 30 miles.

The lake varied in width from 100 yards to 1 mile. It was dotted with islands and long narrow arms of land jutting out into the water. The surrounding low hills were very rocky and strewn with big boulders. The ground cover was tundra, sparsely growing willows, and patches of scrub spruce trees. We were very near the tree line of the North American continent. There were many small lakes, streams, and ponds adjacent to the lake. The caribou, in their migration trek, would not hesitate to cross any of them. Some of us hunted away from the lake, but sooner or later, we found ourselves back at the big lake on some prominence, glassing the surrounding hills for the caribou in their approaches to lake crossings — many, ancient crossings.

Most days, we had what they call "shore lunches." The guides would cook up a fish, a piece of meat, or whatever was handy, on a grate over the coals of dry willows that they would find on the site. An iron skillet brimming with sliced potatoes, onions — the works! These were great. Sometimes, several boatloads of hunters would gather in one favorite spot. At one such gathering, our guide was working over a can of water to use for coffee or tea. He looked up, glanced back down

Bobby Snowball's camp on Lake Tunulik, 1982.

Scott Showalter and Bob Jensen "bringing in the bacon."

the lake and stoically remarked, "There's a bunch of seven caribou down there. The third one from the left has a huge rack." We all looked, saw nothing; grabbed our binoculars, still saw nothing. "No, you looked too close," he said. "Way down there!" Sure enough, we finally picked them up and he was right. The Inuits have incredible eyesight.

Well, the end result was we all took caribou — shots were from 3 feet to 25 yards. Most scored over the 300 minimum for Pope and Young. Two will probably make the Boone and Crockett book. They roughly scored 385 and 400.

The longer we were there, the more the hunting seemed to be concentrated near the lake. When I questioned the overseer about this, he remarked that the guides did not want to backpack the meat any further than necessary. I also got the following story from Bobby Snowball: Years ago the natives lived in small villages along the river. At one such village, there was a shortage of meat. There were no caribou close to the river. Two hunters set out on foot to find the caribou. They went inland several miles before they found the herd. They were then concerned with how to get the caribou to their canoes. Their solution was to shoot two caribou in the front knee joints and herd them to the river! In this modern day, of course, such an incident would be considered intolerable, but to them, it was pure and simple survival. This territory was their "house" — their icebox. They'd get food to the pot any way possible.

Another story: In those same years before the white man came to hunt, there were several villages along the river and lake. Inuit hunters would kill caribou at places along their travel routes, and bury the carcasses on the frozen ground under piles of rocks for future use; mainly when they were on wolf hunting forays, or in moving from one hunting ground to another. The caches were marked by rock pillars, some in the shape of people. They are called Inukshuks.

There was nothing unusual about my hunt. After assuring the guide that shooting the caribou in the water was out, we settled down on a high prominence that jutted out into the lake, where we could overlook several migration trails that came off of the valley rim and into the lake. The object was to "cut them off at the pass" before they got to the lake. Occasionally, a canoe with hunter and guide would cruise by below. It was after one such canoe passing that we spotted six caribou swimming back toward the shore that they came from. They would be landing less than a quarter mile away. The guide knew that they would not stay there very long but would rest, mill around, then head back

Buzzi Cook

across the lake. With the chance that we had time to make a stalk on them, we headed out, literally on the run. I had cover to within about 30 yards. I needed to get closer. Sneaking through the willows apparently created enough noise that one of them heard and came over to investigate. That was his mistake. As he turned broadside to go back with the others, I let loose an arrow. He went down quickly. I doubt if he or any of the others knew what happened. As we approached this beautiful dark animal with the white mane, the others took off down the shore.

We made short work of preparing the carcass for the trip to the camp. With "bird in hand," and a sense of accomplishment, we headed for the "barn." A couple miles down the lake we began looking for my hunting partner, Jack Williams, and his guide where we had dropped them off that morning. We found them in a little bay. Jack was taking pictures of a kill that he had made. Although I had a camera in my pack, it seemed appropriate that, while he was at it, Jack should take a picture of our success also. Why not? However, we later found out that there was no film in his camera!

Soon, with Jack's animal in the boat, we all continued on toward camp — with the wind in our faces, an occasional raindrop, and the hope that the guide manning the boat had a mind's eye map of the shallows along the way. An occasional "tick" of the propeller on a rock, the

Scott Showalter

Roger Hammond makes the shot, 1982. Note the pass-through arrow, beneath the caribou.

The meat rack.

swerving here and there, indicated that we were indeed in shallow waters. At one point, we thought that the boat was going to tip over. Upon reaching camp, noise of the motor quieted down, I asked our guide what had caused the tipping problem. His reply was, "Aw — we rolled on a big fish!"

After having been there once, I am sure that I would do things differently another time. I wouldn't be in such a hurry to fill out. The guides would cooperate if one insisted upon hunting for a trophy. A little more patience on the part of the guides and the hunters could have brought all of us higher-scoring racks. All in all, it was a very good hunt — or maybe I should say "shoot out." The food and camp facilities were very good. Even the linen was changed every day.

QUEBEC LABRADOR CARIBOU UPSHOT

No more do the natives live out in the remote areas. They now spend their winters in modular homes at Fort Chimo and other like towns. Most are subsidized by the Canadian government. The hunting and fishing camps are encouraged by the government since they provide the natives extra money and give them something to do. The Inuit guides receive $50 a day for their services. Now days, without government help in that rough country, it would be very difficult to survive.

Gasoline is $7.50 a gallon. Fuel oil for the houses at Fort Chimo is $4.50 a gallon and a single 2x4 board, 8 feet long, costs $40. The town is also served in the summer months from the Atlantic through Ungava Bay.

We were able to bring out our caribou racks intact. Nordair is apparently the only airline in the northern Quebec area that will allow the rack to come out in one piece. There are many other outfitters and camps in northern Quebec. Hunters should question ahead of time as to the disposition of racks before booking.

I left Boone and Crockett and Pope and Young Record Books at Tunulik. The Canadian overseer pointed out some of the caribou records listed which had been taken at this camp. The guides excitedly remembered the hunters. We hunters went away with the hope that future hunters will find the guides more knowledgeable about hunting and Fair Chase. This could be a problem wherever you go in the Far North, a problem we hunters should be concerned about in helping the natives have a more gainful guiding career, and the hunters a caribou to be proud of.

One laugher on this trip was the antics of the four Safari Club members. They noticed the Boone and Crockett and Pope and Young books that I had left with the guides, and were prone to joke about and ridicule the clubs during happy hour. They were really out to put some heads in the Safari Club records! Well, about the second day, as my canoe was docking at the meat rack, one of the Safari Club members was there to greet me with the remark: "I have something to show you." I followed him to one of the cabins where he pointed to a huge rack. Certainly congratulations were in order. "Do you think that would make the Boone and Crockett Book?" "Yes, with that double shovel and top palmation, it would make anybody's book." "Well," he remarked rather sheepishly, "I would appreciate it if you would measure it for Boone and Crockett and get it entered!"

Surely this scenario has been repeated many times over. Like the early day milk bottles, the cream always comes to the top. Nothing beats the quality embodied in the Boone and Crockett and Pope and Young Club records.

A RETURN TO TUNULIK

1984 saw a return to Bobby Snowball's camp. This time, the hunt would be set up in two different segments. The first one would be September 19 to 26, which ordinarily would be the last because of the inclement weather that sets in about that time. The second hunt would be from September 26 to October 3. It would be questionable, pending weather conditions. Snow would make it impossible for the Twin Otter to land. If weather cancelled it, there would be a money-back guarantee. I was booked to stay for both of these hunts, September 19 to October 3. I was to hunt with a bow on the first and a gun on the second. Having never killed any big game animal with a gun, it was decided that this would be the time. The venerable Dr. Phil Wright, Boone and Crockett Records Committee Chairman, was persuaded to be my hunting partner and perhaps witness my first kill with the rifle. The rifle I brought was one of my antiques — a take-down Bullard, 38-55 octagon barrel, single action, complete with adjustable iron peep sights, vintage 1886, a very beautiful and accurate piece.

It was September 26. The first segment of the hunt was over. I had taken a real nice double-shovel caribou with the bow. Charlie, my guide, had spotted two bulls about a quarter mile away trotting toward us. We were parked on a knoll at the end of a long arm of land extending out into the lake. Charlie indicated that one of them had a double shovel. Sounded good to me and I prepared for a possible contact with these critters. This arm of land is only about 100 yards wide. We were on the left side of the arm facing the caribou as they trotted our way. There wasn't much cover directly in front of me.

I slowly sneaked down off the knob, trying to use the cover of the bushes along the shore line. The animals had the option of going off either side into the lake and probably would. My best shot would be to turn them to their right and make them cross to the other side, thus giving me a broadside exposure. However, I usually shoot left-handed and this would put me in an awkward position. Being a switch shooter, my bow had arrow rests on both sides. I quickly renocked my arrow for a right-hand shot. When they were about 75 yards away, I made a run directly at them, turning them broadside, and while they were running across in front of me, I loosed an arrow that entered the left flank of the double-shovel caribou, and exited just behind the right shoulder on the other side. The critter spun around and came down with all four feet in the air. The caribou, Charlie, and I were all surprised! This was Charlie's first experience with a bowhunter. You can bet this would be subject for conversation at the guide's supper table that night.

The first hunt is over, and the hunters are sitting among the hunting gear and racks waiting for the Twin Otter to arrive. New hunters

Caribou were there for the taking, 1984.

will be coming in and others will be going out. The spirits are high. All were successful and eager to tell their stories to the newcomers. It was getting a bit late and a cloud cover had brought dusk to the area a little earlier than usual. Some of the Inuits were preparing to light flares around the airstrip, if necessary. Finally, the drone of an approaching aircraft directed eyes to a far off speck. It's coming in. The Twin Otter circled once, made the approach, and literally dropped in with the usual whomp! There was a short roll to the mountain of baggage and racks. Yes, the pilot had been there before!

When the door opened, hunters poured out. Among them were my son, Jay, Gail and Dan Martin, and Dr. Phil Wright. The racks on the tarmac produced the usual oohs and aahs, hasty stories were told, and then it was into the boats for the short trip to camp. Next comes the

My Inuit guide, Charlie.

settling-in period, the happy hour, and a dinner of caribou and lake trout. Finally, they were briefed on what's for tomorrow.

When the time came to show Phil my rifle, I gingerly hauled it out of the canvas gun case. I was a little concerned how he would take to this antique firing piece. Would he think I was joking, not serious? He didn't cringe or show any sign of concern. But I am sure he was a bit taken aback. He had brought his favorite rifle, a 7mm Magnum. Well, so much for that. The next few days would tell the story.

The first day out was quite gusty; a strong enough wind for our assigned guides to consider the day not a good one to cover the far reaches of the lake. We did make the short trip across the lake to the far side and did some scouting and glassing, but came back empty-handed. Two gun hunters fishing on the camp side in a lake nearby, got into a small band and two caribou paid the price.

Day three found Phil and me headed full bore up the lake. Our poker-faced guide, manning the power end of the big freighter canoe, was ever so alert, scanning the area for any sign of animals. Phil and I are settled in, our backs to the weather, sitting on our life jackets; not a good thing to do, we were told, by the overseer at an earlier briefing. We were to wear them, because, if for some reason the boat flipped, the colored jackets would help to find our bodies in the frigid water; water cold enough to make one lifeless in about ten minutes! Hunters in the far north are not good insurance risks. I mention this because about

Waiting for the pickup.

The Twin Otter lands for the pickup.

Carol Mauch, Pope and Young World Record Quebec Labrador Caribou, 1984.

five minutes into our trip, without warning, the guide spun our canoe around in a 90 degree turn, almost leaving Phil and me hanging in mid-air and headed over the side. We barely hung on. Without a word or blink, the guide headed for the nearest landing to intercept some bulls coming over the crest of a far-off ridge, the rising sun at their backs.

We quickly dragged the big canoe to a secure rest on the beach. Grabbing our weapons, we hightailed it up a long gradual slope to a rock-strewn plateau, where the herd seemed to be headed. We got in place, none too soon, by some huge boulders that gave us access to watching the oncoming onslaught. Looked like the land was on the move. Perhaps a thousand or so critters! Excitement, you bet! So much so that Phil and I apparently lost our cool. Little did we know, that we were about to be caught up in such a situation that would overshadow our training as judges in sizing up the big one — basically, what it is all about, when with rifle or bow, you are supposed to find one that you can put in the book. No way. Apparently, evaluation went out the window.

It was like we were being attacked by a horde of monsters of the tundra and we were protecting ourselves. We both shot the first keepers that came along. We had committed the cardinal sin of a trophy hunter. It was like I have always said, as a bowhunter, I am a trophy hunter until something else comes along. Neither of our racks were bookers. So much for fun and sport. My firing piece, the old Bullard, had done its job admirably. After bringing ourselves and gear, with meat secured, back to the boat, it was time to unwind and reflect.

My guide was intrigued by my old rifle. I suggested that he try it. I dug in my coat pocket for a cartridge. He loaded and pulled the trigger on a rock out in the lake. Nothing happened! My next bullet, if I had needed it, was a dud! So much for using a 50-year-old box of factory loaded Winchester 38-55s — perhaps a redeeming factor.

Tunulik Upshot

It was noticeable that most of the guides were no longer suggesting that we shoot caribou in the water. They were beginning to understand our ways. Our guide, one of Bobby Snowball's sons, was very obliging. But you can be sure that some of the guides would still try to encourage the newcomers to take a bull swimming in the lake. Quite naturally, the Inuits would revert to their ancestral ways. It would take several years for them to come around fully to the ways of the outside world and the Fair Chase concept.

They killed for meat. Their subsistence hunting consisted of killing the caribou as they made their way over water crossings. They simply boated up to a swimming herd, shot the ones that would supply the best meat, yarded them up, and towed them ashore where they were readied for the winter meat supply.

Through the years, I hunted throughout the Inuit country in several different camps. Each had a different agenda as to how they guided the outside hunters. Some of the ways were culturally related. Some guides would prepare to shoot when animals were sighted — very disconcerting to hear a cartridge being loaded into the firing chamber. Pride in their ability in getting results seemed to be their main concern.

Ungava Bay, Akuliak – 1986

At all camps on Ungava Bay, severe tides had to be reckoned with. You went out with full tide, hunted, and if you weren't staying over in a spike camp, you had to be back at the boat at the next high tide to get off the rocks. The tides fluctuated so much, your boat at low tide could be a mile from the water.

On one sortie, my hunting partner, Myron Storer, and I had been out on the tundra for about four hours, walking and glassing caribou here and there. Our guides were an elder of the Inuit's tribe, Stanley Annannack, and his son, Paulo. During the walk we had glassed many caribou. One especially was really a keeper, but since it wasn't in the direction our guide was committed to, we didn't go after it. A bit further on, we watched three nice heads bed down right on the crest of a ridge facing us. The guides said that they could be approached from the off side of the ridge from us. Sensing that this could be our best stalk of the day before heading back to camp, we approached them from our left, out of sight of the bulls.

When we arrived in the area of the ridge and still out of sight, we found that they had bedded on the top of a rise, facing away from a little gully we could drift into. Probably the shot would be about 15 yards. One problem. We didn't need the guides help or presence on this stalk. We were in a position downwind, where the bulls could be stalked without detection. We asked the guides if they would stay there and let Myron and me go the rest of the way alone. It appeared that the guides understood and approved.

Myron and I, with the wind in our faces, sneaked down the gully and got into position underneath the bulls. Their velvet-covered racks were silhouetted against the sky. A perfect set-up. The bodies would come into view as we worked our way up the slope. Myron was to have the shot, I had the video camera. Myron, at ready, was about to make the shot. The caribou racks and Myron were in my viewfinder. All of a sudden, the bulls jumped up and headed out. Would you believe it! There the guides were walking down the ridge directly toward the caribou, yelling and waving their arms. They had deliberately chased them off! All we could assume at that point, was that the elder guide's pride could not cope with not being a part of the taking of one of those caribou. You never know what's going on in the heads of these folks of the tundra. It was understandable. They had pride. We hunted the surrounding area another hour or so without success.

It was past lunch time. With Stanley, there was no trail lunch. We would have to go back to camp for food. Upon arriving there a couple hours later, we quickly unloaded the cooler they had brought. Cheese and crackers were all that appeared to be inside. We devoured most of that. It's about three o'clock and there would be time for hunting near camp. Suddenly it occurred to me, what's for supper? There was a 12-inch cast iron skillet pan nearby and an almost empty cooler. Nothing else. Stanley, with a shrug of his shoulders, indicated that he had expected us to shoot something for dinner. He had been thinking rifles all the way! We quickly exited the tent and looked at the tide which had started to go out.

"Stanley, can we still make it on the outgoing tide?" Another shrug of the shoulders and we headed for the boat! For the next hour, we frantically poled our way in very shallow waters around boulders, and finally made it to the open water. We had our spike camp experience without even staying overnight!

We arrived back at the main camp to find the Inuits there all scrambling to get into boats, rifles in hand. Someone on a hill above the camp had spotted, out in the bay, a pod of Beluga whales, which I am told are one of the favorite delicacies of these northern folks. We watched with binoculars as the Inuits apparently were shooting into the water. They came up empty-handed. Aside from that, they reported some of the whales were bloodied. They had apparently been attacked by another clan of Inuits further down Ungava Bay.

The next few days found Myron and me beating the tundra with an entourage of guides and their youngsters. Myron took a couple of nice heads with his rifle, one a Boone and Crockett. Although there were a lot of caribou to be had, I finally, on the very last afternoon of the very last day, shot a piece of meat with the guide's rifle — just something to take home.

Ungava Bay, Akuliak Upshot

Such hunts sometimes provide many surprises, many even shocking. Inuits love to eat the lacey fat from the caribou stomachs as they are being dressed out. Two of the teenage girl helpers in the camp kitchen made daily visits to the meat shack as the caribou kills came in. They would, with their fingers, lift the eyeballs out of the caribou heads and eat them raw like they were candy! Perhaps this sort of thing is what you remember from these trips even more than the kills. It's all part of the hunt, great sport, and I will go back.

Each year, as the Inuits experience what bowhunting is all about, they get better and better. And, you always come home with the feeling that you have had an adventure. With the wind in your face and caribou in the hills, win or lose, it's a great experience.

From here, it will be on to Northwest Territories for Central Canada Barren Ground Caribou.

25

CENTRAL CANADA
BARREN GROUND CARIBOU

It's mid-September, 1993. We hunters have just returned from Yellowknife, Northwest Territories. Some of the Central Canada Barren Ground Caribou racks of the Seattle hunters are on a table in our museum. One of my long standing-friends wanders in to examine the spoils and remarks to me, "Well, did you get one?" "Yeah," I reply. "A 39-inch lake trout — a fish." "A *what?* I thought you were hunting *caribou!*"

Fourteen of us, from all parts of the country, had booked into Jaeb's True North Safari Hunting and Fishing Camp. This camp is on 150 mile MacKay Lake, northwest of Yellowknife. Our hunt was for ten days, the latter part of August and into September. Caribou was the priority but, boy, do they ever have fishing! Two of the hunters, Dale Holpainen and Russ Tye were going back for the second time — always a good endorsement for any hunting camp. Both of my sons, Jay and Joe, were there, the first time all three of us have been in a hunting camp such as this at the same time.

The trip from Seattle to Yellowknife via Edmonton was uneventful. We checked into the camp's office and made our way to the Northwest Territories Game Department for the necessary tags. The next morning we boarded the Twin Otter workhorse for the trip to the camp. As we approached the camp, the pilot made the usual getting-in-tune go-around before landing. This is Indian country; Dene, or Dogrib. The land of the stone man-like trail markers called Inukshuks

Glenn with sons, Jay and Joe, and Inukshuks, 1993.

— markers used by the ancestral Dogribs on their treks across this barren land in quest for caribou, wolverines, and wolves.

The lady pilot brought us in with the usual Twin Otter whomp! She taxied to the end of the runway, spun around like she was driving a sports car, and brought us to the unloading area which overlooked a row of hunter cabins and buildings stretched out along the slope toward the lake. There were also three other buildings — a cookshack, a lounge, and a building for showering.

Each one of the hunting cabins could hold up to six hunters with regular beds. They were complete with indoor plumbing, thus avoiding the possibility of wrestling a grizzly bear on a forced potty break. Each cabin sported an oil heating stove. The bowhunters who were to settle down in these quarters for the duration, could best be described as an assortment of characters.

1993 — Left to right: John Evans, Nathan Andersohn, Jack Joseph, my grandson Robin St. Charles, and Billy Ellis.

Rows of hunters' cabins at MacKay Lake.

Float plane bringing in supplies.

One cabin became home to Mississippi "Colonel" Billy Ellis, two rebel cohorts, Max Thomas from Mississippi and John Evans from Tennessee, and Nathan Andersohn from Colorado. Their cabin was immediately identified with a rebel flag.

Dick and Carol Mauch from Nebraska settled into another cabin and immediately turned it into a fish camp with all kinds of fly-tying gear. Dick, a pro fly-fisherman, was thinking grayling and lake trout all the way from Nebraska, while Carol was more concerned with bringing home a rack to measure up to her world record Quebec Caribou.

The three musketeers of <u>Traditional Bowhunter</u> magazine, Tim Conrads, Larry Fischer, and Wade Carstens, didn't waste any time moving in. Wade needed some convincing that caribou existed in huntable numbers, having previously been in two other hunting camps without firing an arrow. And then there were Dale Holpainen and Russ Tye, who, having been there before, knew all the ropes and assured Wade that he was now in the right place.

Jay, Joe, Jack Joseph, and I were the last to settle into our cabin. It was next to the cook shack, perhaps because Jay had made it known that I would probably spend considerable time there nosing around for food.

The next order of business was an orientation of the camp, followed by a briefing with the guides. A happy hour was capped by a sumptuous dinner prepared by the native cooks. Needless to say, the eager hunters got little sleep that night in anticipation of the morrow.

I had talked myself into staying in camp the first day, thus to check out the area and get my feet thoroughly planted in the tundra. The lake was surrounded by low hills with intermittent plateaus of tundra, rock, willows, blueberry bushes, and a few patches of scrub pine, a sign we were near or on the tree line of the North American Continent.

The camps sprung to life early. It seemed appropriate for me to unlimber my video camera and record all the hunters on a first day trek, on their way down the slope to the 16-foot aluminum boats, powered with more than adequate outboards. The guide per hunter ratio was generally one to one unless the hunters themselves decided they would be more happy with one to two. Each of the guides were armed with rifles — the law of the land. Where there's caribou there will be predators — grizzlies.

Carol and Dick Mauch would be going to King Rapids nearby for the fishing. Each would have their own guide, since Carol would be looking for one of those migrating critters. Jack Joseph and Jay were

Jack Joseph and me with ptarmigan, 1993.

teamed up with guides Morris Martin and Ray Simon. My camera did catch Jay and Jack Joseph as they climbed into their boat. Jack, as usual, was "flying with the eagles," an expression his wife, Mary, explained to me later. It's the way Jack was, whether he be at a Pope and Young Convention or on any kind of a hunt with his buddies. Little did we know this was the last time all of us in camp would see Jack alive. He drew on a caribou with his last breath.

It was a pretty subdued gang that gathered for supper that night. Obviously, we needed to talk and loose our pent-up feelings. A meeting was called for later in the lounge. And talk, we did. Emotions ran high. Some of us had been with Jack on other hunts. A consensus determined that he would certainly want us to carry on. All felt a sense of relief. A night Wake for Jack was planned at a time dictated by the elements. Meanwhile, the camp personnel would round up all the pieces of wood in the area for a bonfire. The hunt would go on in full force.

Each day produced one or two racks along with excited hunters and wild stories. Half way into the hunt, Wade Carstens was still without blood on his hands. We all assured him his time would come. Just relax and let it happen. It did! He brought in two racks in one day. One of them turned out to be the best of the hunt!

Yes, caribou were plentiful. There were guide tradeoffs. At times Jay and I would literally putter around the lake with guide Morris. We made a couple of stalks, had wonderful opportunities. These guides were the most disciplined of any of the camps I have been in. You used their abilities if you wanted them, otherwise they would keep their distance, patiently let you hunt on your own to stalk, ambush, or whatever. There were no disconcerting clicks of a shell being chambered, no screams of "shoot-shoot-shoot!" when the caribou were still off 100 yards. If the guides weren't close by, they would always be within sight or earshot if needed. Yes, they did keep track of any wandering or curious grizzlies.

There were sightings of a white wolf. Several wolverines were seen going about their daily tasks foraging for food. One dragged what looked like the leg of a caribou into a pile of huge boulders about 300 yards from us. A prairie, about a quarter mile from the lake shore, had sprouted many clumps of lush tall grass. Further examination disclosed caribou remains within each clump; leftover bone from a migrating herd that had apparently been struck by lightning several years ago. A Peregrine falcon, nesting in a cliff nearby, got the attention of some of us folks from the outside world. Swans were seen and appreciated in

Shore lunch with guide Morris Martin, right.

several of the lake bays. The spectacular aurora borealis was a nightly occurrence — all part of this northern wonderland.

The guide shore lunches, for some of us, were the highlight of the day. There were chosen spots for these on many parts around the lake. The King Rapids was one of them. Quite often, one or two parties would get together. In their travels up and down the lake looking for caribou, there was always time to drop a line and catch a fish for lunch. Otherwise, they would dip into a cooler and haul out a choice piece of caribou meat. Tim Conrads, on the way to a lunch break, dropped a spinning line into the water. He tied on to something that took off with all of his gear, including a badly bent pole. At times, while chasing caribou over the tundra, I would tire and take a break by fishing.

On this particular day, Jay, Morris, and I boated a fair-sized trout, enough to feed more than just the three of us. We headed for King Rapids to join Carol and Dick Mauch and their guide for lunch. Dick was fly-fishing about a quarter mile away. We could see him silhouetted against the horizon whipping the stream, cast after cast. He eventually noticed through his binoculars that we were preparing lunch. Abandoning his pole for the time being, he headed down.

Meanwhile, a willow fire had been set and Morris readied an iron skillet with gobs of lard. When it began to bubble, in went the trout fillets. Dieting was not a way of life for the Dogribs. Another skillet was brimming with potatoes, onions, and the works. By the time Dick arrived on the scene, the only things left were a few potatoes and onions. He surveyed the situation and declared that the whole thing was a disaster, especially how the fish had been filleted! Our happy stomachs did not agree with his assessment. Dick did find enough left on the fish bones to provide for himself, and proceeded to show us how the filleting should have been done.

For a guy who considers happy hour a nap, it was time to respond to compelling reasons that suggested that I get some rest. Lazily trolling with a spoon in a boat sounded good to me. Carol, Jay, and guide Morris took off to intercept an approaching bunch of caribou. Dick went back to his fishpole. He had already caught and released about 30 grayling, keeping a few along with some lake trout. Why he didn't bring at least one down to the lunch, I'll never know.

Ray and I set out with the boat to make several slow, circular passes where the King Rapids water entered the lake. I was using a 3-1/2" yellow lure with five red diamonds on it. It was complete with a hook which looked big enough to haul in a steer — pretty convincing. That, with my foolproof spin reel and 16-pound line, how could I lose? There are no char or salmon in MacKay Lake — only lake trout and the likes of muskies and pike. Each pass over these clear waters seemed to produce a trout. One shallow area where rocks were clearly visible seemed to be the hot spot. After taking three or four trout around 18 to 24-inches, we figured that was probably enough to feed the whole camp for dinner.

But no, let's do it one more time and concentrate on the hot spot. On one pass there was nothing so we had to make another. My lure apparently snagged on the bottom, or so I thought until Ray commented, "I don't think so. *Whatever you hooked is towing the boat!*" Not till then did I set the hook. It soon became apparent we were in for a long haul and a real fight. This fish had soaked up a lot of energy from these ice cold waters. It was certainly not a wimp. The first time it came out of the water and tried to shake the hook, I was not convinced that I would ever land it. "Ray," I exclaimed, "there is no way we would ever get that critter into the boat!" While Ray maneuvered the boat, I continued to try keeping the line snug. My foolproof reel was not much help. Apparently, as a fisherman, I was at a lower level than the reel was supposed to provide for.

A half an hour later the line is circling the boat, back and forth, and under the boat and Ray was doing his darndest to keep the fish away from the propeller. At one point, Ray grabbed the net and made a try, but that only gave the critter more energy and away it went again. It was only a matter of time; the line had overrun the spool and the pole was in shambles. Ray finally got the net under our prize. Not realizing the weight of this critter, he almost went overboard. My hand on the seat of his pants kept him from doing just that!

With the fish on board, we should have headed for the main camp, but no, I just had to "bait" Dick Mauch with it. We went ashore at the lunch site. The trout was secured in the shallows where Dick, without any help from us, would undoubtedly see it. Ray and I patiently waited until Dick gave up for the day. He came down the slope with his catch of grayling and trout, and as he went to freshen them up in water, my monster was staring him in the face. "HOLY SMOKE!" he exclaimed. "Who?" There was no one but Ray and me there. *"For crying out loud, St. Charles, you really did it this time!"* Pictures were taken on the spot and we all headed for camp. There wasn't a big enough scale in camp to weigh it. We estimated it to be about 25 to 27 pounds, 39 inches. Beautiful orange-colored fins and tail complemented the dark speckled body.

Among the caribou racks that came in that evening was one with Carol Mauch's tag on it. She credited Morris and Jay for her success. Moreover, she had found a huge, bleached-out rack jammed in between two huge rocks, perhaps a year or so old. It appeared that the caribou that carried it at one time had slipped or fallen off the small cliff adjacent to the rocks and could not free itself, paying the ultimate price. That pick-up rack scored close to 400!

Came the night for the Jack Joseph Wake. A clear sky, except for a few small, fluffy clouds. Imagine, if you will, a fire large enough to warm a 20-foot circle of folks. There were Dogrib Indians, their siblings, an Inuit or two, and we hunters from the outside, still in hunting clothes. As the fire crackled and sent the sparks leaping through the smoke, a single cloud was drifting across a near full moon low on the horizon. Its light was bright enough to show color on the tundra behind the silhouetted rock Inukshuks.

To get a better perspective of the whole scene, I moved off from the fire about 30 to 40 yards and toward the Inukshuks. Looking back at the far end of the sky opposite the moon, was one of the most brilliant displays of the aurora borealis one could possibly imagine. Curtains of light, wave after wave, criss-crossed the sky and even the stars could be seen peeking through. It was as if some presence had orchestrated this whole scene to fit the occasion. Staring into the flames, you

HOLMES COUNTY
BANK AND TRUST COMPANY

LEXINGTON, MISSISSIPPI 39095   601/834-2311

W. R. ELLIS, III
CHAIRMAN OF THE BOARD

August 28, 1993
Eulogy for Jack Joseph, Sr. Member, Pope & Young Club
By Billy Ellis
McKay Lake Caribou Camp-Northwest Territories, Canada

The arrow is broken and so are our hearts. Our dear friend and bowhunting buddy, Jack Joseph, has taken the last trail.

Jack died near our McKay Lake Caribou camp today. He made his final stalk and shot his last arrow at a big Caribou bull. When the arrow flew from his bow, Jack's soul followed, and he gently slumped to the tundra.

Although Jack fulfilled both his, and every other serious bowhunters desire in the circumstance of his passage; we who are left are only partially consoled for we have lost a true friend and companion of the high trails, and a bright ray of hopeful enthusiasm when the clouds rolled in.

Jack truly loved his friends. At every Pope & Young Convention, Jack always stood at the main entrance so he could meet and greet all of his buddies as soon as they arrived.

Jack phoned me last week, as excited as a kid in a candy store. "Billy, I just wanted to make sure that you're coming on the hunt and to let you know just how excited I am. Although he had not intuition, I guess a rendezvous with Paradise was something to get excited about.

When Jay St. Charles cradled Jack's head there on the tundra, at that moment, a marvelous rainbow lit up the sky over Jack; God's ancient symbol of renewal was fitting for Jack.

The noted English poet, T.S. Elliott once wrote of modern man:
    "they measure out their lives with coffee spoons".

Jack Joseph measured out his life with fine hunting trips and Pope & Young Conventions, along with a legion of friends he made along the way.

Today Heaven is a better place because Jack Joseph is there, but we will never forget his legacy:

    Jack showed us what love, friendship and caring was all about.
    Jack showed us that childlike enthusiasm is not only O,K., it is
    contagious.
    Jack showed us that generosity is more important than fame.

So for now, old buddy, Bon Voyage, but we'll meet you a littler further on up the trail...For you kept the faith and fought a good fight, now heaven's an even better place, since your final arrow's flight.

could almost find yourself in a trance, making you wonder if it was possible to hear the rumble of caribou on the distant hills and the tic tic of hoofs on the rocks.

The faces around the fire were not sad, but rather appeared to be in acceptance of the fact that Jack had left us. The wide-eyed siblings, in awe of what they were witnessing, were especially concerned with the happening. Billy Ellis read aloud a stirring eulogy he had written. Dick Mauch recited, from memory, poetry from the north country ballads of Robert William Service.

All who knew Jack personally stepped forward and told their story. The Dogribs responded with song from their ancestral past. It is truly amazing how death can bring together different cultures, a universal sharing among humans. Yes, Jack was remembered. Gary Jaeb and his wife Bertha announced that he would forever be remembered in their camp — that they have named the bay on MacKay Lake where Jack last went ashore "Jack Joseph Bay," a fitting tribute to a great guy. Always happy, a bowhunter who refused to have a bad time.

As the fire died down, we placed two of Jack's arrows on the ashes and watched the shafts slowly dissolve. With that, the faces gradually faded from the scene.

The hunt continued the next day. Joe and his guide Bobby headed out early. Jay and I with guide Morris would meet up with them later at Jack Joseph Bay — to once again have a presence in the area with a kindred spirit.

As we rounded the rocky shore into Jack Joseph Bay, Morris cut the motor and motioned toward a sizable band of caribou slowly moving down a slope beyond the far shore. Joe's boat was beached across the bay. Apparently a hunting scene was about to unfold. Jay and I confirmed with field glasses that Bobby was to the far right and had the attention of this herd as it moved away toward a boulder-strewn flat below. Joe was behind a big boulder, waiting for an intercept.

As we watched, three bulls broke away from the main herd and headed directly toward the very boulder that Joe was behind. However, he was facing the other way and might not notice them. We literally held our breath, wondering if these bulls would get his attention — they did. He must have heard them. He slowly backed around the rock, with arrow nocked, and waited for them to pass, apparently for the quartering shot. Then the arrow was away and the rear bull bolted for the lake. It didn't go far. A fifteen-yard shot and a 61-pound osage self

Joe St. Charles' first caribou. Left to right: Joe, guide Bobby, Jay, and Glenn.

Dale Holpainen (the tall one), Jay, and I bid goodbye to our host and hostess, Gary and Bertha Jaeb, 1993.

Hunters gather before boarding for trip out. Left to right: Wade Carstens, Glenn St. Charles, Larry Fischer, Carol Mauch, Dick Mauch, Max Thomas, Russ Tye, Dale Holpainen, John Evans, Billy Ellis, Nathan Andersohn, Jay St. Charles, Tim Conrads, Joe St. Charles.

1996 — Left to right: Dick Thrasher, Roy Marlow, Jay St. Charles, R. Bahl, Bill Akers.

bow had done this beautiful bull in. It was now time for congratulations — his first caribou! Jack Joseph would approve.

Most of the fellows filled out their tags. Dick Mauch even put his fly-fishing outfit aside long enough to fill his tag. The MacKay Lake Camp is by far the finest I've ever been in due to our very caring hostess and host, Bertha and Gary Jaeb.

The above picture surfaced as I was about to finish up this chapter. As I look at it, I see more than just a bunch of hunters and a pile of horns. The guys, a more diverse bunch of characters would be hard to put together, even if planned. My son, Jay, took them with him to Jaeb's camp. All used longbows.

Jay, like his dad in the '40s and '50s, makes longbows and has been to MacKay Lake many times. Rich Bahl was on his first caribou hunt and was inclined to take it all in stride — he felt his way into the hunt. Bill Akers lives in the foothills of the Cascade mountains near Seattle, and harvests quality yew for bowmaking. He is also a flintknapper and took, as part of his equipment, an arrow equipped with an obsidian head with which he would attempt to take a caribou.

Roy Marlow, an engineer from Texas, writes many bowhunting articles for Archery magazines. He ordinarily shoots a recurve. I am not so sure he was completely sold on a longbow. However, any doubts he had were dispersed, having witnessed the shooting antics of one who really knows how to shoot a longbow — Dick Thrasher, a retired Boeing executive. Dick started with Boeing as a computer programmer when computers were the size of an upright piano. Dick's wife Sharon, went along to fish and enjoy the camp.

Dick quit bowhunting seventeen years ago over the equipment controversy — archery just wasn't the same anymore. He also dropped his membership in the Pope and Young Club. These past years, he has been making much sought after quality bamboo fly rods. Subsequently, Jay introduced him back into primitive archery and Dick made two 60-pound osage self longbows — beautiful works of art, one called "Caribou Stalker." With that bow he took two Boone and Crockett-size caribou, one at very close range and the other while he was practically lying on his back. He has scrambled into position to intercept a nice bull moving with a herd over the tundra. Lacking any real cover, he laid down in the grass as the bull approached. He let it walk by and when the quartering shot became available, he launched an arrow from a sitting position, hitting the vital spot at 35 yards.

Yes, Bill Akers got a bull with his obsidian point. Roy and Jay were successful. Each took nice heads that would make the Pope and Young and Boone and Crockett books. As for Rich, he had many chances but waited too long for the big one and the weather in the end took away his chances.

The point of this story is that it is another well-documented example of how effective the stick bow can be in the hands of a traditional hunter who is serious about bowhunting. Furthermore, let this be a reminder to everyone that it was the longbow and recurve that proved up the bow as a viable hunting weapon when the Pope and Young records keeping came into being in 1958.

The upshot of this hunt is that Roy Marlow is convinced that the longbow is for real. As for Dick Thrasher, he now claims that he didn't really quit the Pope and Young Club, that he is simply seventeen years behind in his dues!

26
TROPHY HUNTING
AND THE LEGENDS

For those of you who wondered through years of bowhunting why the other guy always seemed to get the big racks, take heart. For every big one taken there are many lesser racks taken. You only hear and read about the big ones. That is the price that trophy hunting has placed upon bowhunting. The law of averages takes care of most of us. However, like any other endeavor, some fellows are better hunters than others. Perhaps a survey that Roy Hoff, publisher of <u>Archery</u> magazine, made in the '70s will give you some insight and solace. He asked the question of his readers: "Who is the best bowhunter in this country today?" After several months of evaluating answers, Roy published the winner. It was a reader who wrote in, declaring himself the best bowhunter, with Fred Bear's time and money. Yes, time and money is what it takes and a lot of hunting know-how.

Howard Hill, Fred Bear, and Ben Pearson were corporate entities and had no trouble with time and money. It was important for sales that they do well in the field. The company PR folks saw to it that they did. Fred commented to me that it bugged him that he was expected to kill something every time that he hunted. He said that if he thought he would get something every time, he would not hunt. Fred and I got skunked on two of our hunts together. His comment was: "You can't win them all!"

Emphasis on trophy hunting came into its own in February, 1958 when the NFAA/Pope and Young Records came into being. Before that,

My friend Duryll is a good sport and a real archer
Howard Hill

Howard Hill

if there was a choice, the bigger rack took the arrow, unless you were a meat hunter and liked the more tender steaks. Many hunters in the early days competed in the numbers game, "who killed the most?"

Let it be known that the legends were not trophy hunters by today's standards. Art Young, Saxton Pope, Will Compton, Howard Hill, Fred Bear, Ben Pearson, and Chet Stevenson all shot and killed everything that came down the pike. They did it the old-fashioned way — no gimmicks or gadgets. The law of averages dictated that some of their kills would be trophies. Most of those that could meet the Pope and Young Club Minimums and Fair Chase Rules were eventually entered. Some were declared world records by their own standards — Pope and Young Club Fair Chase Rules be damned.

Fred Bear put many trophies in the record book. He was a delight to hunt with, fun, and always concerned about the others around him.

As for Howard Hill, he was not one to get close to any organization. He was not particularly interested in entering his trophies. After his passing, his heirs and staunch followers put some of them in the Pope and Young Club Records Book.

Left to right: Art Young, Will Compton, Saxton Pope with his first deer, about 1918.

Saxton Pope and Art Young hunted the early years before my time. Their hunts in Yellowstone Park, Alaska, and Africa are well-documented. They shot many lesser animals, and pictures of them with those animals are common.

Ishi was in a class by himself — strictly a subsistence hunter. He undoubtedly had much influence on Young and Pope.

Compton was a mentor to both Art Young and Saxton Pope. He taught them much in the arts of bowmaking, shooting, and hunting. Pope commented that when the three of them hunted rabbits or whatever, Compton always seemed to get the most.

Chet Stevenson hunted in the era of Art Young and Saxton Pope. This was in the days shortly after the turn of the century and into the '20s when game laws were virtually nonexistent. Deer and elk were hunted commercially. Hides were popular for clothing. Deer and elk meat could be found at the marketplace, or you could get it fresh out of the hills of Oregon directly from deer hunting camps. Chet, at times,

Chester Stevenson at the typewriter in his den.

hunted with them, and in his written chronicles tells about his brushes with moonshiners hiding out in the forests of Oregon. A visit with Chet in his den in Eugene, Oregon, was an unforgettable experience. The walls of his den were covered with archery tackle, and blacktail racks that he had taken through the years. Two of them turned out to be number one and two in the Pope and Young Record Book for several years. They were taken in 1916 and 1921, respectively.

Ben Pearson's trophies that could meet Pope and Young Club Fair Chase Rules are entered in the Pope and Young Record Book.

These greats are not legends because of their exploits at killing game. They did much to bring bowhunting to the forefront as a sport. They carried the message to us with their appreciation of nature and man, their inventions, and their merchandising know-how. They were communicators, and more than anything else, they had one intangible ingredient that is common to legends — CHARISMA!

They lived and hunted when legends were possible. They were pioneers and stand-outs when bowhunting was still considered a sport by all concerned parties. Simply getting the biggest and the most does not a legend make.

27
FAIR CHASE

The accepted definition of Fair Chase by those who care is: *not taking unfair advantage of animals while hunting them in their native haunts.* Boone and Crockett Club and Pope and Young Club have Fair Chase Rules for entry of trophy animals into their records.

Fair Chase is a many-faceted concept — means different things to different people. Most hunters have their own agenda — "fair chase" is whatever they feel comfortable with. Perhaps that is as it should be — to each his own. Those who hunt with concern for our image will be discreet in their hunt and in their stories that follow. The *stuff-it-down-their-throats* advocates will hunt with an entirely opposite look, and write the story phrased in blood and guts.

Recently, I read in one of the national bowhunting magazines, an interpretation which I thought had quite an odd twist: "That hunting animals on the ground was not 'fair chase' — the animals could smell you." How about that!

DANGEROUS GAME

This is an issue that you don't hear much about. It never occurred to us in the early days that bowhunters would be hunting dangerous animals the likes of grizzly, brown, and polar bears. Apparently, we were not prone to look that far ahead. We had enough problems convincing the public and DNR that we should be allowed to hunt any game with the bow and arrow and, later, proving the bow as a viable hunting weapon even on non-dangerous game.

In my opinion, the bow and arrow has its limitations. It should only be stretched beyond the norm into the area of dangerous game, if the bowhunter is willing and able to do it without the backup rifle. I am aware that backup is the accepted way — the bowman wants to live to tell about it — there isn't time to do it the hard way and everybody does it, why shouldn't I? *All arguments are well taken, but do not justify claim to the world of hunting that the bow is a viable hunting weapon in the taking of dangerous game.*

In most other countries where hunting is allowed, a guide with rifle at ready is the law of the land even while hunting non-dangerous animals. Guides are to carry rifles to keep dangerous animals away from you while hunting non-dangerous animals. Most bowhunters prefer to have these guides give them plenty of room to stalk on their own without interference. There is a profound difference when you decide to take on a dangerous animal, an animal that can easily do you in during the attempt. *The guide now becomes your bosom pal — none of this give-me-room-stance — you want the comfort of knowing that the guide with rifle is right there for you if needed. You have literally negated the challenge, the danger and, perhaps, terror. Thus, a kill will mean nothing more than that you shot it. Furthermore, you have exposed the fact that you and the bow are lacking — not a viable hunting combination in killing that dangerous animal.*

When Fred Bear hunted grizzlies and brown bear with guide Ed Bilderback in Alaska, he was not comfortable with the presence of the backup rifle — the look of inadequacy. Art Young and Saxton Pope were not comfortable with the look that came with backup rifles during the hunts in Africa. They killed six lions without rifles entering into the actual kill. However, the rifles were there at ready if needed. Other lions were killed by rifles after a hit by an arrow. They admit that without the rifles, they would not have lived to tell about it. *They were "called on the carpet" for the need of backup by one of the more notable African guides. They came home with advice to the rest of us that the dangerous animals of Africa were not really within the viable limits of the bow and arrow.*

Dangerous animals have been taken by bowhunters without the presence of a rifle nearby. You read about it from time to time. Art Young killed a grizzly in Alaska with no backup. My hat's off to these fellows. I have been asked many times if I have ever killed a grizzly. My answer is no. I don't hunt grizzlies with or without backup — I know my limitations.

Keith Clemmans, Dick Bolding, and I spent a month in Alaska in 1957 without any firearms. Guides were not required. We saw many grizzlies. We weren't hunting grizzlies. We avoided them and they seemed to respect that. Only once did a grizzly wander into our camp. He peeled out of there when he heard the "whirr" of the movie camera. Like I have said before, my dog seems to know when I'm going to give him a bath even when he is not in the same room. Do you suppose these bears sensed that they were not being hunted?

The point of this is: *in today's world, anything we do that appears unsportsmanlike negatively affects our image; an image that is coming more and more under scrutiny.*

28
HISTORY

In the '30s, bowhunting was just the dream of a few. Between 1936 and 1940, bowhunting became a reality. However, we were reminded by our wildlife department (DNR) and the gun hunters that the Indians had abandoned the bow in favor of the rifle, which was a much better provider of meat for the tribe.

Oh, but WE want to elevate hunting to the level of a sport! A "walk in the woods" to challenge the animals in their native haunts. What few animals we take will simply be a climax to a good hunt. This concept apparently had a good enough ring to it to convince the DNR to legalize the bow as a hunting weapon. We were to hunt with the gun hunters in their season. The gun clan was skeptical. The public reasoned that, if man must hunt, the bow would be more sporting and give the animals more of a chance. The Humane Society was our main objector, citing that it was cruel and barbaric. As far as I know, the Humane Society was the only anti-hunting group around at the time. They wanted the use of the bow on animals nipped in the bud.

There were only a few archery magazines in the '30s and '40s. Ye Sylvan Archer was the standout. It was our sounding board and contained bowhunting stories and ads of the tackle vendors.

At first we didn't kill many animals. We really didn't expect to. Bowhunting was new. Not much had been written about bowhunting. We were pioneers. We would write the books. Keep in mind that this was in the days before "fair chase" and trophy hunting. We actually

Washington Bowhunter Irl Stamps, 1936.

stalked and still-hunted. We weren't concerned about gender or size. We shot anything that was legal. Something was better than nothing. We shot lots of arrows and missed a lot. On those early hunts it seemed like the animals played games with us . . . they were curious. "Still-hunting" consisted of slowly covering the area, stopping occasionally, looking, and listening.

A typical "walk in the woods" hunt, 1943: I was hunting mule deer in eastern Washington. Fall colors were on the hills. You could smell the critters in every aspen thicket. I was moving along a steep hillside with longbow in hand, an arrow nocked. As I came out of a patch of buck brush, a wall of brambles confronted me. There was no way I could get through it without making some noise, so, rather than try, I crashed through it, deliberately making as much noise as possible.

It occurred to me that this might attract something, so I took up a crouching position on a vantage point overlooking the "noise" patch, about 15 yards away.

Perhaps five minutes passed. Sure enough, out of a clump of aspens there came a two point with measured step. Obviously, he was curious about the racket. I hurriedly got set. He was wide-eyed, head bobbing, ears flipping. When he nosed the ground the arrow took him where it counted. Yes, I really nailed that critter! A bound or two later he was down. So that's how it was when bowhunting was a sport and accepted by all as such.

Many bowhunters were making equipment in their basements and garages. Theirs was such a slow process they had very little impact on the growth of bowhunting. With the advent of plastics in the early '50s, the equipment picture changed. Now bows could be mass-produced. New designs, recurves, became the latest trend. The archery industry really started rolling and so did bowhunting. With that, our demands for more areas and longer seasons grew. The gun hunters' concern changed to alarm. We were taking over their turf. Between them and the Humane Society, we were beginning to have real problems. There was an increasing number of "reports" of animals running around looking like pin cushions. Even a milk cow was "found" with an arrow in it. The farmer could get $500 for reporting a bowhunter's mistake. The local sheriff shut down the area and a real brouhaha was in the making, until an autopsy on the cow was ordered by the Washington State Bowhunter Big Game Chairman. The autopsy proved that the cow had drowned in a slough it was laying beside!

Now the Director of Washington's DNR, tired of all the rumors, demanded proof — pictures of so-called "pin cushion deer" — and ordered their wildlife agents to come up with something tangible. A picture of a mule deer with an arrow stuck in its side was brought in. Further investigation proved that the deer had been killed by a train! Drag marks of the carcass to a point about 100 yards from the tracks told the real story. The above scenarios were pretty much the same all over the country.

Some of the national sporting goods magazines got into the act. November, 1959 True Magazine printed a repulsive article by a person claiming to be one of us, a bowhunter, and a champion archer-type. The article was called "Butchers with Bows and Arrows." It pictured a deer covered with flies and an arrow sticking in it. Among other things, the writer used answers out of context that Fred Bear and I had

Fred Bear (in light hat) ready to take to the woods with Michigan bowhunters — deer season 1937.

returned from his questionnaire. About the same time, a firearms expert took it upon himself to write an article titled, "Six Guns Versus Arrows," further muddying the waters.

In 1960, the Ravenna Arsenal in Ohio put on a shoot to cull some deer in 900 acres behind cyclone fences. Some overzealous bowhunters took advantage of the situation, and created a "massacre" by killing some deer that got stuck in the fences when they tried to crawl under them. The media had their day!

We were a long time getting over these hits. Although most of these were nonsense, the damage was done — it had been printed. We managed to survive, regroup, and continue our quest for more and better seasons. It was always more. We were never satisfied. Each time we were met with stiffer resistance — more rhetoric on why we should not be out there.

We were "called on the carpet" again and again by everybody concerned. The public demanded that the DNR get answers to the question: Was the bow really a viable hunting weapon? The gun hunters were claiming that we were shooting only does and fawns.

The above concerns brought into focus the Boone and Crockett concept of recording trophy animals. It worked for them — they had credibility. Why wouldn't it work for the bowhunters? Thus the NFAA Hunting Activities Committee brought into being the bowhunter record system in February of 1958. The impressive trophy record is what DNR needed to get them off the hook with the public. Now they had proof that the bow was a viable hunting weapon. However, bowhunters would also have to change their ways. A set of Fair Chase Rules was put into place along with the record-keeping — all brought into being in the interest of preserving bowhunting.

In 1960, the NFAA reluctantly, but graciously, turned over the valuable big game records to an avid group of bowhunters, who became the Pope and Young Club as we know it today. The records brought bowhunting to a new level. Now there was a new standard of measuring the size of animals killed. The old way of gauging by weight, for the most part, disappeared. However, there are still those who judge a hunter by numbers of animals killed.

Production of laminated longbows and recurves gained momentum. The distribution system began having problems with the many bowyers throughout the country. Larger archery dealers selling their production bows, objected to individual bowyers selling their bows direct to customers out of their basements and garages. Industry labeled them "basement bandits," claiming they were taking the "cream" off the profits.

Late in the '60s, the "THING" appeared — the COMPOUND! It got little notice at first. It was difficult to recognize as a bow; wires and wheels yet! Its acceptance was very subtle until Tom Jennings took it under his wing and made it into a real force. Slowly, but surely, most everyone got hooked on it, including me. My archery company even went so far as to design perhaps the first wood-handled compound — the "Buckskin." We had it manufactured at the Martin Archery Company of Walla Walla. The compound was also the answer that industry was looking for to take care of the so-called "basement bandits" — a bow that could NOT readily be made in basements and garages. It was a real mass-production item. The stick bows and recurves began to fade. The race was on as to which compound manufacturer could get there first with the most.

*   *   *

The following text, "Tomorrow: Much More To Do" is from the 1981 Pope and Young Record Book. It pretty much expressed the philosophy of the Pope and Young Club and the state of bowhunting throughout the country at that time.

TOMORROW: MUCH MORE TO DO

by *Glenn St. Charles – 1981*

The uphill struggle for bowhunters from the era of Saxton Pope and Art Young has been difficult. We have come a long way. We have reached our initial goal of proving that the bow and arrow is effective in the harvesting of big game animals. Bowhunters are now respected. Surely the Pope and Young Club's conservation program and its impressive record lists of trophy animals have been factors.

We must consolidate our position and that of all bowhunters by treating our success with reserve and humility. There is much more to do. As the balance of nature becomes increasingly fragile, there will be extreme environmental concern. We share in this concern and, wherever possible, provide help through our conservation program.

It appears that bowhunting has a bright future. However, it is not an unclouded future. As the human population increases, animal habitat decreases. Western states also have the added factor of many diverse groups, all concerned over the available land. Timber, cattle, and other interests have to be served.

The time has come when states must face up to the fact that big game herds in some parts of the continent can withstand little, if any, increased pressure. There is much pushing and pulling between various hunting groups, all vying for the same hunting times and places. Some things will change. States will take longer looks at hunting methods and styles, taking into consideration their impacts on animal resources.

Bowhunters could play a larger role in big game hunting as long as our success ratio remains relatively low and bowhunting equipment remains reasonably primitive. Some sort of balance must be struck, but it should not become a tug of war between the supporters of various styles of hunting in the quest for a place to hunt and game to harvest.

All hunters must face the problem together. There are others waiting in the wings to impose their solutions should we falter in this responsibility, and they would take it (all hunting) from us. We must continue to seek ways to educate the non-hunting public in the importance of game and habitat preservation and the vital role the hunter plays in game management and conservation. The future of big game hunting lies in our ability to persuade the non-hunting public.

Much of our strength lies in our heritage. We all relate to heritage. Our forefathers owned arms for protection and to put meat on the table. A stone axe, a flint head, a spent cartridge, or a steel broadhead . . . all could be found on the same wind-ravaged ridge. All are signs of the hunter, past and present.

If the Pope and Young Club, the Professional Bowhunter Society, the Boone and Crockett Club, the Safari Club International, and the National Rifle Association, just to name a few, are to survive . . . if future generations are to have a hunting experience . . . our heritage concept must be kept alive. We must not let opposing forces convince the public that heritage and tradition are no longer valid reasons to own a gun or bow to harvest a well-managed, valuable, renewable resource, or enjoy our chosen type of recreation.

We must expand wildlife education programs and drive home to whoever will listen that the harvesting of game is necessary, natural, and right. Mother Nature, who opposing forces frequently point to as all-knowing, can be much more cruel than is necessary for the preservation and well-being of life on this planet.

The future is never assured. However, continued protective measures against the threat to our basic hunting rights can go a long way in keeping the future more in perspective, more secure. The earth has predators and prey. We must be certain that hunting does not become one of the latter.

*   *   *

1996 – 15 Years Later, Foresight Lost

Some bowhunters have not treated their success with reserve and humility. Hunters, in general, have lost much of the respect and support they once had from the non-hunting public and the DNR. Likewise, trophy hunting is under fire. Trophies are being taken for the wrong reason. Many hunters are showing less regard for good game management.

To put it bluntly, the animal rights organizations, now over 300 strong, are capitalizing on our poor hunter image and have the attention of non-hunters, the voters who can take it all away from us.

29

A MATTER OF
ETHICS AND IMAGE

This book has taken the reader on a history ride covering bowhunting from its infancy to the present as seen through the eyes and feelings of one who was there — a bridge to the past.

My hunting began in the late '30s, the era that still adhered to the principles of Teddy Roosevelt: that hunting was good for the country, a manly sport that built character and sharpened the senses. The public felt comfortable in accepting that concept since most of their ancestors hunted to put meat on the table. The need for wild animal food gradually faded and hunting evolved into a sport. The DNRs managed wildlife for wildlife's sake and the hunter's sport. The public, at that time, was not into what sport hunting actually entailed — out of sight, out of mind.

Times have changed. No longer are hunters out of sight, out of mind. TV has brought all of our hunting activities right into the living room in vivid color. Simple camo was once acceptable. Today, the public views camo-clad hunters, complete with face masks and hoods, in tree stands with guns and bows at ready, scanning the ground over unsuspecting deer going about their daily lives — combat uniforms, no less, at war with the animals! Sure, this sells merchandise, but it also sells hunting short. We are pictured as killers, gangsters, paramilitary, the look that the public relates to today's violence in the streets. We call hunting sport. The public sees it as killing for fun. The more observing viewers may ask: Where does the hunting come in? Hunting by definition: pursuing animals in their native haunts.

Does sitting in a tree stand over a bear with his head stuck in a barrel of pastry look like fair chase or good sportsmanship to the non-hunters? In my opinion, the voting public doesn't mind that we hunt. It is HOW we hunt that is causing the concern. This concern by the voting public makes them very vulnerable to the views of the animal rights activists — thus the real root of our problems. Wouldn't it seem to make sense that we sacrifice some of our methods for the survival of hunting? Is that too much to ask?

Although Art Young, Saxton Pope, Will Compton, and Chet Stevenson had kindled the sparks of hunting with a bow long before, it wasn't till the late 1930's that bowhunting came into its own. The DNRs were skeptical but bowed to the reasoning of the public that, if man must hunt, the bow would give the animals more of a chance; thus bowhunters became part of the manly sport concept. Howard Hill called it "hunting the hard way." Wouldn't it be great if we could gradually get the non-hunting public back to thinking this way once again?

Today, hunting is struggling for survival, especially bowhunting. It is human nature to react to trouble by pointing fingers — blame someone. The animal rights activists — yes, they are the ones. We anguish, wring our hands and cry for someone to do something. The "stuff it down their throats" and the "don't let them get their foot in the door" advocates cry "they can't do this to us."

Oh, but they already have their foot in the door. However the activists are only part of our problem — an "in your face" problem. Perhaps they have distracted us so much that we have not seen the root of our trouble — our image — how the public perceives hunters. Isn't it possible that we hunters are our own worst enemies? In this light, part of the animal activist agenda would be to keep us distracted so that we don't recognize where we are failing.

What Aldo Leopold wrote makes more sense today than it did fifty years ago . . .

"I have the impression that the American sportsman is puzzled; he doesn't understand what's happening to him. Bigger and better gadgets are good for industry, so why not for outdoor recreation? . . . the sportsman has no leaders to tell him what is wrong. The sporting press no longer represents sport; it has turned billboard for the gadgeteer. Wildlife administrators are too busy producing something to shoot at to worry much about the cultural value of shooting. Because everyone

from Zenophon to Teddy Roosevelt said sport has value, it is assumed that this value must be indestructible."
— Aldo Leopold

Through the years, subtly we have gone from hunting, defined as "a walk in the woods" in pursuit of animals to accepting under the heading of progress, every conceivable gadget and method that the shooting sports industry can devise to kill animals faster and farther. What they have done is compromise our sport by redefining the word "hunting" to accommodate all the new stuff on the market. The question now is: Do we need it when the survival of hunting is at stake? *Surely, it is time for the grass roots hunters to take back their sport and do what they have to do to save it.*

Industry will resist change. They will cite that the price of "turning back the clock" is too high. That hunters are too ingrained in modern hunting concepts for change. Teddy Roosevelt's manly sport, Aldo Leopold's concern, and Howard Hill's hunting the hard way do not fit today's concept of hunting. Perhaps industry would accept subtle change if it were understood that we are not asking that the whitetail hunters throw away their tree stands and discard their camo, but to acknowledge that tree stands don't need to be in the public eye and to soften up the combat look by eliminating the face masks and hoods. Encourage hunters to use camo only while hunting. Keep it off the streets. Perhaps industry could see that these slight changes might be better in the long run in that it would prolong bowhunting beyond their projections.

Having said all this, I can only hope, at best, that time will show that a thread of this dissertation has caught on, that bowhunting is looking more and more like it belongs in the woods. As for the future — for what it's worth, *I believe that the animal rights folks will continue to get more offbeat and self-destruct when the non-hunting public, the voters, tell them to join the human race.* As for hunting? Depends on how the public perceives us down the road. Animals are "in." Killing will not sell. Hunting will be a tough sell. I shudder to think of the alternative to change — 10%, at best, of the population, hunters, trying to cram today's concept of hunting down the throats of 90% of the voting population, non-hunters.

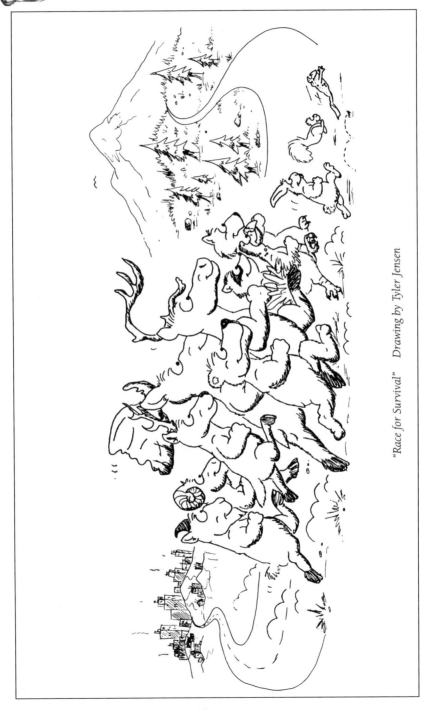

"Race for Survival"   Drawing by Tyler Jensen

Let's recognize that in this crowded world animal habitat is ever-shrinking. We must continue to seek out and support the organizations that can buy, beg, or borrow wildlife habitat, even if it does nothing more than keep it out of the hands of developers . . . those who would pave the earth.

30
EPILOGUE

Good things have been happening this past year — 1997. There seems to be considerable support out there for my stance on how the public perceives hunting. Good writers with no apparent conflict of interest are writing in sporting magazines suggesting that the gadgetry today is not all that great for hunting — how our instincts and senses are being dulled and how our outdoor values are being undermined. ATVs, rangefinders, and use of the G.P.S. positioning satellite, etc., are being questioned. Even the Boone & Crockett Club has picked up on the controversy and is encouraging commentary.

G. Fred Asbell introduced his new book, *Stalking and Still Hunting*, in June 1997 at Cloverdale, Indiana, right in the middle of tree stand America. Margaret and I were there. It's a very good book and brings out the shocking realization that, in all probability, many tree standers do not know how to hunt on the ground and may not even know how to "walk in the woods." Tree stand hunting has been a way of life for them for decades. Every tree stand hunter should read this book, if for nothing else but to find out how much fun he or she has been missing — how much quality time roving the woods in quest of game that they had been robbed of. Most certainly, if a hunting trip to the western states is planned, it is a "must read" book. Yes, westerners do use tree stands where animal movements can be patterned, but by and large, it is mostly stalking and still-hunting.

The midwest and northern whitetail country hasn't always been tree stand country. It is 1960; Grayling, Michigan; NFAA Tournament. Noting the beautiful terrain that seemed to lend itself to bowhunting, I asked the question of Fred Bear: "How do you fellows hunt this country?" "Oh," he replied, "let me show you." We hopped into his car and drove north about 15 miles. He took a little-used road into the hinterland. We travelled down the road a half mile — by swamps, ponds, thickets, and into a forest of paper birch trees, the ground cover, ferns, about two feet high. "Here's where I will be come fall. The leaves will be off the trees. It will be quite crowded the first day or so because it is fairly close to civilization. There will be lots of deer coming out of the swamps. You slowly make your way through the ferns, tree to tree, thicket to thicket, and LISTEN. When you hear arrows hitting trees, you get set. If the sound gets louder, the deer is headed your way. If the sound lessens it means the deer is going away from you." How about that!

Incidentally, in Michigan until 1976, it was illegal to hunt from any elevated stand. For gun hunters, it is still illegal today. Isn't it nice to know that there is still concern out there that the animals get a fair chance? So much for tree stand hunting, guys and gals — get down on the ground and exercise those legs.

There is a lot more to bowhunting than just putting meat in the freezer, rugs on the floor, and trophies on the wall. There is fun stuff; experiences you'll remember long after the meat is gone, the rugs are worn out, and the bugs have done away with your trophies.

Simple camo in the early days was acceptable as the badge of a hunter. I used it, but realized, early on, that movement completely blew the camo cover. I preferred hunting in wool plaids. Once, in stalking a mule deer laying on a hillside nearby, I ran out of cover. It saw me. If I backed away into the thicket I just came out of, I would be out of sight and it would leave. So what have I to lose? I got down on the ground, crawled and shuffled nonchalantly, not directly toward the deer, but so that I would pass in front of him at pretty close range. I occasionally sniffed at bits of brush along the way and avoided direct eye contact. At about 20 yards, I slowly raised to one knee, bow at ready. The deer obligingly stood up as I unloaded a nocked arrow at him. It was a beautiful full-bodied two-point — meat for the pot. The black wool pants and black and white plaid shirt had convinced him that I was just another critter.

A significant approach to improving our bowhunting public relations happened when the Pope & Young Club sponsored what is called

"Discover the Outdoors Camp," where a single parent and a youngster were teamed up in the Colorado mountains. To me, this is a great step in regenerating interest in what real hunters do: "walk in the woods." What better way could there possibly be to bring the bowhunting message directly to the people. Furthermore, the Professional Bowhunters Society sponsored a youth program called "Twenty-first Century Youth Leadership Hunt." It took place at a Texas ranch, where youngsters and their sponsors or parents holed up for several days, for orientation into the outdoors and hunting small game animals. There was some concern at first because of the lack of javelinas as billed. The concern was mainly with the adults, not with the youngsters — who needs anything else when you have rabbits? The ranch owner assured them they could have javelinas by baiting them. There was some concern with the group over the ethics of baiting, especially among the youngsters. They didn't bait — traditional values prevailed. Apparently, it was the youths' decision.

To me, there was a message in that decision that I choose to expand on. Is it possible that a new breed of bowhunter could evolve from these outdoor adventures? Would these youngsters, tomorrow's leaders, practice the true meaning of bowhunting if they were allowed to think for themselves, without being dealt all the hang-ups about hunting from their elders? Could they be the ones to change things around — go full circle, turn back the clock, and once again accept the teachings and concepts of Teddy Roosevelt, Howard Hill, and Aldo Leopold? Think about it. More of these youth camps should be put in place. Leaders will emerge. Wouldn't it make sense to give these leaders their head, get out of their way, and let them take bowhunting into the next century?

I would hope that those of you who have never known the traditional experience will at some time in your life try it, even if for no other reason than you owe it to yourselves and your families. The feel in the hand of a longbow or recurve . . . light, simple . . . the aroma of a cedar arrow . . . the aroma of burnt feathers, of beeswax as you ply it to a linen bowstring . . . sharpen a broadhead and watch the keen edge emerge . . . walk the woods and fields . . . take time to note the sights, sounds, and smells of nature . . . do the stump and cow pie shooting . . . see the shaft fly from a bow without all the "clutter" up front. As you take to the woods in quest of game, do so without a success and trophy mentality. Do the stalking in close . . . do the missing . . . the animals don't mind — your lucky quarry may even sniff the errant arrow. When you make the kill, look upon it with humility and accomplishment — you did it *my* way!

After all this, if you don't feel better about yourselves, tell me about it — go back to *your* way and I'll thank you for trying.

ADVICE AND WISDOM FROM
O'Sage St. Charles

1. Credibility comes from firsthand knowledge, whether writing or speaking. Assumption, rumors, hearsay won't do it.

2. Don't search for a profound justification for hunting. You hunt because the animals are there where you want to be.

3. Hunt ethically and in fair chase. You'll know the feeling when you have done it right.

4. Don't let peer pressure make you a trophy hunter. Be a trophy hunter until something else comes along.

5. Respect the animals in life and in death. A boot in the rump won't do it. A little humility is better. You may be alone, but remember there is a higher Presence.

6. If possible, find a home for all usable parts; the meat, hide, sinew, and hooves. It's called respect. A rack worthy of a mount deserves the best in taxidermy.

7. Do not get caught up in the numbers game. If asked how many animals you have killed, all you need to say is "enough."

8. Remember, everyone is a VIP.

9. You don't really know a person until you have hunted with him.

10. Leaders need credibility. Be an independent thinker. Never let anyone or any entity own you.

31
SHOTS FROM
THE PAST

Glenn's fireplace – a 65-year collection of stuff.

The Chalet hunters Bob Arvine and
Glenn at Nason Creek, 1952.

(CHAPTER 4)

A herd crosses the river in the Olympic Peninsula rain forest.

(CHAPTER 6)

Brooks Range sheep country.
Glenn headed for the top, 1957.

(CHAPTER 10)

*Nason Creek hunters Jay and Glenn with
Pope and Young "Mossback" buck, at the
base of a ponderosa pine, 1959.*

(CHAPTER 16)

*Fred Bear looking down
at "River-of-No-Return,"
the Salmon River in Idaho, 1961.*

(CHAPTER 18)

Cabin in the woods at
Mauch's Ranch, Nebraska, 1982.

(CHAPTER 20)

Hunters at Bobby Snowball's
Tunulik Lake Camp, Quebec, 1982.
Left to right: Buzzi Cook in front of
Dennis Arrowsmith, Dan Martin,
Jack Williams, Scott Showalter,
Roger Hammond, Dick Bean, Dr. Schneider,
Bob Jensen, Gail Martin, Gary Wilgus,
Dr. Strider, Sheldon Showalter, Ron Carpenter.
Kneeling: Carol and Dick Mauch,
Glenn St. Charles, and Ken Bean.

(CHAPTER 23)

*Glenn and 39" lake trout
taken at Jaeb's MacKay Lake Lodge,
Northwest Territories, 1993.*

(CHAPTER 24)

*Pope and Young organizational meeting in
Grayling, Michigan, June 29, 1960.
These fellows made the difference, 1960–1980.
From left, standing: Carl Hulbert, Tobias Flato,
Max Flato, Bob Lee, Russ Wright,
Vic Beresford, Howard Gillelan, Bill Neve,
Don Schram, Ed Marker, Bob Tapley,
Bruce Bourquin, John Downey, Paul Clanin,
Wayne Trimm, and Bill Sparks.
Seated: Chuck Kroll, Bobby Triplett,
Bill Wright, D.F. Vraspir, Glenn St. Charles,
Martin Hanson, Fred Bear, Roy Hoff,
Floyd Hauk, and Larry Whiffen.
Kneeling: J. Tipton Jones, W.T. Berry,
Winston Burnham, Crawford Booth,
Don Vraspir, Bill Stump, and Bob Munger.*

(CHAPTER 27)

Five who made a difference.
Left to right: Chuck Saunders, Earl Hoyt,
Glenn St. Charles, Al Henderson,
Frank Scott, 1986.

Missouri Convention, 1990.
Left to right: Rick Shepard, Gene Eakins,
Jerry Brumm, Marv Cochran, Wayne Allen,
Dale Dortch, Sherry Alkire, Rick Wakeman,
Bill Westphall, Scott Westerly.
Kneeling: Larry Hudson, Glenn, David Alkire.

Mississippi Traditional Shoot at
Billy Ellis' Indian Bluffs Hunting Lodge, 1992.

Billy Ellis, Glenn, and Mississippi photographer Roger Sanford, 1992.

Fred and Henrietta Bear

*St. Charles family with spouses
and grandkids, 1987.
Standing, left to right: William Hughes, M.D.,
daughter Adrienne, Rochelle Hughes with son
Alex, Roger Hammond, Suzanne holding
Sophia Hughes, Jay, Margaret, Glenn, Linda.
Kneeling: Jay's wife Karen with son Robin,
Marge and Joe with daughter Erin.*

Margaret St. Charles doing her thing.

The St. Charles Family, 1990.
Left to right: Margaret, Glenn, Rochelle, Joe,
Suzanne, Jay, Linda.

Glenn St. Charles, 1940.
The days when hunters looked liked people,
acted like people, and smelled like people.

"Ancient Crossing"
Watercolor painting by Charles H. Denault.